To Mike.

Best regards and
enjoy reading this book.

Dr. George Angelopoulos.

GOLD ★ SILVER BRONZE

A DOCTOR'S DEVOTION TO AMERICAN HOCKEY

GEORGE "DOC" NAGOBADS, MD
TEAM PHYSICIAN • 1967-1990

BEAVER'S
POND
PRESS

All photos in this book are from the personal collection of Doctor George Nagobads
with the exception of the following:
University of Minnesota with permission; pages 6, 8, 9, 10, 11, 290, and 306
USA Hockey with permission; pages 12, 15, 28, 39, 40, 50, 60, 74, 77, 78, 90, 102, 108, 118, 126, 133,
134, 150, 164, 174, 180, 184, 190, 194, 202, 210, 224, 233, 240, 246, 256, 262, 268, 280
Cover photo courtesy of Corbis
Photo on page 161, courtesy of AP Images
Photos on pages 21, 22 courtesy of Wilfried Fila, Austria

ISBN 13: 978-1-59298-914-0

Library of Congress Catalog Number: 2014914424

Printed in the United States of America
First Printing: 2015

19   18   17   16   15   5   4   3   2   1

Cover and interior design by James Monroe Design, LLC.

BEAVER'S
POND
PRESS

Beaver's Pond Press, Inc.
7108 Ohms Lane
Edina, MN 55439–2129
(952) 829-8818
www.BeaversPondPress.com

DEDICATION

I would like to dedicate this to my father, Ernests Nagobads
and my wife, Velta Nagobads.

My father taught me a work ethic by saying:
"There is no greater satisfaction for a man than after a job well done."

My wife, Velta, was an ardent supporter in all my endeavors and her supportive
advice was most valuable in all aspects of our life. So often she sacrificed her
own personal comfort for the duties I had to perform.

For all my accomplishments, my deepest gratitude goes to her.

CONTENTS

Hall of Fame, Niagara Falls with Murray Williamson

FOREWORD

by Murray Williamson

One afternoon, at the end of a Golden Gopher hockey practice many years ago, I saw a spindle-legged guy in maroon and gold buzzing around the net, doggedly shooting pucks at goalie Jack McCartan. Intrigued by this stranger's arrival, I skated over to Coach John Mariucci and asked who the heck it was. Maroosh simply said, "That's Doc Nagobads, our new team doctor. University Health Service sent him over." Just then, Doc skated in on McCartan, stickhandled once or twice, and zipped a wrist shot into the net. "He used to play hockey in Latvia and speaks four languages," said Coach Mariucci. "I gave him a locker and a uniform and told him he could skate after practice if he wants." It was that very day that Dr. Visvaldis George Nagobads first skated into my life and the lives of literally hundreds of Gophers, Olympians, and other world-class hockey players, including more than thirty men and women who've been inducted into various national and international hockey halls of fame.

Nine years later I was named general manager of the US National Team, scheduled to compete in the 1967 World Championships in Vienna, Austria. John Mariucci was my head coach, and one of the first things he said was, "You know, Doc Nagobads speaks German, French, and Latvian and understands some Russian. He knows Europe better than any of us. He would make a great team doctor for this tournament." Having recently watched Doc carefully stitch up my own six-year-old son on the infamous kitchen table on which he routinely patched up the Williamson and Nanne boys free of charge, I quickly agreed. Without a

Herb Brooks gala at the Depot with myself, Jack McCartan, and Murray Williamson

doubt, Doc's gentle and gregarious nature would serve our team well throughout training camp and beyond. Doc heartily accepted the invitation and thus began a stellar career in international and Olympic ice hockey that ultimately spanned more than forty years.

The 1972 US Olympic team, which I was fortunate to coach, trained for two years to prepare for the Winter Games in Sapporo, Japan, playing an intense eighty-game exhibition schedule throughout North America and Europe. Doc Nagobads was there every step of the way. His pay was decidedly minimal, but his compensation from University of Minnesota Health Services was all that he needed. His title may have been Team Doctor, but he was much more than that—as much a part of the team as any player, coach, or manager. When it came time to depart for the Games, however, word came down that the US Olympic Committee had assigned a different doctor to the team—a political appointment, if you will. I was aghast and told Bob Fleming, our committee representative, that we weren't going to get on the plane without Doc. Fortunately, Fleming, one of the great people in our lives, worked very hard and arranged for Doc to be named team trainer so he could join us in Japan. Naturally, after we'd all arrived at the Olympic Village, where was Doc while the rest of us were soaking in the atmosphere of the first day's festivities? Pressed into service, of course, off tending to a Canadian figure skater who'd tripped and broken her arm.

The 1980 US Olympic team's gold-medal victory in Lake Placid is the stuff of legend, and goaltender Jim Craig's performance was a huge part of that. In the months leading up to the Winter Games, Craig had been living with Doc, who'd generously given the lifelong East Coast resident a room in his basement while the team trained in Minneapolis. After defeating Finland to win the gold medal, with the American flag draped over his shoulders, Craig famously scanned the crowd, searching for his father. Moments earlier, Craig had shared a hug with Doc, quietly celebrating the monumental win with the man he considered to be his second father.

Later, in the wake of the "Miracle on Ice" celebration, an infamous sports agent who represented a lot of the players arranged for the Olympic team's players and staff to get expensive commemorative rings. Conveniently for the agent, he somehow ended up with a ring while Doc Nagobads did not. Never one to make a fuss or call attention to himself, Doc didn't complain. A few days later, though, Herb Brooks found out, and that was the end of that. The "oversight" was corrected posthaste.

More recently—just four years before the publication of this book, in fact—the World Junior Championships were held in Saskatoon and Regina, Saskatchewan, over the Christmas holidays. The International Ice Hockey Federation (IIHF) was desperate to find an experienced, knowledgeable doctor to head doping control. No other doctor would take the job, so the call went out to Doc Nagobads, pleading for his last-minute assistance. Of course, he was once again ready to help. Eighty-eight years old at the time, this international ice hockey icon agreed to travel north to Canada in the dead of winter to serve the cause. A devoted family man, he nonetheless delayed his Christmas celebration with family until he returned in early January, sacrificing once again for the players, coaches, administrators, and fans of the great sport of ice hockey.

Over the years, Doc has accepted many tributes and accolades with the humility and graciousness that are such a part of his character. Stories of his generosity and selflessness in support of all the people and teams he served over the years are legendary and too numerous to recount in this short essay. Suffice it to say, he did it all for his love of hockey and the people who play it. As he readily admits, hockey is in his blood.

When the call went out to garner support for

Doc's dream to have his journals published as a book, everyone responded with resounding enthusiasm. Doc has meant so much to so many people and touched so many lives that there was a natural, spontaneous outpouring for this beloved man. Perhaps Gary Gambucci said it best when he wrote, "I am hoping it will not only be a tribute to all the National and Olympic teams of the past, but a tribute to a great man who gave so much of himself out of a clear sense of love of hockey and his fellow man." Appropriately, the University of Minnesota hockey team has named an annual award for him: the Dr. V. George Nagobads Unsung Hero Award. George Nagobads's many accomplishments may not be widely known outside of the world of hockey, but he is a hero and lifelong friend to the generations of hockey players who were fortunate enough to know him.

And now, let the stories of the Golden Years of American International Ice Hockey begin.

Murray Williamson

ACKNOWLEDGEMENTS

I am writing this book to help people realize how much enjoyment, professional satisfaction, and great fulfillment of life someone can have by devoting his time and best efforts to help young athletes fulfill their dreams.

I can honestly say that I would not exchange those wonderful twenty-four years of my life for any other professional career. Often people commented: "George, you are such a lucky guy to travel all over the world with that hockey team." Yes, I definitely regard myself as a very lucky man, but when I tell them that all of the traveling was on a leave of absence and without pay, then the reply is: "I don't know if I would like to do that." However, the main enjoyment and satisfaction in my life has been in the camaraderie with those young athletes and the feeling that my work has been appreciated.

My most sincere gratitude goes to all those in the hockey world and the medical profession who have enriched my life and most important, I could not have enjoyed that very full and interesting life without my most wonderful wife, Velta, as well as my two very understanding daughters, Sylvia Lawver and Brigita Kelly and their husbands Joe Lawver and Mike Kelly. They never complained about my extended travels. In fact, they have been very positive and helped me to overcome some very sad moments, like leaving the family at Christmastime. Brigita even said, "Dad, don't feel so bad. Let's have Christmas one week early. Nobody really knows when Christ was born." So, we had Christmas one week earlier and everybody was happy again.

A special thanks to my publishing team, led by Tom Kerber of Beaver's Pond Press, and John Schaidler, Peter Lindberg, and Roger Godin who transformed my journals and writings. And a big thank you to my friends and colleagues who encouraged and assisted me in the preparation of this book.

GOLD ★ SILVER ★ BRONZE

A special thanks to the following individuals who made a financial contribution to make this book possible:

Ahearn, Kevin	Ftorek, Robbie	Naslund, Ron
Bader, Larry	Gambucci, Gary	O'Callahan, Jack
Baker, Bill	Godin, Roger	Ogrean, Dave
Berglund, Art	Harrington, John	Peters, Bob
Boucha, Henry	Howe, Mark	Pleau, Larry
Brooks, David	Janazak, Steve	Rendall, John
Brown, Charlie	Johnson, Mark	Schneider, Buzzy
Bush, Walter, Jr.	Kelly, Brigita & Mike	Sears, Pete
Caracciolli, Jerry	Lawver, Sylvia & Joe	Sheehy, Neil
Caracciolli, Tom	Lewin, Jon	Sheehy, Tim
Christian, David	Logue, Jim	Vairo, Lou
Christiansen, Keith	MacIntosh, Bruce	Verchota, Phil
Craig, Jim	McClanahan, Rob	Williamson, Murray
Curran, Lefty	McElmury, Jim	Williamson, Dean
Currie, Bob	McGlynn, Dick	Williamson, Kevin
Darcy, Randy	Mellor, Don	Williamson, Randy
Eruzione, Mike	Mellor, Tom	
Frauenshuh, Dave	Nanne, Lou	

INTRODUCTION

Dr. Visvaldis George Nagobads was born in Riga, Latvia in 1921, the second of three children. His parents, Ernests and Emma, were both teachers who prized education, particularly foreign languages. Accordingly, George was enrolled in a French-language kindergarten. During his grade school years, a German student named Erika Benefeldt also lived with the Nagobads family under strict orders to speak only German with George and older sister Aina and younger brother Ilgvars—the children. Soon, George was fluent in both French and German and understood some Russian, a trait which proved extremely helpful while traveling abroad with various US national teams.

A naturally athletic and active youngster, George played many sports, including soccer, volleyball, basketball, and bandy. He started playing ice hockey at age ten and joined the club team "University Sports" when he was fifteen. A fast and scrappy forward, he played left wing for "University Sports" throughout his high school and university years.

George began his medical education at the University of Latvia in Riga in 1941 in the midst of the chaos of WWII. In the fall of 1944, upon the Soviet occupation of Latvia, he fled to Germany and enrolled in the University of Giessen near Frankfurt. It was an almost fatal decision. The university campus was close to a railroad station, a prime strategic target for the Allied Command that was bombed frequently and heavily by Allied planes. At one point he almost died while helping a professor evacuate medical equipment from the lab. As the two of them hurriedly carried the delicate instruments to a waiting van, dashing back and forth through a protective concrete *Splittergrabben*, a bomb landed just fifteen feet away, sucking the breath from their lungs and knocking them to the ground as shrapnel ripped into the concrete. Soon thereafter, George transferred

Riga, Latvia, spring of 1939. The family of Ernests and Emma Nagobads.
Standing (L-R): Ernests Nagobads, my father; myself; and Aina, my sister.
Sitting in front: Emma Nagobads, my mother, and Ilgvars, my brother.

to the relative safety of the University of Tubingen, one of Germany's oldest and most prestigious universities, where he graduated with a medical degree— in 1949 and a PhD degree from the department of pharmacology in 1950.

Later that fall, he was working as an x-ray technician for an international refugee organization in French-occupied West Germany, traveling the country by van investigating tuberculosis cases, when he chanced to meet a reverend from Minnesota through a mutual friend. Over a fortuitous lunch, the reverend convinced young Dr. Nagobads that medical jobs were far more plentiful in the US than they were in war-torn Europe where doctors of every kind were flooding into West Germany and France. Nagobads didn't speak any English, but his fiancée Velta did, so the two of them emigrated to the United States in 1951 and were married. He first worked as an orderly at Mount Sinai Hospital in Minneapolis, learning English on the job, but began an internship at the Swedish Hospital just two months later.

He received his license to practice medicine in November of 1954 and began his surgical residency, where he learned the invaluable art of closing and suturing wounds. He joined the University of Minnesota Student Health Center staff in September, 1956 after answering an ad in the paper. In 1958, Dr. Ruth Boynton asked him to serve as team doctor for the men's hockey squad and he jumped at the chance. Neither of them could have foreseen it at the time, but Nagobads served as team doctor for the next thirty-four years, until 1992. In this capacity, he met and bonded with the men who would become a veritable *Who's Who* of US Hockey: John Mariucci, Murray Williamson, Lou Nanne, Doug Woog, and Herb Brooks.

In 1967 he was officially appointed team physician for the US national team. For the next twenty-four years his title may have been team physician, but in reality he was much more than that. Unofficially, he was also the team translator, travel agent, tour guide, chaperone, tournament coordinator, scheduler, nutritionist, concierge, and navigator. Luckily, it's as natural for Doc to go above and beyond the call of duty as it is for him to speak one of the foreign languages he's mastered. He does so without even thinking.

In fact, he is far too modest to tell you himself, but it is difficult to name another person who's had the kind of far-reaching impact on more hockey teams and individual hockey players than Dr. George Nagobads. During his tenure, he served as team physician for five men's US Olympic teams—including the 1972 silver medal team and the 1980 "Miracle on Ice" gold medal winners—as well as fifteen other US national men's teams, two Canada Cup teams, six US national men's junior teams, and the first US women's national team. He also served as the team physician for the Minnesota Fighting Saints of the World Hockey Association from 1973 to 1976 and for the Minnesota North Stars of the National Hockey League from 1984 to 1992.

Since 1986, he has also been a member of the Bavarian Sports Medicine Association in Germany; the (IIHF) Medical Committee and Medical

Supervisor's Group from 1990-2010; the Latvian Sports Medicine Association since 1992; and the USA Hockey Equipment Certification Council, its Executive and Certification Committee since 1997.

His list of awards and accomplishments is as extensive as it is impressive, but a few of them clearly stand out. In recognition of his years of service with international hockey, Nagobads was the 2003 recipient of the Paul Loicq Award, presented by the International Ice Hockey Federation (IIHF) to individuals who embody and promote the spirit of international ice hockey competition in an extraordinary manner, the first person from North America to win the prestigious award. He was inducted into the United States Hockey Hall of Fame and the University of Minnesota "M" Club Hall of Fame in 2010.

More than anything else, however, to spend any time with him at all is to see and experience Doc's passion for hockey and those who play it.

Hockey is in his blood.

On more than one occasion, in the process of compiling this book, he suddenly sprang from his seat and literally ran into the next room to grab a postcard, photograph, tournament program, or his personal calendar to confirm a fact or make a point. To say he is highly organized and detail oriented is an understatement. His ability to remember names, dates, and places is nothing short of astounding. In a debate between Doc Nagobads and Google or Wikipedia, I'd wager on the doctor. He's been there. He lived it. He is the original source. And that, of course, is the joy of the book that follows.

Drawn from years of meticulous notes, journals, and photos that he kept the entire time, *Gold, Silver, & Bronze: A Doctor's Devotion to American Hockey* gives casual fans and students of the game a rare glimpse behind the scenes into the daily life of the players and coaches that comprised Team USA. From the teams that toiled in obscurity thousands of miles from home to those that competed on the world stage under the harsh media spotlight; from the lonely, bitter defeats to the miraculous, uplifting victories that inspired a nation, all of it is here. This is the story of USA Hockey's greatest teams and greatest moments as seen through the eyes of one its great unsung heroes.

John Schaidler
Minneapolis, June 2014

My family in Edina, Minnesota in 2000 (L-R): Velta, my wife; Dr. Mike Kelly,
my daughter Brigita's husband; Brigita Kelly, my daughter; in front of Brigita: her son, Patrick Kelly;
Heidi Kelly, Brigita's daughter; Bill Kelly, Brigita's son; Gigi Lawver, my daughter Sylvia's daughter;
Sylvia Lawver, my daughter; Joe Lawver, Sylvia's husband; and myself.

*1963: Coach John Mariucci with Gopher Team Captain Lou Nanne (right)
and Alternate Captain David Brooks.*

1

John Mariucci,
the Golden Gophers, and the
Start of My International Career

In fall of 1958, the director of the University of Minnesota Student Health Service, Dr. Ruth Boynton, asked me to cover the University of Minnesota men's hockey games as team physician. Having been a hockey player myself, I accepted the assignment with great pleasure. Every day, after work, I stopped by practice at Williams Arena to check for injuries. In those early years, after practice officially ended, I laced up my skates, too, and played shinny with the boys. Naturally, we all got to know each other quite well, and several players from those early teams, including Murray Williamson, Herb Brooks, and Jerry Melnychuk became lifelong friends. Every three-year term brought a new crop of players and new friends. I developed especially close friendships with Lenny Lilyholm, David Brooks, Lou Nanne, Craig Falkman, and Gary Gambucci in the 1960s.

I also traveled with the team and came to know Coach John Mariucci well during the seven years we worked closely together. John was a colorful man of Italian descent from Eveleth, Minnesota, who'd played for the Chicago Blackhawks after his time at the University of Minnesota. He was a tough, unforgiving defenseman. As coach he was equally strict and demanding. Occasionally, when the boys had played a good, hard game, he gave them an easy practice the next day. He also had a good sense of humor. Once, in North

1965-66 University of Minnesota Hockey Squad. Front row (L-R): Chuck Norby, Mark Ryman, Bruce Larson, John Lothrop, Doug Woog, Frank Zywiec, Lorne Grosso, Gary Gambucci. Second row: Jim Branch, Dennis Zacha, Jack Thoemke, Jim Anderson, Bruce Melander, Greg Hughes, Dick Paradise, Mike Crupi. Third row: Head Coach John Mariucci, Student Manager Griff McAuliffe, Bull Suss, Charles Mackay, Jack Dale, Tom Toebe, Rob Shattuck, Jim Marshall, myself, Assistant Equipment Manager Vic Vainovskis. Back row: Chuck Holt, Barry Bloomgren, Bob Goldstein, Jim Jaros, Bob Kohlman, Charles Marvin, Denison Williams, Al Wiederhold.

Dakota, our team played poorly Friday night and lost the game. The next night our team played very well and won. John turned to me and asked, "Doc, did they switch uniforms?" Another time, we played a visiting team from Sweden who were not only tremendous skaters, but also very skilled puck handlers. It seemed like we never even touched the puck. After a while, John said to me, "Doc, drop another puck on the ice so *we* have something to play with!"

The Michigan State hockey team also had an Italian coach, Amo Bessone, who was a great friend of John's. During the Friday night games, they kidded each other across the ice. After the game, John would invite Amo to his house for dinner and offer a toast: "To the winning coach of East Lansing!" John was an excellent cook who made wonderful Italian meals. In

Lou Nanne and David Brooks

those days, after the season was over in May or early June, John would host a cookout for the whole team. When people started to leave, John said, "I never say good-bye to anyone. I always say, 'See you again next year!'" He had a wonderful heart, that man.

John Mariucci was proud that his team was composed mainly of boys from Minnesota. Northern Minnesota, in particular, was known as a hockey hotbed. High schools from Minneapolis and St. Paul, however, also produced outstanding players. Nonetheless, in those days, most other college and university rosters had a high percentage of Canadian players. So, when the US National Team was assembled, most of the players were from the University of Minnesota, products of Coach John Mariucci.

After the 1965–1966 season, John Mariucci left the University of Minnesota and accepted the position of assistant general manager for the newly formed Minnesota North Stars, one of six NHL expansion franchises. I was sad to see him leave, but we kept in close contact thereafter.

In the summer of 1966, John called me and said, "Doc, do you want to come to Vienna with me next spring?"

At first I thought he was kidding and replied, "Yes, yes, John. I'd love to go to Vienna, Paris, Rome, or wherever you want to go!"

John was serious, however. He'd been selected to coach the US National Team at the World Hockey Championships in Vienna, Austria, in the spring of 1967 and wanted me to be team physician.

Unbelievable! I was so happy, it was like a dream come true!

I didn't know it at the time, of course, but that was the start of twenty-four years as team physician for Team USA, a position that opened the door to many wonderful friendships with players and coaches from other states, as well as with players, coaches, doctors, and team managers from countries around the world.

*Spring of 1964, after practice in the old Mariucci Arena
(L-R): Len Lilyholm, Lou Nanne, and myself.*

Herb Brooks—recognition for twenty-one years of service to U of M Hockey teams—March 31, 1979

The US National Team at the 1967 IIHF World Championships in Vienna, Austria.
Front row (L-R): Rod Blackburn, Don Ross, Marty Howe, Bill Masterton, Coach Murray Williamson,
Bob Currie, Herb Brooks, Carl Wetzel. Middle Row: Equipment Manager Don Niederkorn, myself,
Trainer Dick Rose, Lou Nanne, Ron Naslund, Craig Falkman, Dave Metzen, Marsh Tschida.
Back row: John Rendall, Terry Casey, Tom Hurley, John Cunniff, Art Miller, Len Lilyholm,
Gerry Melnychuk, Doug Woog.

2

On to Vienna!

The Perrot–Duval Cup, 1967

Team Roster

In Goal: *Carl Wetzel, Rod Blackburn, Tom Hough*

Defensemen: *Herb Brooks, Bob Currie, Marty Howe, Dave Metzen, Don Ross*

Forwards: *Terry Casey, John Cunniff, Craig Falkman, Tom Hurley, Len Lilyholm, Gerry Melnychuk, Art Miller, Ron Naslund, John Rendall, Marsh Tchida, Doug Woog*

The Amateur Hockey Association of the United States (AHAUS, which became USA Hockey in 1990) selected Murray Williamson as general manager for the 1967 US National Team. Williamson, in turn, asked John Mariucci to be the head coach and also recruited trainer Richard Rose, known to the boys as Doc Rose, and equipment manager Don Niederkorn. Both had worked with Murray the year before and knew many of the players very well. My good friend John Mariucci asked me to serve as team physician. Naturally, I jumped at the chance.

In order to build the roster, Murray selected a core group of standouts from his old St. Paul Steers team. Many of them had experience playing against strong visiting international teams from Sweden and the Soviet Union. He also recruited some young rising stars from top NCAA Division I teams such as the University of Denver, the University of North Dakota, and the University of Minnesota. Many of those players knew each other from league games, and it didn't take long for everybody to gel.

The team was assembled in late October, with a fifty-game exhibition schedule ahead. In the first few weeks, things didn't go so well. Murray and John got into a dispute, and John resigned. Murray took over as coach. I was sad to see John leave, because he'd personally invited me to join him in Vienna and I'd looked forward to enjoying that city with him. Now that wouldn't happen, but life goes on.

After Murray took over as coach, practices got harder and conditioning was a bigger focus. The team got in much better shape. A lot of the players from Murray's old team, familiar with his coaching methods, were happier, and everything went a little bit smoother after that.

Soon after the New Year, 1967, the Austrian National Team embarked on a US tour and stopped in Minneapolis, where we played them. It was an easy game for us, and we won 11–1. The Austrians were good sports, however, and took their loss graciously. Their team leaders, Dr. Dieter Kalt and Rudi Novak, were especially friendly and extended an invitation to our team to come to Graz for an exhibition game when we traveled to Austria for the World Championships that spring. We accepted their invitation with pleasure.

On March 3, 1967, our team left for Vienna, stopping first in Switzerland for exhibition games in Basel, Lucerne, and Geneva. We landed in Zürich at about seven o'clock in the morning and took a smaller plane to Basel, on the northern edge of Switzerland where the German and French borders meet. Locally, Basel is called the Three-Country Town. The Rhine River starts in Switzerland and flows northward, forming the border between France and Germany. This confluence is marked with a missile-like structure where all three flags fly: Swiss, French, and German.

There was no game the first day, but we practiced outside on a rink with soft ice. After practice, we all went sightseeing or just toured around. Since I was familiar with the area, I warned everybody that on the east side of the Rhine, Basel is divided into Swiss and German sections. We were staying in the Swiss part, but a little further north was German territory. There were no obvious signs for the border, and you could easily cross into Germany without even knowing. When you tried to return, however, the Swiss border guard would demand your passport, ask where you were going, and demand to know the reason for your visit. Since we'd had to give our passports to the hotel for registration, we had to be especially careful not to accidentally cross the Swiss–German border.

Sure enough, about thirty minutes later we got a telephone call from the Swiss border patrol. They had stopped two fellows who claimed to be members of the United States hockey team, but they had no identification. I asked their names and politely told the border guard that I would come immediately to clear things up. I went to the hotel registration desk to get the passports of Art Miller, Marty Howe, and myself. Unfortunately, the passports had been sent to City Hall for registration. Now what? *The postcard*! We had

At the airport in Minneapolis before leaving for Vienna, Austria (L-R): Murray Williamson, Don Niederkorn, John Mariucci, Walter L. Bush, Jr., USA Hockey Vice President Dave Metzen, Craig Falkman, Len Lilyholm, and myself.

our team picture on a postcard with everyone's name on the back. I grabbed one and headed out. Just as I was leaving, Craig Falkman and Lenny Lilyholm, two more of our players, asked where I was going. I told them the situation, and they asked if they could join me. Knowing those players well, I said, "No, you guys always make trouble."

"No, no, Doc!" they said. "We'll be good! We'll behave!"

So I took them along on the honest promise that they wouldn't make any trouble. As we got close to the border point, we could see Miller and Howe standing next to the border guard. Lenny and Craig started calling, "Doc, we don't know those guys. They aren't from our team."

"Darn it," I said. "You guys promised to behave! Cut it out!"

I greeted the border guards in German, told them who I was, and explained the situation with our passports. Then I showed them the postcard with the team picture on the front and names on the back. Luckily, despite Lenny and Craig's shenanigans, that was good enough for the guards, and we were allowed to return happily to our hotel, those two troublemakers laughing all the way.

The next day, a Sunday, we were scheduled to play at three o'clock in the afternoon. It was a nice, sunny spring day, and that outside rink was like a puddle of water. We weren't used to playing in such conditions and quickly fell behind 2–1. Murray got a little nervous. Suddenly, I noticed the position of a large apartment building nearby. Murray looked up, and his eyes sparkled. After the second intermission, the sun fell behind that building and the ice started refreezing. In the last period, we caught up easily and won the game 4–2. Everybody was happy about winning our first game.

The next morning we traveled to Lucerne, a very picturesque city on the beautiful shores of Vierwaldstaetter Lake, where we played the same Swiss National Team that we had played in Basel and beat them again, 4–2. We also took a cable-car ride up Mount Pilatus. At the top of the mountain there were two hotels and a lot of snow. In fact, there was so much snow that a tunnel had been dug so people could walk from the one hotel to the other. We had lunch in the more modern hotel, which had large picture windows all around the dining room.

The next morning we boarded a bus for Geneva and drove straight to the ice rink. The rink manager was a Frenchman who only spoke French. Murray told me to tell him that we'd like to practice late that afternoon, if possible. At that very same time, our bus driver, who only spoke German, wanted to know if we were going to unload our gear at the rink or continue to the hotel. So, there I was, juggling three different

conversations with three different people in three different languages. At one point I explained something to Murray—in either French or German—and he listened very intently before finally admitting, "Doc, Doc, hang on. I don't understand a word you're saying." I'd mixed up my languages! We had a good, hard laugh, but we straightened everything out.

On our way to Geneva, I'd told the boys that on a nice, sunny day there is a beautiful view across the lake to Mont Blanc, the highest peak in Europe. Unfortunately, I'd explained, the weather is usually foggy and misty, as it was when we arrived. Nonetheless, almost immediately the guys started asking, "Doc, when are we going to go see Mont Blanc?"

So I went to Murray and said, "Coach, what do you think? Our last day here, after the tournament, we don't fly to Vienna until five in the evening. If it's nice, do you think we should take the team to Chamonix, France, to see Mont Blanc?"

"That's an excellent idea, Doc! I think we should do it," Murray said.

So, I went downtown to travel agency and said, "Sunday, March twelfth, if there is good weather—but only if there is good weather—we would like to arrange for a bus for about forty persons to pick up at the Hotel Montana for a trip to Chamonix starting at nine o'clock a.m."

Meanwhile, we visited the Palace of Nations and practiced at the local rink to get ready for the tournament. As it turned out, there was a big automobile exposition in Geneva in conjunction with our visit. To attract more people to the auto show, the promoters had created this hockey tournament, called the Coup Perrot–Duval, featuring the Swiss National Team, the championship team from Moscow, the championship team from Czechoslovakia, and the US National Team.

Our first opponent was the Soviet Union. We'd played Soviet teams before and knew how difficult it was to stop them once they got their slick passing game going. Therefore, Murray wanted to surprise them by forechecking them so hard at the beginning that they couldn't get into their usual rhythm.

On the day of the game, Murray's strategy worked beautifully. The Soviets were completely confused by our forecheck, and we won the game 4–2, which surprised many people. Now we were in the finals!

On the other side of the bracket, the Czechoslovakians played the Swiss National Team the next day. It was an easy game for the Czechs, and the finals were set: Team USA versus the Czechoslovakian league champions on Saturday, March 11, 1967.

It was one of the most interesting games I've ever seen. The Czechs had seen us play the Soviets and reorganized their breakout and their offensive strategy accordingly. We'd had great success forechecking the Soviets, but not so with the Czechoslovakians. Instead of their usual short passing attack, they opted for long breakout passes, quickly pushing the puck up ice through the neutral zone into their offensive end. We skated very hard to keep up, trading goals the whole night. First, it was 1–0 for the Czechs, then 1–1. Then 2–1 for the Czechs and 2–2. Then 3–2 for us and again 3–3. The Czechs made it 4–3 for them, but we

equalized it at 4–4. Then, a couple minutes before the end of the game, Johnny Cunniff scored our fifth goal, which proved to be decisive.

At that point, a Czech defenseman got so mad that he checked Cunniff very hard in the boards behind the net, causing a severe injury to Johnny's shoulder. After that, our game plan was just to clear the puck out of our zone during the last minutes of the game—and it worked. We held the score and won the game 5–4.

A lot of people were very excited that the American team won the Perrot–Duval Cup, which had never happened before. Many individuals came down behind the bench and gave us notes inviting the whole team to their homes or places of business and letting us know they would be waiting for us outside, but the game was not over yet. I gave all those notes to Murray because I knew that I would have to take John Cunniff to the hospital for x-rays to see if there was a fracture.

Right after the game there was a big, happy ceremony. Our defenseman, Donnie Ross, from Roseau, Minnesota, was voted the tournament's Most Valuable Player. Everybody was in a very happy mood except Cunniff, who was hurting badly. I told Murray that I needed to take Johnny to the hospital and asked where the team was going after the ceremony.

Murray selected the place, and I got the address and planned to join them after we were through at the hospital. It was Saturday evening, and service at the hospital was not prompt. We waited quite a while for the x-rays to be done. Finally, I asked to see the film and said, "We don't need a reading by an x-ray man. I can tell very well what's what, and we won't bother you any longer." They let me see the film, and I was happy to see that there wasn't a fracture, only a second-degree acromioclavicular (AC) joint separation of the shoulder. However, this was very bad news for our team. Johnny would be out for at least a week or two and probably would miss some early games at the World Championships in Vienna.

After Johnny was through at the hospital, we took a taxi to the party. Everybody was happy about our win and having a good time, but I could see that Johnny could not get comfortable. I asked Johnny if he would rather go home and rest. He said, "Doc, I don't think I am enjoying this party very much." So we hailed a taxi and went home early from the party.

I was surprised when I woke up the next morning. My room had never been so bright! *What was happening*? *Could it be that the sun was shining*? I went to the window, and sure enough, the sky was bright and clear. It was a beautiful day. The bus would be here in one hour to take our team to Chamonix to see Mont Blanc!

I knew the boys had gotten home from the party around four or five in the morning and were sound asleep. *Now what*? I showered and shaved quickly and went to wake up Murray. I said, "Murray, what are we going to do? The bus to Chamonix will be here any minute."

"We should go, we should go!" said Murray.

Quickly, we both went door-to-door and woke up every player. Most of them moaned and groaned, pleading with us to let them sleep, but I said, "You guys asked me every day when we would see Mont Blanc. Today is the day. Get up. We are going to see Mont Blanc." The only player I gave a choice was Johnny, who said that he was really uncomfortable and needed to stay home and rest.

At about ten minutes to nine, the bus arrived. While boarding, I reminded everyone to take their passports because Chamonix is in France, and there would be a passport check at the border. Finally, everyone was on the bus and we started our trip. Later, as we approached the border, I said, "Please have your passports ready. We need to show them to the border guard." Right away, Ron Naslund said, "Doc, I'm sorry. I thought I had my passport in this jacket, but I don't. It must be in my other jacket." *Oh boy, here we go*! But that good old postcard was our savior again.

As we stopped at the border checkpoint, I spoke to the border guard in French and told him that we had just won the Perrot–Duval Cup in Geneva and didn't want to leave without seeing Mont Blanc and Chamonix. I buttered him up with compliments and gave him a postcard as a souvenir. Then I explained that one of our players didn't have his passport and showed him Ron Naslund's picture on the postcard. "We have only two or three hours to see Chamonix," I said in French, "please let him go, and we'll be back in three hours." The border guard finally relented but cautioned, "You absolutely need to be back within three hours because a different guard will be on duty after that." We promised to be back on time, crossed the Swiss–French border, and started winding our way up one tight hairpin turn after another to Chamonix.

As we entered the town, massive Mont Blanc was on the right and Mount Breve was on the left. There is no skiing on Mont Blanc, but there is on Mount Breve, where a cable car runs up the steep cliff from the ground station to the upper station. Of course, our resident practical joker, Donnie Ross, had to scare everyone to death by saying, "Hey, guys! Look at that huge rock by the cable car! Last year an airplane hit and the damn thing went down, killing everyone!" The trouble was, Donnie was right, but I couldn't say that because then nobody would want to take the cable car up to the peak. So, I quickly fabricated a story that there was such an incident in these mountains, but not here. Nobody knew the area anyway, so I made up the name of a fictitious village and was able to calm some of them down. When we arrived at the ground station, though, most of the players were still hesitant to take the cable car and said they would rather browse around in Chamonix. In the end, just six or seven players decided to go.

Naturally, as we were waiting in line for the cable car, Donnie Ross pointed to the big wheel and the metal cable on which the cable car hung. "Look, look," he said, "that damn cable is so old and worn out it will break any minute!"

I said, "Donnie, would you please shut up? These cables are inspected regularly and are very safe!"

Eventually, our group made it up to Mount Breve, where we had a majestic view across the road to Mont Blanc. The sun was shining, and skiers were enjoying the day. We took some pictures and relaxed with a cup of coffee in the restaurant at the top of the mountain. Everybody enjoyed the beautiful scenery, but we couldn't stay too long because we had to be back at the border by three o'clock.

As we got back down to the ground station, Craig Falkman turned to me and said, with a worried look on his face, "Doc, I don't have my passport anymore." My heart sank. I asked him what could've happened. He said, "I think when I used the restroom up at the restaurant, it fell out of my pocket." We immediately turned around and took the cable car up to retrieve it. As soon as we reached the top, we went to the bathroom Craig had used. No passport. I said, "People here are very honest. Let's go to the counter at the cafeteria and see if anyone turned it in."

"Yes," said the woman at the counter, "someone found an American passport in the bathroom, but we gave it to an American skier to take to the American Embassy in the morning."

I said, "We have a flight to Vienna at six o'clock. We need to find that skier!"

They were very cooperative and sent out the ski patrol, as well as asking over the loudspeaker for the skier with the passport to return to the restaurant immediately. A few minutes later, though, we couldn't wait any longer or we would miss the border crossing at three o'clock, when our border guard went off duty. I told the woman to tell the American skier to bring the passport to the airport as soon as possible.

Craig and I returned to the ground station, knowing that Craig couldn't board the plane without his passport. Meanwhile, the bus driver was very upset, knowing how much he needed to hurry to make it back to Geneva on time. We quickly got on the bus, and the driver sped off, taking those hairpin turns at high speed. Players started screaming, "Doc, Doc, he's going to kill us!" I did my best to keep everyone calm, but suddenly a big truck with a load of logs groaned by on the inside as we took the outside curve. *Just don't look down*, I thought, and we made it. *Whew!* By the time we hit the border, everybody was exhausted and sound asleep. But now I had two players without passports. Luckily, the same border guard was still on duty. I thanked him for his kindness and held my breath as he entered the bus. Everyone was sleeping. He looked around and laughed. "Yes, yes," he said, "they look like real champs!"

We returned to the hotel, quickly packed our bags, and left for the airport, where we waited for Craig's passport as the minutes tensely ticked by. Soon they started boarding the plane, but the skier still hadn't arrived.

I suggested to Murray that we explain our situation to the airport supervisor. My French language skills helped again as I explained the problem to the supervisor, who was very understanding and helpful. "Okay," he said, "I will let Mr. Falkman board the plane to Zürich, but there you will need to change planes for your flight to Vienna. As soon as you land in Zürich, call me. If by then I have the passport, everything will be fine. I'll call Austrian Airlines to tell them I have the passport, and they should let Mr. Falkman board the plane to Vienna. I will also call Vienna to tell them I will send the passport on the next available plane. They will need to arrange for a customs officer to escort Mr. Falkman through passport control in

Vienna." It sounded like a good plan. "But," said the airport supervisor, "if I don't have the passport when you land, Mr. Falkman will be stuck in Zürich until I get it." Murray and I were very thankful, and we all boarded the plane.

The moment we landed in Zürich, I ran to the telephone and called the airport supervisor in Geneva. Thankfully, he said, "Yes! I have a passport for Mr. Craig Dean Falkman!" Oh, God, we were all so happy! I asked the supervisor how could we reimburse him for all this wonderful help. We would be glad to send him a check right away, but he answered that he was very happy to help and we didn't owe him a thing. Of course, before we boarded the plane to Vienna, Murray asked me not to tell Craig the details, that the customs officers were set to escort him personally off the plane and directly through passport control. It would be a big surprise. Everybody was happy, knowing Craig's passport was found.

Shortly before arriving in Vienna, the pilot said, "Ladies and gentlemen, we are approaching Vienna Airport. Please remain seated once we land, since local security guards will be coming aboard to escort a passenger out. Only after that can other passengers move and exit the plane." Everyone started buzzing, wondering what the pilot meant. Was there a prisoner on board, or a criminal? Murray and I sat quietly, not blinking an eye. We landed in Vienna, and everybody waited for the security guards to come.

Sure enough, two stern-looking military men came onto the plane. The stewardess announced, "Mr. Craig Falkman, please come over here." Craig was surprised

At the airport in Vienna on Sunday, March 12, 1967 (L-R): Jerry Melnychuk; Len Lilyholm; Dick Rose; our stewardess, holding the Perrot-Duval Cup trophy; myself; Tom Hurley; Art Miller; and Murray Williamson.

and nervously asked, "Excuse me?" The other players all wondered what the heck Craig had done. In the back of the plane, Murray and I started laughing. Finally, I got up, went to Craig, and explained, "This is because you don't have your passport. These guards are here to escort you through passport control and customs. Meet us on the other side. Everything is fine." Craig slowly smiled, relieved, and got up to join his military escorts.

As the rest of us started to disembark, the pilot congratulated us, announcing, "We are happy to have had the winners of the Perrot–Duval Cup on board, the American National Hockey Team, who won the championship game last night in Geneva! Congratulations!" Everybody applauded. Then Doc Rose, some of the other guys, and I lifted our stewardess onto our shoulders and carried her through the airport while she held the Perrot–Duval Cup aloft. Everybody was laughing, celebrating, and having a good time. We were greeted like heroes in Vienna!

Captain Bob Currie, Marty Howe, and myself in front of Opera House in Vienna

3

My First World Championships
Vienna, Austria, 1967

After our adventure, it was nice to finally arrive at the Intercontinental Hotel, where all of the teams were quartered. The location was perfect, right across from City Park, where the beautiful Johann Strauss Monument stands. City Park is also where a lot of people with children stroll and promenade, chatting and enjoying the city, in a relaxed and happy mood, as the Viennese usually are.

Our first game was set for the following day, an exhibition against a Czechoslovakian team from Bratislava to celebrate the opening of the new Stadthalle, the Viennese civic center. The game was good and clean. We won 6–4 and were happy to have won our first game in Vienna.

The next day we went to Graz, where the Austrian National Hockey Federation had invited us to play when they'd visited Minneapolis in January 1967. The Austrians provided a nice bus to bring us to Graz, a well-known university city in the southeastern corner of Austria. The road there wound through the vineyards of Gumpoldskirchen and over the hills of Semmering, a region famous for its ski slopes and resorts.

Back in Minneapolis we'd had an easy game against the Austrians. Naturally, we thought this game would be easy too, and we treated it almost like a practice. Even Murray toyed with the idea of suiting up and playing. That never happened, however, because we got a big surprise. The boisterous crowd encouraged the home team, who played very well, and they got off to an early lead. We had our hands full catching up, but we managed to win the game 5–4. After the game, we took the bus back to Vienna. We now had two more days to practice and prepare for the World Championships.

On Saturday, March 18, we played Sweden in our first game of the tournament. It was a good, hard game, and we were lucky to come away with a 4–3 victory. It was a good start, and we were very happy about it.

After getting back to the hotel, the boys all went to their rooms to get a good night's rest. Meanwhile, Murray and I went down to have a beer at the famous Grinzingkeller, in the Paulus Stübel, with our good Austrian friend Rudi Novak.

The next day, we played the Soviets. We knew it would be a difficult game, and it was. We lost 7–2, but our boys put up a good fight.

Monday was our day off. After a light morning practice we decided to go see the world-famous Lipizzaner stallions at the Spanish Riding School, as it's known locally. It's an often overlooked fact, but there is a great deal of Spanish history interwoven with that of Austria's Hapsburg Dynasty. Through marriages to French and Spanish wives, the Austrian monarchy became rulers of the Holy Roman Empire in the early 1500s. In 1526, Ferdinand I became the ruler of Austria and brought considerable Spanish influence to the Austrian court. His son, Maximillian II, established the Spanish Riding School in 1580. In 1735, under Emperor Charles VI, construction of

the new Winter Riding Hall was completed, and the Lipizzaners perform there to this day. In fact, as the riders enter, they lift their bicorn hats in a salute to the portrait of Charles VI that hangs in the elegant Court Box.

The smooth, athletic movements of the powerful horses were mesmerizing to watch. Everyone was duly impressed and greatly enjoyed the show. We returned to the hotel relaxed and in very high spirits.

The next day we played Czechoslovakia, one of the strongest teams in the tournament. We played hard but lost the game 8–3. We were not discouraged, however, because we'd played hard against a very strong opponent.

After a tough game, it was nice to have the next day off. It was a crisp, sunny spring day, so we all decided to visit Schönbrunn Palace, designed by the famous Viennese baroque architect Johann Bernhard Fischer von Erlach in 1695. It was a lovely afternoon.

That evening I had plans to go to the opera *Tosca* with Rudi Novak. I was very excited to see the beautiful Vienna Opera House and decided to take an early dinner at our hotel. The boys would eat a bit later.

As I sat down and looked at the menu, I heard a commotion in the lobby. Carl Wetzel and Herbie Brooks were cooking up a practical joke to play on Doc Rose and Don Niederkorn. Carl was pretty good at disguising his voice, so he called Doc Rose's room pretending to be a Swedish hockey equipment manufacturer who wanted to see some American protective equipment. He would appreciate it very much, he said, if Doc Rose and the equipment manager would meet him in the lobby to show him some equipment. Afterwards, they would all go out to dinner together.

The first time Carl called, Rosie said, "Carl, I know it's you," and hung up the phone. Carl called again, but Rosie hung up again. So Carl called Murray and told him what was up. Murray always liked a good joke, so he went along with the prank and they both ganged up on Rosie. Murray called Doc Rose and said, "Rosie, what are you doing? The Swedes are complaining that you won't cooperate with them. Stop screwing around!"

A few minutes after that, Wetzel called Rosie again. Suddenly, he was very cooperative and said, "Yes, sir. Yes, sir. I'll be right down."

By now it was time for me to leave for the opera. As I left the hotel, I saw Rosie and Don sitting in the entrance hall with a bunch of hockey equipment, patiently waiting for some mythical Swedish official. Meanwhile, Herb and some of the other players were giving Rosie and Niederkorn grief about not joining the team for dinner. Rosie and Niederkorn waited and waited, but nobody ever came. After a while, they knew Wetzel and Murray had tricked them, but by then they'd already missed dinner. All of us, at one time, were the butt of Wetzel's, Brooks's, or Don Ross's practical jokes.

The game against Canada was hard. Most of the players from both teams knew each other well from junior leagues or college games, which kept the scoring low. It was a rare treat to watch Carl Brewer, however, a reinstated amateur who'd won three consecutive Stanley Cups with the Toronto Maple Leafs

from 1962 to 1964. He was a natural playmaker and the most dangerous player, by far, on the Canadian team.

Going into the last period, the score was tied 1–1 and it looked like it might end that way. Suddenly, Donnie Ross's stick got a little too high, and he was called for crosschecking. The Canadians scored on the ensuing power play and the game ended 2–1, an unfortunate way for us to lose the game.

The next day was Good Friday, a very quiet day in Austria. All of the shops were closed, and there were no shows or concerts. We spent the day relaxing at the hotel, walking, and window shopping. I read the local paper, which praised our game against Canada very highly. They complimented both teams, saying, "It was very nice to see a hard, clean, well-played game."

On Saturday, March 25, we played East Germany. The East German goalie was hot, and they played a great defensive game. We couldn't find a way to score, and the game ended 0–0. We were disappointed we didn't win, but at least we didn't lose.

Easter Sunday was a crisp, sunny spring day. Since we didn't play the Finns until 5:00 p.m., everybody wondered which church service to attend. There are many beautiful churches in Vienna, but Craig Falkman and Len Lilyholm wanted to join me at historic Saint Stephen's Cathedral, built in 1144. It was burned and rebuilt several times over the years and exhibits a variety of architectural styles. The atmosphere was festive, and we enjoyed the sermon and singing greatly. After we left Saint Stephen's, we also visited the Franciscan Church with its twisting, orange-brown marble columns, beautiful stained glass windows, and lavish wall paintings.

On the way home, we went for a stroll through City Park. The air was fresh and brisk and we enjoyed it wholeheartedly. After lunch, we rested and got ready for the game.

Carl was fantastic in goal and we beat the Finns 2–0. Now, we were very happy because there was only one game left, against West Germany, widely considered to be one of the weaker teams in the tournament.

That night, Rudi and some other Austrian friends suggested that we celebrate with dinner at the Csardasfürstin, meaning "Gypsy Princess," a well-known traditonal restaurant named for the Emmerich Kalman operetta which premiered in Vienna in 1915. They made reservations, and we walked down Schwarzenbergplatz to the nice little restaurant. As soon as we walked in, a band greeted us with traditional music. All of them were dressed in red, white, and green, the colors of the Hungarian flag. The restaurant manager welcomed us and showed us to our table in a cozy corner. First we had a glass of a Kremser Schmidt white wine. Then each of us ordered our meal of lamb, veal, or pork with paprika and other Hungarian spices. The meals were served on wooden plates or—for those who'd ordered more traditional Hungarian dishes—presented in a black, cast-iron kettle like those that hang over an open fire.

After a while, the band came to our table. It is customary to ask them to play your favorite tune and then reward them with money or drinks for their performance. I asked our waiter which drink was their favorite, and he told me that they liked cherry brandy the best. So, I ordered a round of cherry brandies at the next intermission, and they were our friends for the rest of the night. This was a wonderful finale to our Easter Sunday. We were still humming some of Kalman's famous tunes as we walked back to our hotel.

The next day we didn't have a game. Since it was our last free day, Craig, Lenny, and I walked down to the Rathskeller, the beer hall in the basement of City Hall. We went to the smaller, common room, where people were eating, drinking, and singing to Schrammelmusik, a popular style of Viennese folk music. After finding a nice little table, we ordered some house wine and Wiener schnitzel. We enjoyed our meal and the music and had a good time.

After a while, Craig said, "Look, Doc, isn't that Murray over there?" Sure enough, it was our coach and general manager, Murray Williamson, in the room across the hall, enjoying dinner with some Austrian friends.

Lenny said, "Why don't we ask the Schrammel musicians to play a special song for Murray?" Craig and I thought it was a great idea. When the musicians arrived at our table, we made our request, gave them a tip, and said, "See that table over there? Go play them a song and say, 'This is a special request for Murray.'" Then we watched to see what would happen. Sure enough, the musicians went to Murray's table and played the song we'd requested. After playing it, they said, "This was especially for Murray." You could see Murray's excitement. He started looking around, trying to figure out what was going on. We were across the hall, just laughing our heads off. After a while, Murray spotted us and waved as if to say, "Oh, you sneaky fellows!"

The next day was our last game, against West Germany. During the morning skate it looked to me like Johnny Cunniff was moving his shoulder and arm pretty well. The soreness and swelling were gone. Johnny was begging me, "Doc, please let me play this game. I feel really good." I didn't see why not. The West Germans were one of the weaker teams, so I let him play.

Things started quite well. We did not have much action at our end of the rink. Carl Wetzel was just standing around his net. Suddenly, action increased around our net, and then Carl went down, grabbing his head. Some players called me over, saying, "Doc, Doc! Carl got hurt!" I got on the ice and saw that Carl had a little cut on his head. I said, "Carl, you need a couple stitches." He said, "No, no, Doc, not now. I feel fine. Just bandage it." He was alert, not knocked out or drowsy. I wrapped a big bandage around the wound and let him play until the end of the game. After the game, I took him to the first-aid room and put a few stitches in his head. We won the game 8–3 and were very happy to have started and finished with a win.

The game was over at about 7:30 p.m., and the banquet was scheduled for the next day, so we had the whole evening to ourselves. Murray thought it was a good time for the whole team to celebrate. Where should we go? No other place than Grinzing, that little suburb of Vienna full of small, cozy wine restaurants.

Most of those places have gardens that are lit with lamps and lanterns, making it very intimate and pleasant. It was an early spring day, and the weather was not very warm yet. We had made reservations for indoor seating, and the host had a nice, big corner table for all of us in a nicely decorated room with a very festive and relaxed atmosphere. The other patrons greeted us, and we all had a wonderful time. We tasted the young wine, as is the custom, and listened to Grinzing songs and some other Viennese tunes. Soon everyone was in good and friendly spirits, and we had a wonderful time on our last evening in Vienna. We couldn't have left that wonderful city without visiting in Grinzing and feeling that Viennese spirit of friendship.

Wednesday, March 29, was the tournament banquet at the Rathaus (city hall). I had plans to leave for Kitzbühel, in Tyrol, right after dinner. Trainer Doc Rose and Doug Woog, then a player, were set to join me for a few days. After packing our gear, we went to the banquet, which was well organized and festive. We had a great meal and were happy for our goalie, Carl Wetzel, who was honored as the best goalie of the tournament. We ordered a bottle of good wine to celebrate Carl's award. It was the icing on the cake for the whole championship.

1968 US Olympic Hockey Team on the way to Grenoble, France. In front (L-R): John Cunniff, Larry Pleau, Herb Brooks, Pat Rupp, Craig Falkman, Jack Morrison, Lou Nanne, Bob Paradise, Paul Hurley, Larry Stordahl, Jim Logue, Doug Volmar, Murray Williamson. On the steps, from seven o'clock and up: Jack Dale, Bob Gaudreau, Don Ross, Dick Rose, Don Niederkorn, Bruce Riutta, myself, Tom Hurley. Not pictured: Len Lilyholm.

The 10th Olympic Winter Games

Grenoble, France, 1968

Team Roster

In Goal: *Patrick Rupp, James Logue*

Defense: *Robert Gaudreau, Paul Hurley, Lou Nanne, Robert Paradise, Bruce Riutta, Donald Ross*

Forwards: *Herb Brooks, John Cunniff, Jack Dale, Craig Falkman, Tom Hurley, Len Lilyholm, Jack Morrison, Larry Stordahl, Larry Pleau, Douglas Volmar*

During the Winter Sports Medicine Conference in Madison, Wisconsin, in January 1967, Dr. Merritt H. Stiles asked me to join his staff for the 1968 Winter Olympic Games in Grenoble, France. Meanwhile, USA Hockey, together with the US Olympic Committee, had selected Murray Williamson as coach and general manager. Williamson, in turn, chose Doc Rose as trainer and Don Niederkorn as equipment manager, as well as requesting me as team physician. I was thrilled by the invitation, but weeks of official negotiations with the US Olympic Committee followed before I finally got the official assignment.

The hockey team itself was assembled in September to play a pre-Olympic

Munich Airport with Lou Nanne

tour of Europe and Canada and then reassembled on October 16, 1967, for training camp at the Metropolitan Sports Center (MSC) in Bloomington, Minnesota, home of the NHL expansion Minnesota North Stars.

The boys made good progress in October and November, practicing and playing hard as the Thanksgiving break approached. Since several players were far from their homes on the East Coast or Michigan, my wife Velta and I invited them to Thanksgiving dinner at our house. On the way home from that day's practice, the boys and I picked up a lot of milk and some other refreshing drinks. Meanwhile, Velta had prepared a big turkey with all

the trimmings, as well as a large ham. It was a great Thanksgiving dinner and made the boys very happy.

A heavier schedule, with more international games, followed in December. Our first game, against the Canadians in Winnipeg, was on December 13. We were lucky to come away with a 4–4 tie.

We played two games against the Soviets on December 17 and 19. The first was in Duluth and the second at the MSC. The Duluth rink was small, which worked in our favor, and we dominated play throughout much of the game. Late in the third period, the score was tied 3–3. Then, with about six minutes left to go, a Soviet player speared Craig Falkman with the blade of his stick. Falkman retaliated with an elbow, and the referee called a two-minute penalty. Up to that point, we'd really outplayed the Soviets and had them on their heels. We felt it was just a matter of time before we scored the go-ahead goal. Suddenly, with the Soviets on the power play, the game changed completely. Sure enough, they scored to make it 4–3. In the last minute of play, we pulled goalie Pat Rupp and they scored on the empty net. The gamed ended 5–3 in favor of the Soviets.

On the way back to Minneapolis, referee Gordie Lee was on our flight. We were so mad at him that we wanted to throw him off the plane. I asked him, "Gordie, how could you do that to us? Why didn't you call the Soviet player for spearing? That's why Falk threw the elbow!" Gordie said, "I didn't see the spear, Doc. I only saw the elbow. I had to call it." It was very unfortunate to lose the game that way because we were so close to winning.

Two days later we played the same Soviet team at MSC in Bloomington, a much larger rink. With the extra room to maneuver, superstar Valeri Kharlamov—who in 2008 was one of just six players voted to the IIHF Centennial All-Star Team—really put on a show. At just twenty years of age, Kharlamov was already one of the fastest skaters in the world and an extremely skilled puck handler. He did things with ease that seemed impossible for others. As Mike Eruzione said, after facing him several years later, "It seemed his feet never touched the ice." The boys played very well, but we lost the game 3–2.

After the game there was a banquet. The captain of the Soviet team, Vitaly Davydov, who spoke some French, came up to me and asked to speak with our captain, Lou Nanne. So, I introduced Louie to Davydov and acted as interpreter. Davydov, who'd already won a gold medal in Innsbruck in 1964, told Lou that the United States had talented players, but lacked teamwork. Lou smirked and said, "We can only work so much *on the ice* because we have to work *off the ice*."

At that time, well before NHL players started competing in the Olympics, national teams were comprised of amateurs. It was common knowledge, however, that the Soviet players were "professional amateurs," officially employed by the Soviet army. They were also given preferential treatment, such as access to better housing and cars, and allowed to shop at nicer department stores. This was a constant source

of aggravation for North American players like Louie, who felt the system was unfair, rigged in favor of the Soviet "Red Army," as the team was known. Now that Nanne had the chance to voice his opinion, he wasn't going to miss it.

Checking medications at the Dispensary with Dr. Daniel Hanley.

Davydov responded simply, "Louie, you don't work when you play hockey for the US National Team."

Louie said, "Oh yes we do. Don't you?"

Davydov said, "No, when I play for the National Team, I don't have to work."

Louie seized his chance. "Then you're a professional," he said.

Davydov answered, "No, no, I am *not* a professional with a big salary like Bobby Hull. I get a teacher's salary."

At that moment I interrupted politely and said, "Davydov, okay, you get your teacher's salary, but you also get special privileges, too, like a better apartment, a car, a special shopping card, and friendly customs

February 1968, Kitzbühel-Tyrol, Austria (L-R): Len Lilyholm, Herb Brooks, Karen Brooks (Dave Brooks's wife), Dave Brooks, and myself.

agents who never check your bags when you return from a trip abroad."

Davydov looked at me with surprise and asked, "How did you know that?"

Louie interjected, "Doc is from Riga, Latvia, that's why he knows those things."

So Davydov spoke to me in Russian, but I continued in French, saying, "No, I understand, but I cannot speak the Russian language very well."

At the end of our conversation, Davydov once again stressed the need for more frequent practices and teamwork. We just smiled and said, "Yes, yes, we will try to do that."

On January 7 and 9 we had two final games in Duluth against international teams before leaving for Europe. The first game was against Sweden. Our team played very well, and we won the game 6–1. Two nights later we played Canada. It was a much harder game, and we lost 5–2.

So, after two weeks of practices and exhibition games, we flew to New York for outfitting before continuing on to Munich. We took a team picture in front of our Lufthansa jet, but Len Lilyholm was on the phone with his wife, Carol, who had just given birth to their second daughter, Gretchen. Eventually, Lenny boarded the plane, we all congratulated him, and the plane took off for Munich.

The next morning, however, we couldn't land in Munich because of very thick fog. Instead, we flew to Nuremberg and took a bus to Munich. The day after that, we took another bus to Bad Tölz, a pretty little town in the Bavarian mountains, for a game against the West Germans. We won the game, but we didn't enjoy it at all because the West Germans were quite chippy, hooking and slashing our players with their sticks—a sign of things to come.

Monday, January 29, was our day off. After an early practice, Herb Brooks, Lenny, and I drove to Kitzbühel in Tyrol, Austria, where Herb's younger brother, David, played hockey. It was a nice, sunny day, and the drive was very scenic as we wound over the Bavarian mountains and through the Tyrolean Alps. David and his wife, Karen, were very happy to see us. We walked through the town, went to see the hockey rink where David played, and had lunch at a typical Tyrolean restaurant. Afterwards we returned to Bad Tölz and had a very relaxed evening with the rest of the boys.

The next day we drove to Garmisch-Partenkirchen, another beautiful Bavarian town near the Alpspitze and Zugspitze, two of Germany's picturesque peaks, for our second game against the West Germans. The chippiness continued, escalating, in fact, until a West German player speared Herb Brooks in the stomach. Herb retaliated by pounding the West German into the boards. The referee blew the whistle and gave Herb a two-minute penalty for boarding. Herb argued the call but went to the penalty box. At that moment, the West German player skated over to Herb, stuck out his tongue, and made a nasty comment. Herb dropped his gloves and went after the West German player. Suddenly, out of nowhere, the West German goalie joined the fray and hit Herb over the head with his stick. That was the final straw. Johnny Cunniff jumped on the West German goalie and started beating him up very badly, prompting a bench-clearing brawl. In order to regain control, the referees suspended the game and gave us many

penalties. After lengthy conferences with the coaches of both teams, the game was started again, but we had to play shorthanded for the duration. Ultimately, we lost the game, but we knew the West Germans could never play like that at the Olympics in Grenoble.

The next morning we returned to Munich and then went on to Geneva to play the Canadians. People in Geneva were very excited about the contest and expected a hard, physical game, which wasn't the case

With Len Lilyholm (left) and Don Ross in front of the Olympic Medical Dispensary.

at all. Players from both teams knew each other well from playing together at various universities and colleges in the United States. I also knew the Canadian team doctor very well, and we always helped each other when we could. The game was exciting and

L-R: Jack Dale, Herb Brooks, Dick Rose, Lou Nanne, myself, Len Lilyholm, Doug Volmar, Bob Paradise.
At the Olympic Village in Grenoble.

clean, with the advantage shifting continuously back and forth. Finally, the Canadians won the game 6–5.

On the morning of February 4 we boarded the bus to Grenoble. Winding through the narrow streets of some of those picturesque French villages, we often wondered if our bus would fit! We arrived at Grenoble in the afternoon and unloaded into our new quarters. I was stationed in the Infirmerie Olympique together

with two other doctors and two trainers of the United States medical team. Two young, pretty French girls served as our interpreters and assistants.

The next morning, the team practiced early while I attended a medical meeting. This was the year doping control began, so we were briefed about all the new rules and regulations. Two hours before each game, the team physician was required to submit a list of players who had taken any medications during the last three days. Then, after each game, two random players from each team would be tested. In those first three years, the rules and regulations, and especially the sanctions for a positive doping test, were much stricter than they are today.

The spectacular opening ceremony of the tenth Olympic Winter Games took place on February 6, 1968. After the teams had entered the stadium, led by their respective flag bearers, five parachutists in the five Olympic colors landed in matching Olympic rings on the stadium grounds. The Olympic flag was raised, and the runner bearing the Olympic torch ignited the Olympic flame. Finally, the French president, General Charles de Gaulle, officially opened the games by releasing colorful balloons and white pigeons. Many people had to cover their heads in a hurry!

Later that evening we played our first game against a very strong Czechoslovakian team. We knew the game would be tough because they were not only very good skaters, but also very skilled technically. We lost the game 5–1.

The next day, February 7, our opponent was Sweden. We were playing well, with a 2–1 lead in the second period, when Craig Falkman, one of our best forwards, ran into the boards and dislocated his right ankle. As I ran onto the ice, I saw that Craig's right foot was almost ninety degrees out of its normal position. He was in tremendous pain. "Craig, clench your teeth," I told him, "I have to get the foot back in the right position."

I stabilized the ankle with one hand, grabbed

Craig Falkman, with foot bandaged, with myself.

the skate with my other hand, pulled down hard, and turned the foot back to its normal position. Craig's pain was somewhat relieved, but now I was concerned that I could have chipped off a piece of bone in the process. Craig was taken off the ice by stretcher, and another US Olympic team physician, Dr. Daniel Hanley, volunteered to accompany him to the hospital.

After Craig's injury, our game plan was completely disrupted. Our top scoring line, with Larry

Pleau at center and Len Lilyholm and Craig Falkman at the wings, was gone. Murray tried to juggle the lines, but nothing worked and we lost the game 4–3.

After the game was over, I tried to get in touch with the hospital to check on Falkman's injury, but the Frenchmen in the first-aid room couldn't get me the right hospital on the phone. Finally, I got ahold of Dr. Hanley. He told me there was no fracture, only badly injured ligaments, and that Craig's right leg was in a cast.

In the middle of the night, Craig's roommate, Herb Brooks, came to the Infirmerie Olympique and said, "Doc, can you come over? Craig is in agony." Immediately I thought it had to be pressure from that cast. I couldn't find a cast cutter, so I grabbed a large bandage scissor and ran over to Craig's room. Sure enough, the toes of his right foot were blue. It was an ordeal to get that cast off with my pocketknife and a bandage scissor, but I did and his pain was relieved almost completely. I stabilized the injured right ankle for the night with a heavy elastic bandage, using the cut-up cast for support, and gave Craig a couple of Tylenols for pain. The next morning, Craig came to the Infirmerie Olympique and our orthopedic doctor applied a new bivalve cast that could be better adjusted for tightness and stability. I advised Craig to keep his right foot elevated during the night and to take a couple of Tylenols at bedtime.

On February 9 we played the Soviets. They were the clear Olympic favorite, led by their newest star, Anatoli Firsov, a very fast skater and excellent stick-handler with a good, hard shot. The game was very difficult, and we lost 10–2. After the game, two players from each team were required to go to doping control with their doctors. When we arrived, the Soviets were already there, and one of their players, Alexander Ragulin, was swearing ferociously. Our two players had already gone through the doping control procedure, but Ragulin couldn't produce any urine and was still sitting there, cursing, when we left.

On the morning of Sunday, February 11, I got a call from the medical staff at the luge track in Villard de Lans. Because of a scheduling mix-up, they were short staffed and needed help. I grabbed my medical bag and hailed a taxi, but the driver was from Paris and didn't know the streets of Grenoble very well. Luckily, I'd walked around town before and remembered the signpost for Villard de Lans.

As soon as I arrived, the trainer from the luge team explained what had happened to the schedule. Originally, the plan had been for the women to go first. Because of bad weather, however, officials in charge of the luge event decided to start with the men. Our men were thus unprepared when they were awoken earlier than planned.

As I walked down to the luge track, an American luger walked up with Band-Aids all over his face. He looked pretty bad. I asked incredulously, "What happened to you?"

He said, "I thought the women would go first. I was sound asleep when they woke me up. I was still half-asleep when I started down the track. On the first curve I lost my sled and was thrown off the track. I landed in a bush and scratched my face. It looks worse than it is. I am fine, but my sled hit an Italian spectator and broke his leg. Boy, was he mad about that!"

In any case, the men had already finished and the women would be starting soon. Our trainer pointed out the most dangerous part of the run, and we walked over to that section of track. I had my movie camera with me and wanted to film the US women's runs. We knew the US women would follow the Italians, so I decided to practice the shot and make adjustments by looking through the viewfinder at the final Italian woman's run.

I followed her through the viewfinder as she sped down the track through the S-curve. Suddenly, she lost her balance. The luge was shaking side to side as she hit the U-curve, and she was thrown from her sled, which hit her hard. Our trainer started yelling, "Doc! Doc, this girl is badly hurt!"

I ran over to her. She was unconscious and bleeding from the neck. Two French first-aid men came with a stretcher, and all three of us jumped onto the track. We tried to control the bleeding and lifted her onto the stretcher to take her off the track. The American trainer yelled, "Get off of the track! An American woman is coming!" Apparently, they didn't have any walkie-talkies to coordinate the runs. The Frenchmen pushed me off the track, but only one of them had time to follow. The second Frenchman was out of time. As the American luger sped closer, he squeezed himself tight to the inner wall on the lower part of the U-curve. Seconds later, the American woman zipped by. Later, we asked the American luger if she had noticed anything unusual in that curve. "Oh, yes,"

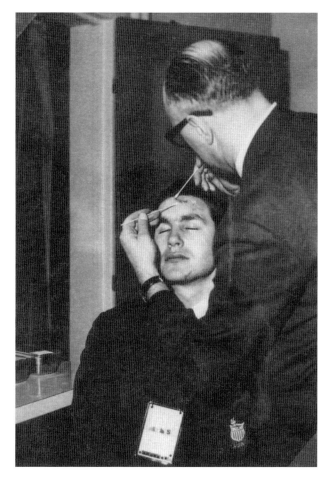

Rechecking a forehead wound on Tom Hurley.

she said, "all that blood made me a little nervous!" We said, "But what about that man who was on the inner wall of the curve?" She said, "No, I didn't notice him. That would have made me extremely nervous."

Tragically, the Italian woman had suffered severe internal injuries. She was taken immediately by helicopter to the hospital in Grenoble and flown back to Italy that same day for more emergency surgical treatment, but we found out later that she didn't make it. It was the most serious and tragic injury I have ever witnessed in a winter sports event.

Later that same afternoon we had a game against Canada. It was a close but friendly game. In the last period, the score was tied 2–2 and looked like it might end that way. However, near the end of the game, Canadian defenseman Marshall Johnston's shot hit Herb Brooks's skate and bounced into our net. The Canadians won 3–2. Johnston, a good friend of Herb, came over to him after the game and said, "Thanks, Herbie, for the tip-in." Herb didn't think that was very funny, but that was how we lost the game.

On Monday, February 12, I went to check up on Craig. His wife, Sandy, had arrived and that helped to keep his spirits up. We played the West Germans that afternoon. Exactly as we had predicted, the West Germans were forced to abandon the chippy style that they had used in Bad Tölz and Garmisch-Partenkirchen. We completely controlled the game and beat them 8–1.

After a few days off, we played East Germany on Thursday, February 15. It was a much harder game than the one against West Germans. Lou Nanne got another laceration across his chin. When I told him to be careful out there, he said, "Doc, those guys have their sticks in my face all the time." He got quite a few lacerations on his face during that tournament. It seemed like one was not yet healed before he got the next one. I think I put about forty stitches in Louie's face in Grenoble. Still, we were able to handle the rough stuff by the East Germans and won the game 6–4.

Saturday, February 17, was our last day in the Olympic Village and also our last game. We played a strong Finnish team against whom we'd always had good, hard games. We scored first, but they scored a fluke goal later and the game ended 1–1. We placed sixth in the final standings. Everyone was disappointed, but without a doubt, Craig's injury was a major factor. Our line combinations were never quite right. Even Herb Brooks, who centered Larry Stordahl and Tom Hurley, was switched to defense. Our previous harmony was completely disrupted.

Once the tournament concluded, Lenny, Don, and I said good-bye to our teammates, caught a late train for Zürich, and flew to Munich to meet Peter Koch, who took us touring and skiing in Tyrol in the fresh winter air. We greatly enjoyed the Tyrolean specialties, including good glasses of red Kalterer See and after-dinner dancing. In fact, one of my fondest memories is when they played "Baby, Baby, Bala, Bala." Everybody walked in a line through the dining room, into the kitchen, down to the basement, and back up to the dance floor again. It was a wonderful, festive end to my first Olympic Winter Games. I kept asking myself, "Was this all a dream, or did it really happen?" It was so wonderful!

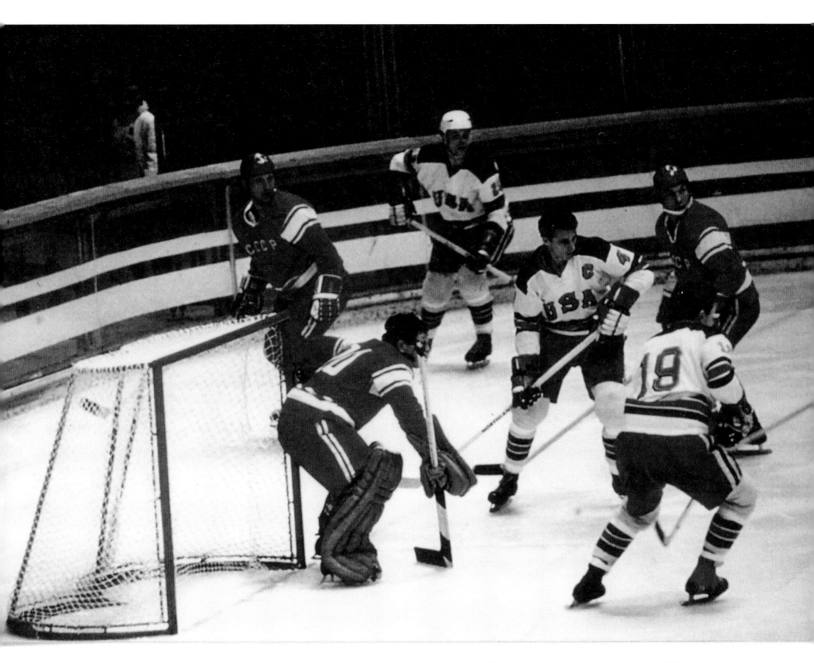

Game: USA vs. USSR, February 2, 1968 (L-R): Viktor Kuzkin, Viktor Konovalenko, Larry Stordahl,
Herb Brooks, Alexander Ragulin, and Tom Hurley.

1970 World Championship, Pool "B" in Bucharest, Romania. Front row (L-R): Gary Johnson, Larry Stordahl, Len Lilyholm, Coach Murray Williamson, Manager Hal Trumble, Don Ross, Doug Woog, Carl Wetzel. Middle row: Myself, Henry Boucha, Bob Lindberg, Craig Patrick, Jim McElmurry, Charlie Brown, George Konik, Wally Olds, Trainer Dick Rose. Top row: Keith Christiansen, Ozzie O'Neill, Mike Greenleaf, Gary Gambucci, Bryan Grand, Chuck Norby, Gary Schmalzbauer. Not pictured: Herb Brooks, Bruce Riutta, Peter Fichuk, and Pete Markle.

5

Behind the Iron Curtain

Bucharest, Romania, 1970

Team Roster

In Goal: *Carl Wetzel, Mike Curran*

Defense: *Charles Brown, Gary Johnson, George Konik, James McElmurry, Bruce Riutta, Donald Ross*

Forwards: *Henry Boucha, Herb Brooks, Keith "Huffer" Christiansen, Gary Gambucci, Bryan Grand, Len Lilyholm, Robert Lindberg, Pete Markle, Ozzie O'Neill, Craig Patrick, Larry Stordahl*

The AHAUS administration was not happy with our sixth-place finish at the Olympic Winter Games at Grenoble. Never mind that Craig Falkman's injury in our game against Sweden had taken him out of the rest of the tournament. Even though Murray had juggled the lines from that point forward to the best of his formidable abilities, AHAUS decided to put the management of the national team in different hands for the 1969 World Championships in Stockholm, Sweden.

Under new leadership, the team finished in last place and the United States was relegated to the B Group for the 1970 World Championships in Bucharest, Romania. Swiftly changing course yet again, in the summer of 1969 Robert

41

Fleming, chairman of the United States Olympic Ice Hockey Committee, instituted a long-range, three-year program and appointed Murray Williamson and Hal Trumble—who knew each other from the University of Minnesota—as coach and general manager, respectively. By then, Murray had been away from the team for a year and had to act quickly to assemble a lineup for the rapidly approaching World Championships in February.

The team assembled for the first time in December 1969 for a few days' practice. With so little time to prepare, the players hardly knew each other when they played their first two exhibition games. Shortly after that, everyone returned to their respective teams and reassembled again just two weeks before leaving for Europe.

On Wednesday, February 18, we reunited in New York. Before boarding the plane for Zürich, I briefed the players about Romanian politics and culture. I told them, "This isn't going to be like Switzerland, Germany, or Austria. This is a country behind the Iron Curtain. Things will be very different, with much stricter rules and regulations. Police and soldiers will watch and observe you. They may even follow you at times. Be very careful with money. Don't ever exchange it on the black market. That's one of the worst crimes over there. And for God's sake, don't talk nonsense or make stupid jokes. Even that will get you in trouble."

After landing in Zürich, we took a train to Geneva through the beautiful Interlaken mountain district. When we arrived at about noon, we were all

Taking home the Cup of the Championship (L-R): George Konik, Murray Williamson, Herb Brooks, Pete Markle, Bob Lindberg, Larry Stordahl, and myself.

very tired from the long trip and rested before our late afternoon practice.

The day after that we practiced at an outdoor rink. The weather was typical for Geneva—cold, damp, and misty. Our team manager bought stocking caps for the players. That same evening we played the Swiss National Team and beat them easily, 5–2.

On Saturday, right after breakfast, we took a bus to La Chaux-de-Fonds, close to the French border. The team from La Chaux-de-Fonds was champion of the Swiss league, led by the best Swiss player, Michael Turler. Everybody in town was excited to see the game. The arena was packed with rambunctious, vocal spectators. The game was much closer than the one the night before, with the outcome still in doubt until we scored a last-minute power-play goal, clinching a 4–3 victory.

On Sunday, February 22, we were scheduled to take a bus to Zürich for our flight to Bucharest. Our goalie, Carl Wetzel, was often a big practical joker, but he took his religion very seriously. I told Murray that Carl needed to go to church before we left for Zürich. At first Murray must have thought I was joking. He was very concerned that we wouldn't be back in time. I told him I wasn't joking and assured him that we would make it. Carl and I flagged a taxi and asked the driver to take us to the nearest Catholic church.

After the lengthy service, we needed to get back to the hotel quickly. It had snowed the previous night, and the streets were covered with deep, slushy snow—not a single taxi in sight. We ran through the wet, heavy slush all the way back to our hotel. We made it with just enough time to change into warm, dry socks.

On the bus ride to Zürich we heard frightening news on the radio: a bomb had been found on an Israeli plane bound for Tel Aviv. Naturally, as Americans traveling abroad in our official red, white, and blue team gear, we were quite nervous about our flight to Bucharest. At the Zürich Airport, our bus drove straight to the runway and we boarded the plane without passing through the terminal. The takeoff was a little rough, which added to our nervousness. Thankfully, the flight soon smoothed out and we relaxed, enjoying the scenery of the Alps, the Dolomites, and the valley of the Danube River.

Upon our arrival at the Bucharest Airport, it was clear we were in a different world. Indeed, we were behind the Iron Curtain. There were no smiling faces. Everybody looked serious and grim. Numerous police officers and soldiers with machine guns patrolled every inch of the airport. Still, some of the more mischievous boys couldn't resist. Ignoring my preflight speech, they started joking around that I was car-

George Konik receiving the MVP award
of the tournament.

rying hidden money. Luckily, we got through all of the checkpoints and drove to our hotel. Out on the street we could sense Bucharest's former glory in its wide boulevards and stately buildings with beautiful architecture.

Len Lilyholm with Highest Scoring award.

welcomed us to their city. One was a younger student who spoke English quite well. The other one was older, an engineer who spoke little English, but was friendly and helpful to us. The younger one wasn't friendly at all. In fact, he even refused to translate the newspaper, especially if it said something good about us. We distrusted him from the start, especially after we caught him searching the desk in Murray's room.

On Monday, February 23, we had our first practice. The arena was an old, heavy stone building, and the locker rooms were cold and damp. Later that afternoon we were issued our credentials and returned to the hotel for dinner. Murray called a team meeting and passionately stressed the importance of getting off to a good start. Our first game was against Japan, who'd recently completed a very successful exhibition tour of Canada and was regarded as a favorite.

The game was the following morning. Our boys got up early and seemed nervous and concerned. Nobody joked around. On the bus to the arena everyone was quiet, thinking about the game. I had never been on a quieter bus in my life. Nobody said a word. The same intensely quiet mood prevailed in the locker room. Once they hit the ice, however, they were like a bunch of tigers. They blitzed the heavily favored Japanese, and we won 11–1. It took a big load off our minds.

We played Bulgaria next, an easy game that we won 19–1. The line centered by Herb Brooks, with Larry Stordahl and Len Lilyholm on wings, had a heyday. Even Brooks, who was a great playmaker but never much of a goal scorer, tallied a hat trick. During

After we checked into our hotel, the Old Glory, the boys noticed an unpleasant smell and asked me, "What is that?" It was mold! Many years ago, the Old Glory had been quite nice. Now it was badly run-down and had an overpowering musty smell. In some of the rooms, in fact, the wallpaper hung down in shreds.

Once we were settled in, our hosts and interpreters

the handshakes after the game, one astonished Bulgarian player asked Herb to trade sticks with him. He was convinced Herb's stick was full of magic! Even the Romanian newspaper said the next morning, "The United States team is in a class by itself!" Everyone relaxed and had fun.

Thursday, February 26, was a day off. After breakfast I met our older, more friendly host, who asked if it was true that one our players was an architect. I said, "Yes, that's Len Lilyholm." Our host's son, it turned out, was studying architecture himself and wanted to learn about such programs in the United States. I said, "Fine, I'm sure Mr. Lilyholm would be happy to talk to your son. Have him come to the hotel, and we'll find a good place to talk."

"No, no," said our host, "my son cannot come here. That would be no good for me. You and Mr. Lilyholm must come to my apartment. I can't even walk with you on the street. Meet me at two o'clock in the cafeteria across the street. I will wait for you there. As soon as you arrive, I will get up and leave. Then you must follow me, but not too close. I will lead you to my apartment. Stay thirty or forty feet behind me."

I said, "Yes, yes, we can do that."

After practice, I explained the situation to Lenny, and at two o'clock we went to the cafeteria. As we entered, our host got up and left. We didn't look directly at him, but we noted which way he went and started following as instructed. He went around the corner and into a grocery store. There were many people around, and we almost lost him. Then he left the store by the back door, went through a courtyard, and stepped out onto the street again. We followed him around another corner and down the block. Finally, he went into an apartment house. Two flights up the stairway, he was there waiting for us. He had a tiny apartment, but he was happy to not have to share it with anyone else.

Lenny talked to the son and explained architecture programs in the United States: how many years they took, what the various programs involved, what the exams were like, and so forth. We had a nice chat with them. As we were ready to leave, our host explained a more direct route back to our hotel. We had no trouble with his instructions, but we couldn't help glancing over our shoulders to see if we'd been followed.

After lunch, Murray asked me if there was a nice restaurant nearby for dinner. I told him that Bucharest is often called "The Paris of the Balkans" and suggested that we ask the vice president of the Romanian Hockey Association for a recommendation. He was frequently at the information desk and was always very friendly and helpful. Murray thought that was a great idea and suggested that we invite him and his wife to dinner.

I found the vice president, extended our invitation, and told him we were looking for a restaurant like Csardasfürstin in Vienna. He said, "Oh, ja, ja, Csardasfürstin. I know very well what you mean. We used to have many nice restaurants just like the Csardasfürstin, but now they are all closed. People in Bucharest don't like to go out anymore because you never know who is sitting at the next table. If you talk freely over a glass of wine, you could be in trouble the next day. All the nice places have closed." I saw the tears in his eyes as he remembered happier times, saddened by present conditions.

He then composed himself and said, "Thank you very much for the invitation, but my wife will be unable to join us. I have a friend with a car who can take all four of us to a very nice Gypsy restaurant a little way out of town. We will have a nice dinner there."

We met at the hotel at 7:00 p.m. His friend's car was really quite small. There was barely room for four people, and I immediately understood why the vice president's wife could not join us.

The restaurant was called Două Cocosi, which means "two roosters" in Romanian. It was about five or six minutes outside of Bucharest proper. It was a typical Romanian restaurant where all of the waiters were dressed in traditional red, yellow, and green costumes. A table at the center had been reserved for us, and we were briefed about their specialties. I ordered barbequed chicken prepared with traditional spices, and it was delicious. While we were eating, musicians came to our table and played traditional Romanian songs. It was a lovely evening, and we thanked our hosts very much when we arrived back in Bucharest. They were also very happy to have shared their traditional Romanian culture.

On Friday, February 27, we played Yugoslavia. It was a tougher game than the one against Bulgaria, but we still won easily, 5–1.

On Saturday we played West Germany. They played a good defensive game, and we had to work much harder to score than against the other teams. We won the game 5–2 and were happy and relaxed. Only three games remained, against Romania, Norway, and Switzerland, none of which were very strong teams.

Sunday, March 1, was a very special day. The crew of the *Apollo 12* moon mission was visiting Romania, amid much fanfare and heavy security. A group of us went out to meet them at the airport, but military security was everywhere and we couldn't get close to them. That evening, however, a big dinner and dance party were held in honor of the astronauts, and our team was invited.

Earlier, Murray had received the Ugly American Award, given every day at lunchtime to a member of our group who'd said or done something to embarrass one of our European hosts. The award was a little red devil with black horns, and whoever won it was forced to carry it everywhere for the next twenty-four hours. So, of course, Murray had it with him at the party. After the dinner, the dancing started and the bandleader announced, "The next dance is ladies' choice!" A beautiful Romanian woman came to our table and asked Murray to dance. All of us applauded, but Gary Gambucci and "Huffer" Christiansen quickly said, "Murray! Don't forget your award!" All night long, Murray had to dance with the little red devil in his hand.

The next day we were all relaxed and feeling quite well liked by the locals. Of course, the boys were also happy about all of the games they'd won. They were so giddy, in fact, that they'd gotten a bit too enthusiastic about exchanging money on the black market. They were laughing at me and saying, "Doc, why are you so suspicious? You worry too much." Then came the big bomb! Defenseman George Konik had arranged with a local fellow to go to his apartment to exchange dollars for Romanian leu for a very high rate. Immediately after the transaction, as soon as George left the apartment, two big policemen grabbed him, confiscated his leu, and drove him to the police station.

Luckily, while getting the report, the chief of police recognized Konik, who was very popular among the local spectators and often followed by groups of fans after our games. The police chief asked, "Aren't you George Konik, who plays for the US hockey team?"

George answered, "Yes, yes, that's me!"

The police chief said, "No! That cannot be! Do you know what this means? Six months in prison!" He paused, "But I can't do that to you. I will let you go, but you must give your friends this message: this must never happen again."

George returned to the hotel, shaking and as pale as a ghost. He told me the whole story, and I said, "You need a drink! Let's go to Murray's room." Murray gave him a glass of cognac while George told Murray what happened. We were all very relieved that the chief of police was such a big hockey fan.

A few nights later, the American ambassador invited our team to his house for dinner. Murray told him the story about George's close call with the police. The American ambassador said, "You don't know how lucky you are! A couple of years ago an American businessman was caught exchanging money on the black market. He was in prison for six months!" Finally, everyone understood that I wasn't kidding when I'd told them that life behind the Iron Curtain was serious business.

On Monday evening we played Romania. The atmosphere was warm and friendly. The fans cheered for the home team, of course, but they showed our team great respect. I think they liked supporting us as a way of opposing the Soviets. In any case, it was another easy game and we won 9–1.

Tuesday, March 3, was a day off for all of the teams, so the Romanian Hockey Association organized a trip to the old Peleş Castle in the Transylvanian Alps, the former summer residence of the Romanian kings. On the bus ride to and from the castle we saw groups of poorly dressed peasants with wheelbarrows and shovels. Others cut large pieces of wood from fallen trees along the roadside. Even little old ladies were doing manual labor. Our boys saw how hard life was here in the country, and it made them realize how good we had it back home.

On Wednesday, March 4, we played Norway and won the game 9–2. Now we had only one game left, against Switzerland. We played them on Thursday, March 5, our last full day in Bucharest. We easily beat them 12–3. We'd won all seven of our tournament games!

The award presentations started immediately after our last game. The Norwegian team took third place, and the German team took second. Then Herb Brooks and Donnie Ross, our captains, went up to receive the championship trophy. Don took the cup,

Captains Herb Brooks and Donnie Ross accept the championship trophy.

and Herb got a big bouquet of red roses. Of course, it wouldn't be Herbie if he didn't do something sneaky. So he skated over to the dignitaries' box, where the only lady was sitting, and presented the red roses to her. She kissed him on the cheek, and the crowd roared with applause. Herbie skated back to join us with a big smile on his face that lasted the rest of the day.

After we'd skated a victory lap with the cup, we went down to the locker room, where the big celebration started. Hal Trumble, as team manager, had arranged for a case of champagne. Everyone clapped and cheered and enjoyed our tournament victory.

But I had work to do.

In the final period of that final game, Lenny Lilyholm had gotten a stick across the nose and still needed stitches. We both decided it was best not to go to first aid, but instead to suture it up right there. So Lenny sat down on the bench, and I got out my sewing kit and cleaned and sutured the wound while Carl Wetzel and Larry Stordahl poured a bottle of champagne on our heads. Never had I sutured up a player like that before, but the wound healed up well.

After our locker room celebration, we went to the adjacent building for another award ceremony in which individual awards were presented. Our players won five out of six:

George Konik—Most Valuable Player
Len Lilyholm—Highest Scoring Player
Carl Wetzel—Best Goalie
Craig Patrick—Best First Year Player
Bob Lindberg—Best Student Player

A Yugoslavian player got the youngest player award, but our players won everything else. On top of all that, our team was also awarded the Fairplay Cup. Our boys were jubilant.

Later that evening, Hal Trumble and Murray Williamson announced the biggest surprise of all: to reward us for our hard work and celebrate our championship victory, we wouldn't go home tomorrow, but would instead embark on a three-day Roman holiday!

Friday, March 6, was a very emotional day. Throughout the whole tournament, the Romanians had been exceptionally kind, polite, and hospitable. They liked our team very much. They even gave us the big cup to take home, instead of the usual replica copy. Of course, we promised to send it back. Many Romanian fans even came to the airport to say goodbye. As our plane taxied down the runway for takeoff, they ran along the fence, waving to us. We had a good feeling that we had gotten the United States back into the A Group for the next world championship.

1971 World Championships in Bern and Geneva, Switzerland. Front row (L-R): Carl Wetzel, George Konik, Coach Murray Williamson, Manager Hal Trumble, Gary Gambucci, Mike Curran. Middle row: Myself, Dick McGlynn, Craig Patrick, Jim McElmurry, Henry Boucha, Tim Sheehy, Pat Westrum, Trainer Don Niederkorn. Top row: Len Lilyholm, Rich Brown, Ron DeGregorio, Craig Falkman, Peter Fichuk, Kieth Christiansen, Kevin Ahearn, Dick Toomey. Not pictured: Tom Mellor, Don Ross, Paul Schilling, and Bruce Riutta.

World Championships

Bern and Geneva, Switzerland, 1971

Team Roster

In Goal: *Carl Wetzel, Mike Curran, Ron DeGregorio, Dick Tomasoni*

Defense: *George Konik, James McElmurry, Richard McGlynn, Tom Mellor, Bruce Riutta, Don Ross, Pat Westrum*

Forwards: *Kevin Ahearn, Henry Boucha, Rich Brown, Keith "Huffer" Christiansen, Craig Falkman, Pete Fichuk, Gary Gambucci, Len Lilyholm, Craig Patrick, Paul Schilling, Tim Sheehy, Richard Toomey*

The 1971 World Championships were scheduled to be played in Switzerland from March 19 to April 2. The first round was to be played in Bern, with the second in Geneva. The US team was assembled in Minneapolis under the direction of Murray Williamson during the final week of October 1970. A heavy schedule of fifty-one games was set, with most games to be played against Western College Hockey Association (WCHA) teams, minor league squads, and some local amateur teams.

We started with a few good wins, but then one day at practice, Herb Brooks said, "I can't do this anymore. I can't keep playing and working. I'm no good for the team, and I'm no good for my work."

I said, "Herb, what's the problem?"

After the games in Bucharest, Herb had taken a position with the St. Paul Companies selling insurance. He said that he was very busy with work and felt like when he was working, he was letting down the team, but when he was with the team, he wasn't doing his job. He couldn't devote himself 100 percent to either one and felt like he needed to quit playing hockey. He was a perfectionist. That's just the way he was. Murray tried to convince him to stay, but was unsuccessful. Herbie's departure was a blow to the team, but we had to press on without him.

To make matters even worse, one evening Kevin Ahearn, Tim Sheehy's roommate, called me by phone and said, "Doc, Timmy's in terrible pain. Abdominal. It's brutal. Can you see him?"

I said, "Sure, I'll be there right away," grabbed my medical bag, and ran over to their apartment. Sure enough, Tim had all the symptoms of acute appendicitis. I needed to act quickly to find a surgeon to perform an emergency appendectomy. So I called Dr. John Linner, for whom I had great respect, and told him the situation. "Sure, I can do it," he said. "Take him to the Swedish Hospital right away. We'll operate tonight." So I took him to the Swedish Hospital and assisted with the procedure. Tim's appendix had been very close to rupture, but the operation went well, and

the next morning he was much better and made a good recovery.

The day after that I got a telephone call from Timmy's sister, who gave me a hard time for taking Timothy to a non-Catholic hospital. I said that I was sorry and apologized for overlooking that detail, but reminded her it had been an emergency. I had nothing else in mind but getting her brother the very best care. Later, I called Timmy's parents and apologized to them, too, for taking Timmy to a Lutheran hospital, but they were very nice and thankful and told me not to worry about what their daughter had said. So everything was all right, and three weeks later Timmy started skating again. A couple of weeks after that he was back and ready to play.

Then, just as Timmy was returning, we were struck by injury again. Craig Falkman suffered a concussion in a game against Denver and was hospitalized before coming home. I arranged for a neurosurgeon, Dr. Lyle French, to see Craig and perform an EEG. Craig had a minor concussion, and we certainly couldn't let him practice or even skate until all of the symptoms had disappeared. It was another hard blow to the team, but all of us patiently waited until Craig's recovery was complete.

By the end of January our team was doing quite well. On Friday, January 29, we lost to Michigan Tech 5–4, but we beat the University of Wisconsin 7–1 the following day. However, February 23, a little over three weeks later, is a day I will never forget.

That night we were set to play in Omaha,

Nebraska. Murray wanted me to come because he expected a rough game. The team left Minneapolis by bus at noon, but I knew I had a very busy day at University Health Service and had arranged a flight to Omaha after work. The weather was cloudy and rainy, with a storm rolling in. The first part of the trip, from Minneapolis to Rochester, Minnesota, was bad. The small, two-engine, thirty-six-seat plane bounced around a lot, and a few people even got sick. I considered getting out in Rochester but then decided the worst was probably over. *It could only get better*, I thought, so I stayed on the plane.

The next leg was even worse. Takeoff was really rough. The plane was thrown from side to side and tossed up and down. It even felt, at one point, like we'd hit the ground any moment. People screamed and vomited as I kept asking myself, "What are you doing here? You have the most wonderful wife and two charming little daughters at home. What are you doing, you idiot?!"

After the plane finally landed, I thought, *My God, if these pilots can control this plane in such a terrible weather, then those little jitters we sometimes feel on big jets on overseas flights don't mean a thing.* I was so relieved.

The game went well. There were no injuries, and we won 5–3. Then it was time to return to Minneapolis with the team. I was very happy and thankful to be taking the bus and not another plane.

Before we left for Europe, Craig Falkman had another EEG at the University of Minnesota Hospital.

The results showed no problems, and I was relieved to know that he would be ready for the tournament.

On Wednesday, March 10, we left for Europe. First we flew to Prague, where we would stay for three days and play two exhibition games. The Czechoslovakian team was very strong, as always, and a solid favorite to win the World Championship.

When people think of ice hockey's origins, naturally they think of Canada. It is well documented that McGill University students organized the first true hockey game on March 3, 1875, at the Victoria Skating Rink in Montreal. Two years later, a McGill University student named William Fleet Robertson invented the hockey puck by cutting off the top and bottom of a hard rubber ball to make a disc. That same year several McGill University students codified the first seven ice hockey rules. A little further south and a few years later, an early formalized hockey match took place between the Baltimore Hockey Club and Johns Hopkins University.

Over in Europe, however, games similar to ice hockey were known from much earlier times. In the sixteenth century, Flemish and German artists such as Hendrick Avercamp, Pieter Bruegel, and Anthonie Beerstraten painted scenes of popular ice hockey–like sports. Bandy, played with a hard round ball and a curved stick similar to a field hockey stick, has been played in northern Europe since the eighteenth century. In fact, the game is still quite popular in Sweden, Russia, Finland, and other northern countries.

Canadian-style ice hockey was brought to

Europe by Canadian students at Oxford University in the late 1880s. By 1903, Great Britain had a five-team league, and the Prince's Club of London was the premiere team in all of Europe. Canadian hockey soon spread to Germany, Czechoslovakia, France, Belgium, Austria, Switzerland, and other countries. In Czechoslovakia, Canadian-style hockey became especially popular, and teams started forming in many small towns throughout the country.

The first European Ice Hockey Championships were played in 1910 at Les Avants, Switzerland. The Czechoslovakian team did not participate because they didn't feel adequately prepared. The wait served them well, apparently, and in 1911, and again in 1914, Czechoslovakia won the European Championship.

After World War I, Czechoslovakia won the European Championship on several more occasions. Historically, Czechoslovakia had outstanding teams and very good players. Personally, I remember a young Czechoslovakian student named Jaroslav Drobny who came to Riga in the late 1930s to teach us the fundamental skills and strategies of the game. At the time, he played for CLTK–Prague, centering a line between Karl Robetin and Vaclaw Fryzek. He was a rising ice hockey superstar in the late 1930s and early 1940s, but he became a world-class tennis player in his later years.

In 1948, a Czechoslovakian team coached by Josef Herman went to Moscow to teach the sport to the Soviets, who were to become so dominant throughout the 1960s and 1970s. At that time, however, the Czechs

were the top of the top, in a class by themselves. It was with a bit of reverence and trepidation, then, that we stepped off the plane into the Prague airport.

Our guide and interpreter, Jiri Trnka, greeted us warmly. From the first moment I met him, I was impressed by his intelligence and class. I felt pleasant and relaxed around him. He spoke fluent English and was enjoyable to be with. He was an artistic painter who came from a very well-known noble family in Prague. For several centuries prior, his family had owned a large, beautiful property on the left bank of the Vltava River, near the famous Charles Bridge. The communist government had nationalized the property, though, so Jiri and his family lived in a modest apartment on the outskirts of Prague. Jiri took us to our hotel, where we unpacked and relaxed for that evening.

After practice the next day, Jiri wanted to do something special for Murray and me. He asked if we'd be interested in seeing the best Czechoslovakian crystal store in Prague, the Moser Shop, and become members of the prestigious Moser Club, a unique and special privilege.

Murray and I both knew that Czechoslovakian crystal is some of the best in the world, and membership in the Moser Club sounded interesting indeed, so we instantly said yes, we'd like that very much. Then we asked Jiri, "Are there any particular rules and regulations that we should know about?"

Jiri said, "Well, the store manager, Mr. Emil Slama, will demonstrate at the initiation ceremony by pouring cognac into a speeding glass as it spins around the table. He would be most appreciative if you could bring along a bottle of good French cognac."

We said, "No problem! We can get it from the bar right here at the hotel." So while Murray and I picked up the cognac, Jiri arranged everything with Mr. Slama, and the three of us walked downtown to the Moser Shop.

Upon our arrival, Mr. Slama greeted us and we presented him with our bottle of good French cognac. His face just lit up like a light. He started showing us the store's beautiful crystal and china, explaining shipping procedures, should we decide to buy anything. After that, he let us wander around the store with Jiri and excused himself to go make preparations for our initiation into the Moser Club. The prices were much better than they were at home, and those crystal glasses were some of the best in the world. Murray and I each bought several and arranged for them to be shipped home.

Soon after that, Mr. Slama opened a heavy, dark red velour drape and asked us to enter a special room with a round table in the middle. It was dimly lit and elegant, the only light coming from specially illuminated colored crystal glasses and other pieces in the cabinets that lined the walls of the room. Mr. Slama said, "I would like you to come to the *altar* now." He walked us over to a corner of the room and opened the door of a wooden cabinet. *Oh my God*, it was breathtaking. A special lighting effect brought out the brilliance of a dozen or so gigantic cognac snifters of different shapes and styles. Each had an evocative name such as Longfellow, Slim Lady, Stout Gentleman, Big Berta, Long Face, Moon Face, and so on.

Mr. Slama took down one of the snifters and carefully placed it on the round table. The glass started spinning in a circle around the table. We were afraid it might tumble off. Mr. Slama sensed our concern and said, "Don't worry, it won't run off the table." It looked like a normal round table, but obviously it wasn't. It must have been specially built for the initiation test. Meanwhile, Mr. Slama told us that to become members of the Moser Club, we would have to pass a test. He said, "I will give each of you one of the large cognac snifters, according to your face or your build. You have to pour a glass of cognac into the spinning snifter."

Murray was lucky: he got Big Berta, with a wide opening, and had no trouble passing the test. I was given Stout Gentleman, however, with a much narrower opening, and I spilled cognac all over the table. Nonetheless, I somehow got enough cognac into the glass to pass the test.

Then all four of us, Mr. Slama, Jiri, Murray, and I, poured some additional cognac in our glasses and returned to the altar. There we made a toast to long-lasting friendship by chiming all four of our glasses together at the same time. Each one produced a unique sound, like the chimes of different-sized bells. The secret to producing such exceptional sound, we learned, is to strike the widest part of the glass, not the rim. Needless to say, we had to empty our glasses and enjoy the fine cognac. Murray and I signed the membership book and wrote a few lines alongside the names and signatures of some very impressive members, including prominent world dignitaries.

Murray and I felt very honored to be members of the prestigious Moser Club and were very grateful to Jiri for arranging this special event. As we were leaving, Mr. Slama told us that there was only one request attached to club membership: every time you visit Prague, you have to stop by and say hello! You don't have to buy anything, just show your face again. After returning to the hotel, we invited Jiri to join us for dinner and talked about our wonderful experience at the Moser Shop.

The next day we played the Czechoslovakian A team. Almost immediately, we fell behind 4–0. After the first period, though, our playing tactics changed. Murray told the boys to be more physical. Unfortunately, soon after that, it became a very rough game, and the Czechs didn't like it one bit. Their coaches were upset, the fans started booing, and the referees started calling one penalty after another. It was an unpleasant situation. The Czechoslovakian players didn't come close to our net again, but they still managed to score four goals in the last two periods, and we lost the game 8–0.

The next day we played the Czechoslovakian B team. It was a closer game, but we still lost 5–3.

A banquet followed the last game, but it wasn't pleasant at all. The Czechoslovakian officials were upset and said that it had been a very unfriendly

exhibition, which they did not expect from the American team.

The next morning, March 15, we flew from Prague to Geneva, where we beat the Swiss All-Star Team 12–3 the following day.

On Wednesday, March 17, we took a bus to Bern, where the first round of the World Championships were scheduled to be played. We stayed at the Hotel Gurten-Kulm on a hill on the outskirts of town. The only way to get there was by mountain railway. It wasn't at all convenient for shopping or sightseeing, but the Russian team was also quartered there. I knew the Russian team physician, Oleg Belakovski, from previous World Championships and now, seeing each other every day at the Hotel Gurten-Kulm, we became good friends.

On Friday, March 19, the World Championships began. We had a light, early morning practice and then got our credentials. Our first game was against Czechoslovakia. The Czechoslovakian team seemed afraid that we would play rough like we did in Prague, so they played a conservative, careful game. Meanwhile, we were very lucky. Whatever we did seemed to work. Gary Gambucci, Henry Boucha, Craig Falkman, and Len Lilyholm, in particular, just couldn't do anything wrong. We took control of the game and won 5–1.

The next day we faced the Swedes. It was a close game, but we lost 4–2.

Sunday, March 21, was a day off. After practice we stayed in town for some sightseeing. Bern is the capital city of Switzerland. It has a lot of nice administration buildings and is famous for having a bear pit. The bear is also the symbol of their town insignia. After sightseeing we returned to our hotel for dinner and a good rest.

On Monday, March 22, we played the Soviets. We held our own for the first period, but soon after that the roof caved in on us and we lost 10–2.

Without a day of rest, we played Finland the next day. Still tired from playing the Soviets, we lost 7–4.

Wednesday, March 24, was another day off. Team spirit was down, and the staff decided we needed a change of scenery. We had to do something—anything—to get the boys out of our isolated hilltop hotel. We contacted our Swiss friend Paul Haenni, who suggested that we visit his watch factory in Biel, about fifty miles northwest of Bern on the shores of Lake Biel, near the French border. Everyone on the team was excited about the idea, so we rented a bus and drove to Biel. At the factory, most of the workers spoke French, but Mr. Haenni and some others spoke very good English. The tour was quite extensive and very interesting. We could see the boys loosening up as they enjoyed observing the fine workmanship. We returned later to Bern in a much better, more relaxed mood.

Unfortunately, during practice the next morning, goalie Mike Curran injured his ankle. It was too tender to play on anymore, so we declared him unable to play and took him off the team roster. A reserve goalie was called to come over from the United States, but

for the moment Carl Wetzel was our only goaltender.

Our last game in Bern was on Thursday, March 25, against West Germany. I don't know if our boys underestimated the West Germans or were overconfident, but the mood in the dressing room before the game was not serious. In fact, I overheard some players talking about scoring hat tricks, which I didn't like at all. Once the puck dropped, sure enough, the West Germans came ready to play while we started flat. Before we knew it, we were down 3–0 in the first period. The West Germans kept all the momentum, and our boys got frustrated. We scored two goals in the third period, but that was not nearly enough and we lost 7–2.

We left for Geneva the next day for the start of the second round.

We played our first game in Geneva on Saturday, March 27, against Czechoslovakia. This time they weren't intimidated and played their usual style. They beat us easily, 5–0. To make matters worse, Len Lilyholm separated his shoulder and was out for the rest of the tournament, a terrible loss for our team.

We played Sweden the next day. It was a close, hard-fought game, but we were leading 3–2 with about seven minutes to play. All of us started thinking, *Finally, we might win a game.* Then, unfortunately, the Swedes scored two quick goals and we lost 4–3. It was heartbreaking.

We had the next day off, and the movie actor William Holden was in town. Together with some American expatriate friends, he hosted a reception for us at a local golf club. Everyone enjoyed the afternoon very much and returned to the hotel in far better spirits.

The next day we played Russia. Our boys played very well, but in the last period our strength started lagging. Then Craig Falkman took a slapshot on the ankle that slowed him down considerably. We lost the game 7–5.

Our players were physically and emotionally drained. On top of that, Craig Falkman's ankle was markedly swollen, and he could barely walk. In the locker room the next day, before our game against the Finns, he cut a piece out of his skate boot so his swollen ankle would fit. But our boys were just too tired. The Russian game had taken so much energy that they didn't have legs for the Finns. Then Carl Wetzel, tending the goal, lunged for a loose puck and injured his head. At least he wasn't knocked out and didn't show any signs or symptoms of a serious head injury. I quickly stitched up his scalp, bandaged his head, and let him finish the game. We lost 7–3.

It was good to have the next day off so we could rest and concentrate on West Germany, our last game of the tournament. Because of the goal differential, we knew we needed to beat the West Germans by five goals or more to avoid finishing in last place.

The game started great. We were playing well and leading 5–0 after the second period. Our frustration mounted, however, when the Germans scored a goal in the third period and we couldn't put the puck in their net. We won the game 5-1, but we'd finished in last place. Now we would have to win a tough qualification game in order to play in the Olympic Games the next year.

Why did this happen to us? We had such a good, talented team. Injuries? Maybe. Lenny was knocked out of the tournament with his shoulder separation after the first game of the second round, and Craig had taken that slapshot in the ankle against the Soviets. Those were two very costly injuries for our team. Scheduling? Possibly. That wasn't the best for us either. If we'd had a day of rest between the games against the Soviets and the Finns, we would have had a better chance to beat the Finns. Strategy? I don't know. Some people might say, "Why did you play so hard against the Soviets? You needed to save some energy for the game against the Finns where you'd have a chance to win." But you can't just tell your players to slow down and take it easy during an international tournament game. If it's an exhibition game, sure, then you can tell your players, "Look, this game doesn't mean anything. Save your energy. We need legs when the tournament starts in a few days. This is just practice for us." But during a tournament our boys play with heart every single time. I think it's the American way. Look at our last game against the Soviets. The spectators had a heck of a time. The Soviets only beat us 7–5. What a game to watch!

On the morning of Saturday, April 3, right after breakfast, Len Lilyholm and I, together with his wife, Carol, said good-bye to the team and left for Austria. We drove across the whole of Switzerland, all the way from Geneva to the northeastern corner of the country. The scenery was beautiful, and soon we started relaxing. Lenny and I even managed to get in a little skiing on Hahnenkamm Mountain before we parted ways. Lenny had to be careful with his separated shoulder, but he was a good skier and managed it well. After all that frustration in Geneva, skiing in the clear, crisp mountain air was a very nice way to relax.

A few days after I got home to Minnesota, Gary Gambucci came to my house and brought me a beautiful Swiss desk clock from Geneva, a gift from all of the boys, he said, for my dedication and care. I thanked Gary very much and placed that beautiful clock on my desk, a lovely reminder of the 1971 World Championships in Bern and Geneva.

1972 US Olympic Hockey Team in Sapporo, Japan. Row 1 (L-R): Peter Sears, Co-Captain Keith Christiansen, Coach Murray Wiliamson, Manager Hal Trumble, Co-Captain Tim Sheehy, Mike Curran. Row 2: Trainer Bud Kessel, Bruce McIntosh, Jim McElmurry, Larry Bader, Frank Sanders, Ron Naslund, Wally Olds, Charlie Brown, Tim Regan, myself. Row 3: Mark Howe, Craig Sarner, Tom Mellor, Henry Boucha, Dick McGlynn, Kevin Ahearn, Rob Ftorek, Stu Irving.

7

Olympic Silver Medal

Sapporo, Japan, 1972

Team Roster

In Goal: *Mike Curran, Tim Regan, Peter Sears*

Defense: *Charles Brown, James McElmurry, Richard McGlynn, Bruce McIntosh, Tom Mellor, Wally Olds, Frank Sanders*

Forwards: *Kevin Ahearn, Larry Bader, Henry Boucha, Keith "Huffer" Christiansen, Robert Ftorek, Mark Howe, Stuart Irving, Ron Naslund, Craig Sarner, Tim Sheehy*

The formation of the 1972 US Men's Olympic Hockey Team was again delegated to General Manager Hal Trumble and Coach Murray Williamson.

In the previous two or three years, Murray had become quite friendly with the great Soviet coach Anatoli Tarasov. In fact, in the spring of 1971, during the World Championships in Switzerland, Coach Tarasov had invited Murray to come to the USSR to tour the infamous Red Army athletic facilities and watch the Soviet hockey team train. Murray eagerly accepted and made arrangements to travel to Moscow for the first two weeks of August 1971. Soon after that, Murray returned with a number of new ideas for practice and conditioning programs.

A brand-new model for preseason training, including a tough new dry-land regimen and competitive exhibition schedule, was beginning to take shape. Many of these innovations, first introduced by Murray and inspired by Coach Tarasov, would evolve and carry forward to the 1980 Miracle on Ice team and beyond.

Tryout camps were held in Massachusetts, Michigan, and Minnesota during the last week of August and the first week of September. After the team was selected, there was a ten-day training camp in Bemidji, Minnesota, before a forty-seven-game domestic schedule began.

Our first two games were against the American Hockey League's Cleveland Barons on September 23 and 24. We won 5–3 and 6–2, respectively. Then, on September 30 and October 1, we played the Omaha Knights, the New York Rangers' farm team. Both games were very rough, but we managed to win the first by a score of 5–2 and tie the second 4–4.

These games were quite physical, and the injuries started to mount. It seemed like every other game a different player got hurt. In the early part of our schedule, nine of our players went down, including Tim Sheehy, who was hospitalized with a bad ankle injury. This time, however, I was lucky to have access to my orthopedic consultant, Dr. Harvey O'Phelan, a good old Irish Catholic who practiced at St. Mary's in Minneapolis. Tim's sister, Sheila, was very happy with that. Tim stayed in the hospital for a week and needed rehabilitation for two more weeks after that. Despite our injuries, we still maintained a favorable win–loss record heading into the Christmas holiday.

On December 26 we were scheduled to depart for Broadmoor World Arena in Colorado Springs. Our last two practices were held on Christmas Eve and Christmas Day, leaving no time for the boys to travel home to see their families. So I talked to Velta about once again inviting the players from the East Coast to our home for a holiday dinner after practice on Christmas Eve. She was very enthusiastic and mentioned that our daughters would also be home that evening. It worked out perfectly. After dinner, we presented a little gift to each of the players, who had to sing a little song or tell a funny story before opening it. It was a beautiful Christmas Eve party, and everyone had fun.

After practice on Christmas Day, Murray invited the entire team and staff to a party at his house. It was a brief but much-appreciated break. The next morning we flew to Colorado Springs for the start of a round-robin series of games against the Russian National Team and the Czechoslovakians. It was at this tournament that I first met the talented Czechoslovakian forward Jiří Holik, then an engineering student, with whom I later became good friends.

We played the Soviet Nationals first. We knew they were very good, and they blitzed us 13–3. Maybe Coach Tarasov wanted to send Murray a message about what his team could do. To be honest, it was shocking, especially to our goalies, who faced more than sixty shots.

The next day we played the Czechs. It was a much better game, and we won 7–5.

On the third day the Soviets beat the Czechs 8–3.

Unfortunately, my friend Dr. Belakovski did not travel with the Soviets this time. Instead, his young assistant, Dr. Igor Silin, was team physician. So, I introduced myself to Dr. Silin and made his acquaintance. He told me that his parents were both from Leningrad. "What a coincidence," I said, "my mother studied at the University of Leningrad and can still speak pretty good Russian." I invited him to visit with us when he was in Minneapolis. He was pleased with the invitation and said he would definitely like that.

On the way back to Minneapolis I met the Czechoslovakian team physician, Dr. Marian Kartushek, and Coach Stanislav Nevesely. It turned out that all three of us were avid tennis players. So, when we arrived in Minneapolis, I arranged for a doubles match and invited Dr. Kartusek, Coach Nevesely, and Jiří Holik to a New Year's Day breakfast at my home. They happily accepted, and I picked them up at their hotel.

At the breakfast table, I asked if we should toast the New Year. They thought that was a good idea, so I got out some cognac and the Czechoslovakian crystal glasses I'd bought in Prague. They recognized the crystal immediately and said, "This is the proper way to have a cognac for the New Year." After that, everyone relaxed and the conversation flowed around the table. It was a nice way to start the year.

On the evening of January 1 we played the Soviets again. It was another lopsided game, and we lost 11–1.

Since the Soviets were off the next day, I suggested to Dr. Silin that he come over to my house to visit with my mother in the early afternoon. He agreed. At that time, for security reasons, the Soviets never traveled alone. There had to be at least two of them at all times. So, when I went to the hotel to pick him up, Dr. Silin was joined by Russian player Viktor Vikulov. I took them both to my house for a cup of coffee, and they had a nice conversation in Russian with my mother.

Later, we went shopping downtown. They were interested in buying winter coats for their wives, and Dr. Silin was looking for an outfit for his four-year-old son. He found one he liked very much, but the price was more than he wanted to spend. So I asked the girl at the counter and Dr. Silin if they were sure it would fit. When both of them said yes, I took the outfit and said, "Then this is a present from my family to your boy." At first, he said, "No, no, please," but I could see that he was quite happy about my gesture.

As the girl packed up the outfit, I gave her my Dayton's credit card. Viktor elbowed Dr. Silin and said, "This is not the place for us to shop." I immediately knew what he meant, because I knew the Soviet system. In Russia, there are stores where only the privileged can shop, using special cards. I started laughing and said, "No, no guys, this isn't a privileged store. We Americans don't carry much money. We buy things with credit cards, and they send us a bill at the end of the month." Then I spotted a woman paying with cash and said, "Look, look, she is paying with money. This store is for all kinds of people. It's not a privileged store." They reluctantly believed me and started looking for coats for their wives.

They had a team meeting later, so they quickly found what they wanted and we hurried back to the hotel. Viktor was especially nervous about not being late. We got there in time, but as we neared the hotel, Dr. Silin said, "Please keep those packages for us until tomorrow." Privilege store or not, they didn't want the others to know that they'd been shopping.

We played the Czechoslovakian team that night. Again, we were stronger and won 6–3.

On January 3, the Czechoslovakians played the Soviets. I don't know if they were tired from shopping the previous day or what, but the Soviets didn't look good at all. In contrast, the Czechoslovakians looked smooth and every shot seemed to score. The Czechs beat the Soviets 6–1 for the last game of the tournament.

After the game, a party for the players and their friends and families was held in the MSC media center. My wife and I were chatting with Dr. Kartusek and Jiří Holik when Dr. Silin approached. My wife turned to Dr. Silin and said, "I am sure, Dr. Silin, that you know Dr. Kartusek, but do you know Mr. Jiří Holik as well?" Dr. Silin gruffly answered, "Yes, yes, I know too much of him," as if to say, *I don't need to be introduced to the man who scored a hat trick against us tonight.* But the evening was very friendly. Everybody mingled, and we wished each other good luck in the upcoming Olympic Games.

Before leaving for Sapporo, however, we played the Soviets twice more, once in Philadelphia and again at Madison Square Garden. We lost the first game 9–3 and the second 11–4. The games were great conditioning, though, and we returned to Minneapolis for the last of our domestic games, finishing our preparatory

stage with some impressive wins.

On January 21, we left for Denver, Colorado, to be outfitted with our Olympic gear and get our identification cards before continuing on to Japan. Our general manager, Hal Trumble, had arranged a farewell party at the Minneapolis airport and invited our wives, girlfriends, and family members to bid us good-bye. It was a very nice, festive departure.

On Monday, January 24, we flew to Japan. We stopped to refuel in Anchorage, Alaska, and everyone got out for a little walk around the airport. Later, as we climbed into the sky, Mount McKinley looked like a majestic, snowcapped castle among the purplish clouds of sunset.

As we approached Sapporo, the pilot announced that there was a blizzard and thick fog covering the city. We'd have to land in Tokyo. Two hours later we landed at Tokyo Airport and were taken to a modern high-rise hotel. It was our first taste of Tokyo and all those millions of people. We had a good Japanese meal and traveled to Sapporo the next morning.

The storm had ceased, the sky was clear, and we had a very good view of the rough, mountainous Japanese landscape on our way to Sapporo. As we flew over the island of Hokkaido, however, where Sapporo is located, the land flattened out and the ground was covered with snow. A bus took us from the airport to the Olympic Village, which was very festive and neatly decorated with the flags of the participating countries. Unfortunately, we didn't get much time to enjoy the Olympic Village because we needed to return to Tokyo for a pre-Olympic tournament the next morning. There were three teams competing: Czechoslovakia, Poland, and the United States.

Back in Tokyo, we were taken to the Takanawa Prince Hotel, a beautiful high-rise building. Equipment Manager Buddy Kessel and I were room-mates. When we got to our hotel room, we thought that there must have been a mix-up. The room was so beautiful and spacious, we thought it couldn't be for us. But after all that travel, we were tired and ready for bed, so we decided to stay and enjoy it.

A few hours later I was awakened by a strange, rumbling-shaking noise. Buddy woke up, too. He said, "Doc, I think someone's at the door." But I'd heard such a noise once before, many years ago, as a student in West Germany. Back then, I'd thought it was trucks rumbling by, making the windows shake, but when I got up and looked outside, the streets were empty. This was the same sensation. "Buddy," I explained, "no one's at the door. We're having an earthquake!"

At breakfast the next morning, our English-speaking Japanese host assured us that those little tremors were nothing to worry about and briefed us on Japanese customs. As we conversed, we were sur-prised to hear birds singing throughout the dining room. We didn't see any birdcages and were confused. Our host explained that there were "mechanical birds" in the columns. Their singing made breakfast time very pleasant.

Our host also explained that there is no tip-ping in Japan, other than at restaurants. "We all have jobs," he said, "and are proud to be paid for our work. Nobody is on welfare. Even old people work. An older lady may be assigned to go to the park to observe flowerbeds, for example, every day, or once a week, depending on her health. This is how we compensate older people."

In those years, there were sometimes student pro-tests—and even riots—in the United States. We asked if they had a similar problem. Our guide laughed and said, "Well, no, not really. Our police take care of that. If somebody has been to a police station once, they will not want to go again."

During my month in Japan, I saw many signs of this authoritarian attitude. People have this image of the militaristic Germans. I lived in Germany for seven years, and I know what the Germans are like. In my opinion, the German militaristic attitude is child's play compared to the Japanese version. In Japan, every order is strict and there is no back talk. If a superior tells you something, you simply bow and accept it.

One day, in the Olympic Village, we experienced this firsthand when we wanted our bus driver to take a detour to pick up some of our players at the post office. The bus driver said, "I have orders to go this way. This is the way I go." Later, Buddy Kessel said, "Doc, every-thing is so controlled and highly organized, they keep us on pins and needles." I said, "Buddy, don't worry. We'll tell them *yes, yes,* and do what we want anyway."

Our first game was against Poland. It was an exhibition game, not part of the Olympics, so our boys were relaxed and we won 7–5.

We played the Czechoslovakians the next night, but we had the whole morning free. Three of our play-ers—Sheehy, Dick McGlynn, and Henry Boucha, who

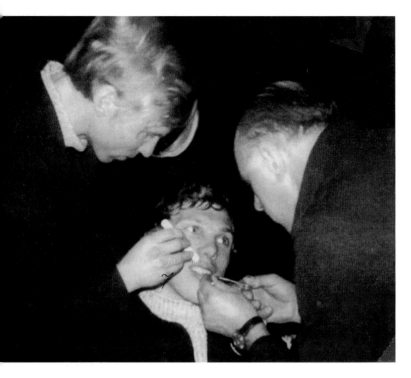

Removing stitches from Stu Irving's lip;
Rob Ftorek assisting.

had recently been in the army—knew about a canteen on the outskirts of Tokyo where they could buy electronics much cheaper than at home. They asked Coach Williamson if they could leave for a few hours to get their shopping done. Murray was a bit leery. "Are you sure you'll it back in time for the pregame meal at three o'clock?" he wondered. "We'll be back by two," they assured him. "Okay," Murray said, "but don't be late."

So the boys left for the canteen on the outskirts of town, and Hal, Murray, and I went downtown to Tokyo Tower, where we had a beautiful view of the city. After a little sightseeing, we returned to the hotel for the pregame meal. It was 3:00 p.m., then 3:30, but Boucha, McGlynn, and Sheehy still weren't back. Another hour went by. Murray was getting nervous, wondering what could've happened.

At 5:00 p.m, we had to leave for the arena. They still weren't back. We got dressed and ready for the pregame warm-up. Still no sign of those three. Now Murray was really upset and worried about those players. Then, just as warm-ups ended, the three of them rushed in, huffing and puffing, short of breath. They said, "Oh my God, Murray! Please, please excuse us. You don't know what happened."

The Japanese are extremely polite, but that doesn't always work in your favor. If they don't understand what you're saying, often they will bow, smile, and agree with you just to be nice.

After shopping at the canteen, the boys went to the railroad station to catch the train back to Tokyo proper. They weren't sure which direction to go. As a train approached, they asked someone, "Does this train go to the center of Tokyo?" The stranger bowed and said very politely, "Yes, yes." So the three of them got on the train. A few minutes later, they were headed further into the suburbs, and it was bye-bye, Tokyo.

Now they were out in the woods, couldn't speak Japanese, and nobody spoke English. Eventually they found somebody to point them in the right direction, but quite a few hours had passed and they got to the arena just fifteen minutes before game time. Murray was upset. They hadn't eaten or rested, and Boucha and Sheehy were our main scorers. Our guys did not play that well, and we lost the game 4–1. No more pre-game shopping trips after that!

We returned to Sapporo the next day and were greeted at the airport by a young Japanese student who was our guide for the rest of time we were in Sapporo. His English was okay, but it could have been better. Every once in a while we couldn't make him understand what we wanted or he couldn't express himself as well as he liked. But we got along all right, and everything was fine.

One particular problem everyone had in Sapporo was very slippery snow. It sounds strange, I know, but the snow in Sapporo was much slipperier than normal. Even the Swiss ski team complained.

At the foot of the giant slalom course there was a lake that never froze. It was a warm, spring-fed lake, and steam constantly rose from its surface. The steady precipitation and mist from that lake must have been oily or something, making the snow especially slippery. Our team in particular had endless problems with that snow. On top of everything else, the boots we were given in Denver had slippery soles. In the first few days of the Olympics we suffered three serious injuries due to that snow. First, the United States Olympic Committee liaison officer, Richard Dunnham, slipped and fell, fracturing his ribs. Then the treasurer, Julian Roosevelt, slipped and fractured his arm. Finally, I fell and fractured two vertebrae.

What the heck was going on here?

The day before the opening ceremony, Buddy and I were walking around the Olympic Village. On the path that ran from our dormitory to the dining room,

Buddy noticed a steep slope with three or four steps cut into the upper half, but nothing on the lower part. Buddy said, "Doc, look at this path. I think someone's going to get hurt here." I said, dismissively, "They just need to be careful."

Oh sure, I had to go and open my big mouth.

That was exactly the spot where I broke my back that evening.

Walking up to dinner, Huffer Christiansen, Mike Curran, and I took the path to the dining room. I was the first to go down the slope. At the bottom of the steps, I put my foot down and, *whoa*! My feet went flying. I fell and hit my back on the last step, the wind knocked out of me. I groaned and gasped for air.

Huffer and Mike said, "Doc, Doc, stay quiet, we'll get an ambulance. Don't move!"

I said, "No, no, just let me catch my breath. I'm sure I'll be all right."

For a minute or two I had a hard time breathing, but then it got better, and with some help from Huffer and Mike, I got up again. As we entered the dining room, our chief medical doctor, Larry Crane, looked at me and said, "George, you look a little pale." I laughed and said, "Larry, I don't feel too good. I had a little spill and hurt my back."

Especially during the first week, I had considerable difficulty getting my shirt on and off. Raising my arms was hard, and I couldn't sneeze. As soon I took a deep breath, my back hurt so much it took away the sneeze reflex. When I got home three weeks later and still couldn't sneeze, I knew something wasn't right. I got an x-ray, and sure enough, I had compression fractures of two vertebrae: the thoracic third and fourth!

But that wasn't even the worst thing that happened because of that slippery snow. One of the best Canadian figure skaters tried to step over a chain and slipped. She fell and broke her arm. She was one of the favorites, too, expected to place well in the competition, but now everything was over for her. Knowing how much time, effort, and money figure skaters at the Olympic level spend to get ready for competition, it was heartbreaking.

On the day of the opening ceremony, everyone got dressed in their parade outfits. The day was sunny and warm, but breezy. My back still hurt, so I watched the parade on TV. It was a beautiful thing, but when our boys got back, they were exhausted. They said walking through the snow in those slippery boots was the hardest workout they'd ever had. So Hal Trumble took all of our boots to a shoe repair shop and had rubber soles put on. That was a blessing. Now we could walk again without being afraid of falling down with every step.

The day after the opening ceremony was a very important day for us. We had to play the Swiss in a qualification game. Everything came down to this. Win, and we were in. Lose, and we were out. We'd prepared hard and we knew that we could beat the Swiss, but we were nervous about the game. Would we make it into the Olympic Games or not?

We scored first, but the Swiss came right back and tied it. Back and forth it went, and by the end of the second period the score was 3–3. But the boys clearly understood the seriousness of the situation and came out charging in the last period. We scored two more goals, and the game ended 5–3. It was a big load off our shoulders. Now we could compete for an Olympic medal.

Our first opponent of the tournament was a very strong Swedish team led by eventual NHL superstars Anders Hedberg, Borje Salming, and Ulf Nilsson. We lost the game 5–1 but were not disappointed. We had played well against a strong, talented team.

We had the next day off and practiced at a different rink. After practice we noticed a little magnetic hockey board that we could use at the Olympic Village to go over our game plan. Buddy said, "The bus is right next to our window. Murray, go outside. I'll hand you this board through the window." Murray said okay, and Buddy quickly passed him the board. We filed onto the bus for the trip back to the Olympic Village and everything seemed to be fine. But just as we were ready to leave, a Japanese official knocked on the door and said, very politely, "Mr. Kessel, Mr. Kessel, please, we would like to have our magnetic board back." Buddy whispered to me, "How in the world did they see that? Nobody was around." I said, "They must have radar or something. They know everything that happens." First, we tried to act innocent. When that didn't work, we said, "We don't have one of these in the Olympic Village. It would be a nice way to review our game strategy. We'll bring it back at our next practice." But the Japanese fellow said, "No, no, we need our board back. You have to make special arrangements to use such a board at the Olympic

Village." So we reluctantly gave the board back.

Interestingly, at that point in the games, the US women had won six medals already: three gold, one silver, and two bronze. Meanwhile, the US men had yet to win a single medal. Every day in the dining room, our team got a lot of heat from the US women.

The next morning we had a short practice to get ready for the game against Czechoslovakia. We had lost to them, 4–1, in Tokyo and knew they were very good.

Magnetic board or not, our preparation paid off. That game against the Czechs became the upset of the tournament. We beat them 5–1.

Our goalie, Mike Curran, was absolutely fantastic, the hero of the game. There was one save in particular that I will never forget. The Czechoslovakians had a power play. Their big, strong defenseman, František Pospíšil, skated in and blasted a shot at the net. It screamed toward the lower corner. Pospíšil raised his arms, already celebrating the goal. But Mike stretched out his left foot, and the puck hit the tip of his toe, glancing up and out of play, an unbelievable save. Pospíšil banged his stick on the ice so hard he broke it. When you run into a hot goalie like that, you can try whatever you want, but you still won't score.

In fact, everything worked out for us. The only injury was a slapshot to Huffer Christiansen's little toe. I applied ice packs right after the game, and he kept his foot elevated all night. The next morning, however, his little toe was swollen and quite tender. I decided to get an x-ray to see if it was fractured, so I took him to the medical center.

After taking the x-ray, the Japanese doctor came out with the film and said, "Everything is fine." I said, "Do you mind if I take a look? I would feel better that way." The doctor said, "Sure, you can see them," and put them on the view box. I looked at them and noticed a fracture line at the base of the phalanx of the fifth toe. I said, "Doctor, you said everything is fine, but there is a fracture line at the base of the prox-imal phalanx." The doctor replied, "No, the sides of that bone are okay. There is no shifting of anything." I said, "Yes, this is not a displaced fracture, and the bone should heal properly, but from what I can see, this is an undisplaced fracture of the proximal pha-lanx of the fifth toe."

At that moment, our chief medical officer, Dr. Daniel Hanley, walked into the room, so I asked him to look at the films. He agreed it was an undisplaced fracture. I told the Japanese doctor, who insisted there was no fracture. Dr. Hanley said, "George, don't argue with him. We'll treat it as an undisplaced fracture." So we thanked the Japanese doctor and took Huffer to the American dispensary. There, I taped his little toe to his fourth toe for stabilization, and that was that. The fracture healed without any problems.

That same afternoon we went to see the men's giant slalom race. We took the shuttle bus to the hill and saw the steaming lake. Spectators were trying to get up the hill to find a better place to watch the event. Ropes had been tied from tree to tree to help people pull themselves along, but the snow was so slippery, almost everyone was crawling on all fours. It was ridiculous! I had my movie camera and took some footage of it so that my friends at home would believe me. Finally, we found a good spot where we could see the skiers heading into the final stretch toward the finish line. We even saw Gustav Thöni's gold-medal run.

The next day we played the Soviets and lost 7–2.

In any case, that day will always belong to the three Japanese ski jumpers who won medals in the 70-meter event. Yukio Kasaya won the gold medal, Akitsugu Konno won the silver, and Seiji Aochi took the bronze. It was the first time ever that a Japanese skier had won an Olympic medal in ski jumping, let alone all three. The excited Japanese fans and Olympians waved their flags, cheering and celebrating everywhere we went. One of the most excited was my old friend Hitoshi "Mel" Wakabayashi, former center for the 1964 NCAA national champion Michigan Wolverines. After a stellar college career, Mel had moved to Japan, where he played professionally and worked with the Japanese National Team. His younger brother, Osamu "Herb" Wakabayashi, was on the current team's roster, in fact.

Almost as soon as I'd arrived in Japan, Mel had wanted me to meet his parents, who lived in Sapporo, and join them for dinner, but we'd yet to make arrangements. Now, giddy from the day's events, he extended an invitation to join them all at a restaurant, and off we went. We spent a happy evening, eating, drinking, celebrating, and remembering those good old days when Mel's Michigan Wolverines played my Minnesota Golden Gophers.

The next morning, February 10, we took a little walk to prepare for our crucial game against Finland. We knew if we lost the game, there was no chance for a medal, but if we beat the Finns, we had a shot at the bronze. When we arrived for the game, everyone was ready to play. Just fifteen seconds into the game, Craig Sarner scored on a pass from Henry Boucha and we took a 1–0 lead. Finland scored to tie it about four minutes later, but Boucha regained the lead on a pass from Sarner, and the first period ended 2–1 in our favor. The Finns never scored again; we added two more goals and won the game 4–1. We were ecstatic. Even Stu Irving's forehead laceration couldn't put a damper on the day.

After my experience with the Japanese orthopedic "specialists" in the x-ray department, I decided that when I dealt with the Japanese medical staff again, I would be a plastic surgeon. Now that I needed to suture up Stu's forehead, it was time to play that card. When we arrived at the first-aid room, the Japanese were very polite and helpful, as usual. They offered a doctor's assistance, but I said, "Thank you very much, but I am a plastic surgeon and will take care of my patient myself."

I had my own suture kit and started preparing the wound. Three or four of them gathered around me as I put on a pair of sterile gloves and readied for "plastic surgery." When I noticed how interested they were in my work, I described the things I'd learned from plastic surgeon Dr. Sam Balkin, who'd trained me during my surgical residency. Slowly, I explained every step of the procedure, carefully stitching the wound to get minimal scar formation the way that I'd been taught.

When I was through suturing the laceration, they all bowed and said, "Thank you very much. It was a very nice lesson in plastic surgery. Thank you very much." I'm not sure if they really meant it, but that's the Japanese way. They are always very polite.

After we got back to our quarters, Murray said, "Doc, let's go out for a beer." My back was feeling a little better, so I said, "Fine, let's go for a beer."

We took the subway to downtown Sapporo and found a nice, typical Japanese restaurant. The waiter took us to our table, where we sat on the floor with our feet dangling into a sunken space. As we got settled, he asked what we wanted to drink. We told him we wanted a beer, and he said, "Would you like to have a little beer or a large beer?" So, we ordered two large beers and—oh, my God!—the mugs were so big we couldn't even finish.

We sat there for quite a while, talking about our games and calculating our chances for a medal. We had one game left, against Poland, a game we should win. Of course, the Swedes still had to play Finland and the Soviets had to take on the Czechs. A lot of it depended on what happened in these games.

The only bad combination for us would be if the Czechoslovakians and Swedes both won. Then, the Czechoslovakians would win the gold medal, the Soviets would win the silver, and the Swedes would take home the bronze. In any other combination, we were assured a medal. If the Soviets and the Swedes both won, the Soviets would get the gold, the Swedes would win the silver, and we would get bronze. But, if

Russia beat Czechoslovakia, as expected, and Finland upset Sweden, Russia would get the gold, the Czechs would take the bronze, and we would win the silver medal.

In any case, we still had to beat Poland.

Our last game at the Olympics was set for February 12.

We'd beaten Poland in Tokyo just days before the Olympics began and knew that we should win. Still, we didn't want to take them lightly. So we came out strong from the start and soon had a comfortable lead. No matter what the Poles did, they couldn't seem to score, not even when they were awarded a penalty shot in the last period. Mike Curran, our goalie, stopped the first attempt, but then the referee ruled that he'd come out of the crease too early and awarded another try. Mike stopped that one, too, and everyone started laughing, suggesting the shooter get a third try. During the last minutes of the game we scored our final goal of the tournament, and the game ended 6–1, an easy victory for us.

The celebration began.

Hanging behind our bench was an American flag. Dick McGlynn took it down and brought it into our dressing room. Everyone was happy, knowing we had a good chance for a medal. But, sure enough, after a little while the Japanese arena attendant knocked on our locker room door and said to our equipment manager, "Mr. Kessel, Mr. Kessel, we would like to have the USA flag back."

Buddy looked the rink attendant in the eye and said, "I don't know what you're talking about. Leave

2010 Hall of Fame induction get-together with myself, Bus Driver, Keith "Huffer" Christiansen, Mike Curran.
Back row: Don Mellor, Murray Williamson, Tom Mellor, Frank Sanders, Craig Sarner, Ron Naslund,
and Dick McGlynn.

me alone." For a brief moment it was silent, but the rink attendant could see that the situation was hopeless. Alone in the locker room with a team full of rambunctious hockey players, he knew he'd never get that flag back. He shook his head and quietly left. The room exploded with cheers. Big Frank Sanders and Craig Sarner—who grew up together in St. Paul—were smiling and laughing their heads off, giving Huffer Christiansen grief about how the two of them always cleaned up the mess after their feisty captain's frequent infractions.

Later that evening, we heard the news that Finland had upset Sweden. Now it was clear that we'd win a medal no matter what. Murray met the Finnish coach and took him out for a drink. The boys went out in different groups, and Buddy and I went out for a beer.

On the last day of the competition, we were only spectators. Our whole team went to the ice arena to watch the Soviets beat Czechoslovakia.

We'd won the silver medal!

The award ceremony started right after the USSR–Czechoslovakia game. At that point, we realized Bruce McIntosh wasn't wearing his white turtleneck sweater like everybody else. Luckily, I had mine, so we exchanged shirts on the spot. Now everything was perfect. I had my movie camera with me, so I went down to the ice to film our boys as they lined up and received their medals. It was very emotional. At one point, I couldn't even see anything because there were tears in my eyes. We were all so proud to see our boys with silver medals around their necks.

After our last game, Dick McGlynn got the USA flag.

Soon after that, the closing ceremony started. It was quite exciting and interesting to watch, but I thought I'd better get back to finish packing. When I returned to the Olympic Village, I ran into my good friend Oleg Belakovski, the Russian team doctor. Oleg said, "Georgie, where have you been? I have been looking for you all evening! We have a very good party going. Come over, and let's celebrate our gold and silver medals."

"Oleg, I have to pack," I said. But Oleg insisted that I come for just five minutes. I said, "Okay, but

The presentation of the Olympic Hockey silver medal.

only for five minutes."

We went to his apartment, and sure enough, the Soviets were really celebrating, drinking vodka out of tea glasses and eating caviar and all kinds of other food. They poured their tea glasses half-full of vodka and drank them straight down, "bottoms up."

We toasted their gold medal, our silver medal, our friendship, and on and on. After a while, I knew I had to get out of there. So I got an idea and said, "Oleg, you wanted some penicillin and Band-Aids. Buddy is almost packed. If we wait another five minutes, we won't be able to get them."

Oleg said, "Yes, yes, I want those things! Let's go!" And we grabbed our coats and left. Back at our apartment, Buddy was far from finished, but Oleg didn't seem to notice. Buddy packed him a big box full of medications that were hard to get in the Soviet Union: antibiotics, cough syrup, cold tablets, and those Band-Aids he liked so much.

After Oleg left, Buddy and I finished packing and went to bed. Just as we were falling asleep, somebody knocked on the door. I thought it was one of the boys who couldn't sleep or had a headache. I said, "Buddy, the aspirin is there, as well as the sleeping pills. Just give them what they need."

Buddy came back from the door and said, "Doc, it's that Russian doctor. He says he has something for you."

I thought, *What does he want this time?* and went to the door. There stood Oleg with a big Russian samovar—a huge, traditional metal teapot—in his arms. He said, "Georgie, you gave me all that penicillin, I give you this samovar."

I said, "Oleg, I'm all packed up. I have so much to carry already. There's no way I'll get that thing home."

But Buddy came over and said, "No, no, Doc, take it. I'll help you get it home." So we took the samovar, which had elaborate inscriptions in Russian all over the top of it.

The next morning it started to rain, and all that beautiful snow turned to slush. The bus ride to the airport was difficult and slow. To make matters worse, the rain turned to a wet, heavy snow. As we boarded the airplane, there were four men on the wings brushing off the snow. But as fast as they brushed it off, more snow kept coming. After a three-hour delay we finally got out of there. When we got to Anchorage, however, the pilot announced that they were having trouble getting the landing gear down. For a while there was even talk of an emergency belly landing. Finally, they got the landing gear to work and we landed safely in Anchorage. After all of that, unsurprisingly, the pilots wanted a different plane to fly to Chicago. We waited for an hour for a new Pan American plane to arrive from Seattle.

On the flight to Chicago we got a telegram from President Nixon congratulating the United States hockey team for winning the silver medal. It was a long, tedious flight, but we were all very happy about our victories and Olympic medals. The speed skaters, who were also on our plane, were very happy too, since the women's team had won four medals (two gold, one silver, and one bronze) and broken records as well. Some of them were from the Illinois area, and when we arrived in Chicago, there was a big crowd of fans at the airport, cheering and celebrating.

On our way through customs, one of the agents pulled out the samovar and asked what it was. Buddy told him the whole story and showed him the inscriptions in Russian. The agent just laughed and said, "Okay, carry it through."

A few minutes later, however, we had a little scare with our large trunks, which usually aren't inspected. A different customs officer noticed Buddy struggling with the big, bulky cases and said, "Just a minute, just a minute. What are these?" Of course, those big trunks were jammed with the souvenirs the boys had asked Buddy to pack. Not wanting the customs officer to start digging through everything and asking more questions, Buddy took his own sweet time fumbling through his pockets, looking for the keys. Luckily, by that time, a supervisor had come out of his office and asked, "What is all of this?"

Buddy said, "It's the US Olympic team's hockey equipment."

The supervisor told the customs agent, "Let it go, let it go," and waved us through. Thanks to Buddy's masterful stalling techniques, we were safe again.

On the trip from Chicago to Minneapolis, thankfully, we had no more trouble and were greeted at the airport by a large, enthusiastic crowd congratulating us on winning the silver medal.

One night, not long after we got home, Murray

Russian samovar (metal teapot) received in exchange for Band-Aids and penicillin.

came over to my house to have a glass of wine and some cheese. While we ate and drank, we chatted about the Olympic Games and everything we'd been through. Then Murray said, "Doc, this is it for me. I'm not going to coach the United States Olympic hockey team anymore. This is as high as anybody can get it. Who's going to beat the Russians . . .?"

We sipped our wine.

"I want to start a junior team," said Murray. "Our twenty-year-old kids can compete with their twenty-year-old kids. If they train just like the Russians, they have a chance. I want to focus on junior hockey."

I said, "That's a great idea." Then he asked me if I would be the team doctor. I was looking for a new challenge, so I said, "Murray, sure. I'm happy to help you anytime. If you need something, I'll be there!"

Soon after that, Murray started organizing a new junior team to compete in Upper Midwest and—eventually—in international tournaments. The future was going to be very, very interesting.

1997 team reunion. Sitting: Peter Sears, Co-Captain Keith Christiansen, Coach Murray Williamson, Manager Hal Trumble, Co-Captain Tim Sheehy, Mike Curran. Standing: Bruce McIntosh, Tom Mellor, Jim McElmury, Craig Sarner, Frank Sanders, Larry Bader, Ron Naslund, Kevin Ahearn, Wally Olds, Stu Irving, Charlie Brown, myself.

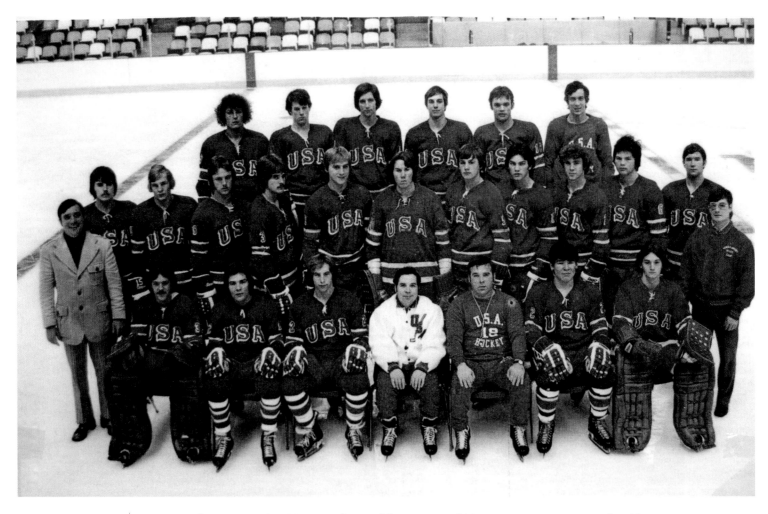

1973/74 US National Junior Hockey Team at the World Invitational Tournament in Leningrad, USSR.
Front row (L-R): Mike Dibble, Mark Lambert, Steve Roberts, Manager Murray Williamson, Head Coach Andre
Beaulieu, Gary Sargent, Frank Zimmerman. Middle row: Assistant Coach Mike Radakovich, John Shewchuk,
Tom Funke, Dave Hanson, Craig Hanmer, Paul Holmgren, Steve Short, Mike Wong, Tom Ulseth, Trainer Al
Mathieu. Top row: Dan Bonk, Greg Woods, Dave Geving, Jim Warner, Buzzy LaFond, Jim Kronschnabel.
Not pictured: Tom Madson, Earl Sargent, Public Relations Representative Jim Antonopoulos, and myself.

First Junior World Tournament

Leningrad, USSR, 1973–1974

Team Roster

In Goal: *Mike Dibble, Frank Zimmerman, Dave Heitz*

Defense: *Dave Geving, Craig Hanmer, Jeff Hymanson, Steve Roberts, Gary Sargent, Greg Woods*

Forwards: *Dan Bonk, Tom Funke, Dave Hanson, Paul Holmgren, Jim Kronschnabel, Buzzy LaFond, Mark Lambert, Tom Madson, Peter Roberts, Earl Sargent, John Shewchuk, Steve Short, Tom Ulseth, Jim Warner, Mike Wong*

The first international Junior Hockey tournament, for players aged twenty years and younger, was held in Leningrad, Russia from December 26, 1973 to January 4, 1974. Murray Williamson was the general manager, Andre Beaulieu was head coach, and I was once again team doctor. Although it was technically an invitational tournament, in essence it was the Junior World Championships because all of the major ice hockey–playing nations competed: Canada, Russia, Czechoslovakia, Sweden, Finland, and the United States.

The US Junior Team first practiced on November 22, 1973. A mere two days later we played a citywide junior all-star team in Winnipeg, Manitoba, where we got off to a good start with a convincing 8–2 victory. Over the next three weeks we practiced and played exhibition games in and around Minneapolis.

On December 17, 1973, we flew to Toronto and took a bus to Peterborough, Ontario, to play a couple of exhibition games against the Canadian juniors before heading to Europe. That evening at dinner, I thought it would be wise to caution everybody about the danger of contracting diarrhea from the water in Leningrad. So, after we'd finished eating, I stood up and said, "Gentlemen, you know we are going to Leningrad. What you probably don't know is that the city was built on a swamp by Peter the Great in 1703. Why is this important? Because the water there contains large numbers of the parasite *Giardia lamblia*, which gives people extremely bad diarrhea, abdominal cramps, and loss of strength. If you get sick, you won't be able to play for many days. Don't drink water from the faucets. Don't put ice cubes in your soft drinks. Don't even open your mouth in the shower. Only drink bottled water and soft drinks. Brush your teeth with bottled water. The smallest amount of tap water can make you violently ill. You must be very careful."

That same evening, I met the team doctor for the Canadian National Junior Team. We talked about how to make the water safe in Leningrad and got some four-gallon plastic containers and Halazone tablets to purify the water at practices and games.

The next afternoon, we played the Canadian junior team and lost 6–4.

The morning after that we took a bus to Toronto and practiced there. We'd planned to take another bus to Montreal the following day and then fly to New York, but it had started snowing so hard that we decided to scrap that plan. Instead, arrangements were made for a flight to Montreal, which left us little time for our connecting flight to New York. It was still snowing very hard when we boarded the plane in Montreal. As I settled into my seat, I looked out at the tarmac and noticed our bags on a luggage cart. I got Murray's attention, and he looked out the window and said, "Goodness gracious, those are our bags! What's happening? Why aren't they loading our bags?"

After we were told that our bags wouldn't be on this flight, Murray decided that Andre, who spoke French, and our public relations man, Jim Antonopoulos, should stay in Montreal to make sure that our luggage got on the next plane to New York. The rest of us flew to New York, where we boarded the plane to Prague. Our transatlantic flight was smooth and problem free, but as soon as we got to Europe, it was foggy and snowing again. We couldn't land in Prague. We had to continue on and land in Bratislava, where we spent several hours at the airport and railroad station.

After dinner at the railroad station, we boarded a train for Prague. It was very crowded, and the seven-hour ride was exhausting. We finally arrived in Prague early the next morning and went straight to the International Hotel, where everybody rested.

Later, when our luggage arrived, Murray's suitcases were missing, as were all of the hockey bags. We'd finally made it to Prague, but didn't have our gear and couldn't skate. That night's game against Czechoslovakia was canceled. We were all very disappointed. In order to get some exercise, we organized a gym workout the next morning.

On the afternoon of December 22, the boys went sightseeing. Murray and I decided to visit the Moser Shop again with our gracious host, Jiri Trnka. The three of us said hello to Mr. Emil Slama, as club membership required, and bought a few more of his beautiful crystal wine glasses.

We'd hoped that by the morning of December 23 our equipment would arrive, but it still hadn't come. The Czechoslovakians were upset and canceled the second game. Later that afternoon our gear finally arrived, but everything was wet and Murray's suitcases were still missing. We took the bags back to our hotel, and I helped our trainer, Allen Mathieu, unpack everything and spread it out to dry on the floors of our rooms and in the hallways. Our gear was everywhere. Those players who could wear skates practiced on an outside rink. Other players were forced, once again, to work out at the gym. It was a sad, unhappy situation. We'd lost two days to the luggage delay and missed both of our games in Czechoslovakia.

On December 24 we practiced in the morning and had a team lunch afterward. Some players were talking, saying they wanted to go to church for Christmas Eve. Jiri said, "Boys, this is maybe a little bit difficult for you to understand, but Christmas is not very popular with our government. We are not really allowed to celebrate Christmas, especially at church. After dinner this evening, we might try to see if a church is open, but please don't make any funny remarks. You never know who is watching, and we can get in serious trouble if you start making ridiculous comments." The boys said they would behave and wouldn't cause any trouble.

After a very nice dinner, Jiri, a group of players, and myself tried to locate a church. The streets were deserted. We found a church, but it was closed. Jiri said, "I hoped to find an open church, but this year is especially strict." We walked a little further along the empty street and took a streetcar back to the hotel.

On Christmas Day, we had breakfast at 7:30 a.m. and boarded the bus for the airport. At the airport security checkpoint, a big, heavyset woman with a militaristic appearance told us, "You are overweight. Nobody gets on the plane until you pay $700 in overage fees."

Murray said, "What? This is ridiculous! We never pay overages. When your team comes to our country, we never charge you like this. I want Miro Subrt, the vice president of the International Ice Hockey Federation and chief ice hockey official of Czechoslovakia, to come here and settle this problem."

Mr. Subrt came to the airport, but the woman was still very strict and said, "You can talk about hockey all you want, but you can't tell me how to run the airport. These people will pay $700 or they don't get on the plane."

I looked at Murray and saw a devilish spark in

his eyes. He took out his checkbook, slammed it on the counter and said, "Fine! We will pay. I'm sorry we caused so much trouble. We'll even pay $50 more for the trouble. Here is a check for $750."

The woman took it and said, "Fine. This is okay. Everything is all right. You can get on the plane."

Then I saw Murray run to the phone booth. He came back with a grin on his face. Later, I asked if he canceled the check. He said, "Of course I did, Doc. You think we were going to pay them?" I laughed and thought, *That's my boy.* I knew he would do something like that.

The flight to Moscow was easy. A short two hours later we met Valery, a young man in his mid-twenties, who was going to be our guide and interpreter during our stay in Leningrad. He spoke such good, fluent English—with a Brooklyn accent!—that we all looked at each other and knew it didn't come from a book. He must have lived in New York for a year or more to learn that dialect. Valery told us to get our bags and leave them in a secure room because we would fly to Leningrad later that afternoon. In the meantime, a bus would take us into town for lunch at a hotel near Red Square.

After lunch, a group of us went to Red Square and walked around for an hour before boarding the bus to the airport. It was a funny feeling. I had heard and read a lot about Red Square, but actually being there, looking at Saint Basil's Cathedral and the Kremlin Wall, it was all a bit surreal.

The weather was quite foggy. Valery said, "Because of the bad weather here in Moscow, our plane hasn't left Leningrad. We will have to wait and see. When the weather improves, it will be on its way."

So, we waited and waited, one hour and another. It was getting late. Finally, Valery said, "The weather is still not good. We will go tomorrow. I will arrange a hotel, so you can have a nice dinner and good night's sleep here in Moscow. Tomorrow morning we'll get you back to the airport and fly to Leningrad."

What else could we do? We got returned to the hotel and had dinner.

After dinner, Al, Andre, Jim, and I walked over to Red Square again. Then we returned to the hotel to find that our rooms were large, with high ceilings and old metal beds. But the mattresses were comfortable, and I got a good night's rest.

The next morning we left for the airport right after breakfast. The weather was a little bit better, but still somewhat foggy and misty.

The streets of Moscow seemed quite wide, but maybe they looked that way because there were very few cars. Big, long apartment buildings, five or six stories high, lined the streets. Some of them took up whole blocks.

At the airport, we were told the same story again: the plane hadn't left Leningrad because the weather was bad here in Moscow. We waited for two hours and started getting tired.

Now, I can't speak Russian fluently, but I can understand almost everything. The loudspeaker announced that there were flights arriving from Frankfurt, Vienna, and Stockholm. I went to Valery and said, "Why are you telling us that our plane can't land in Moscow? The loudspeaker just said that planes are coming in from Frankfurt, Vienna, and Stockholm. How come our plane hasn't left?"

Valery said, "Those are international flights, big planes with instruments. Your plane does not have instruments and flies by direct vision only. That's why it can't come in."

I told Murray this, and he said, "No way! We are not taking a plane that is navigated by direct vision only!"

He went to Valery and asked if what I'd said was true. Valery replied, "Yes. Our domestic flights are served by planes without instruments. That's the way it is."

Murray said, "No way. We won't fly on the plane like that. Get us a train to Leningrad."

So Jim Antonopoulos found a good, fast train that left at 3:00 p.m. We would be in Leningrad that evening. Then Valery said, "I don't think it will work out. Things have to be arranged, and it doesn't happen that quickly."

Jim said, "We still have three hours' time! More than enough to make arrangements. All they have to do is attach a couple of cars. The route starts here in Moscow. The train is already waiting."

Valery was still not sure that we could get on that train. Jim got mad and said, "Valery, you just don't want us to see your countryside. That's why you don't want us to get on that train."

Valery shrugged it off and said, "Well, you said it, not me."

In the end, we took an overnight train called the

Red Arrow, which was fast and had sleeper cars. It was scheduled to leave Moscow at 10:00 p.m., with arrival in Leningrad early the next morning.

After dinner, we got our bags and took a bus to the Moscow railroad station. The sleeper car was comfortable, with good sleeping arrangements. I shared a compartment with Al. After we'd settled in, Al went to check on Mike Wong, who'd injured his knee, leaving me alone in our compartment. A few minutes later, Valery stopped by. I noticed a little grin on his face as he said, "Well, how is the doctor?"

I said, "Very well, thank you. This is a nice, comfortable train."

Valery said, "Only the best for the Americans." He paused a moment, then asked, "So, tell me, Doc, why in the world would you leave your beautiful Riga?"

I said, "Valery, maybe you're too young to really understand—you weren't even born at the time—but thirty years ago it was wartime. The University of Riga was closed. The only way I could continue my medical education was to go to another country, so I went to Germany."

Valery looked me in the eye and said, "Bullshit." A sly smile spread across his face, and he started to tell me the story of my family, my father, the Latvian Resistance, my father's dissidence, and my own personal history. He knew it all, every detail. I wasn't particularly surprised, but it was an uncomfortable situation, to be sure. I didn't know quite how to respond, so I decided to be blunt.

"Valery," I said, "if you know all of this, why do

you ask me such questions?"

Valery shrugged it off and said, "Well, okay, Doc. Let us forget the whole thing."

I breathed and said, "Okay, fine," and we didn't talk about such things anymore. Then Valery asked me to go get Murray so that we could all have a drink. He said, "You know, we have a very good cognac in Russia."

I said, "Yes, yes, I have heard that."

Valery went to get the cognac while Andre, Murray, Jim, Al, Assistant Coach Mike Radakovich, and myself assembled in Murray's compartment. I told them what had just happened and that it was more clear than ever that Valery was a KGB agent.

Valery came back with a bottle of cognac and several glasses. After he'd filled the glasses with cognac, he said, "I would like to make the first toast to the great country of the Soviet Union!"

We all looked at each other and thought, *What do we do now*?

Murray put down his glass and said, "I won't drink to that."

Valery took it in stride and said quickly and nonchalantly, "Well, okay, let's drink to a good tournament."

Murray said, "Okay, fine, I will drink to that."

Valery didn't try that trick again, and soon after we all went to our compartments and had a good night's rest.

The next morning, when we woke up at 7:00 a.m., we were already in Leningrad. After we got our luggage, a bus took us to the newly built Hotel Leningrad

on the shores of the Neva River. The rooms were small, but modern and clean. The elevators didn't always work, but that didn't bother us too much. I roomed with Andre, who had a larger room that we used for meetings and such.

After resting for a while, we practiced at 11:00 a.m. The stadium was also newly built and fairly modern, with nice locker rooms. My first concern, of course, was where and how I could fill the four-gallon containers to prepare safe drinking water. In the equipment room, the faucet was in a good spot, so we got a little table and filled both big plastic containers. I put in the Halazone tablets and started the purification process. Everything was arranged. When practice finished, we ate lunch and got our credentials.

We didn't have a game on the first day of the tournament, so I went to the kitchen to talk to the chef about our team's meals. I asked Valery to join me because my Russian was not very good. Valery was a good translator, but the chef didn't have much to offer. Breakfast, especially, was going to be a problem. They had all kinds of porridges, but no fruit juices or ham and eggs. They didn't even know how to scramble eggs! And the only fruit they offered was an occasional apple, which didn't look the best. As far as lunch and dinner, I knew that our boys were not big fans of lamb or fish, so pork was the best choice. We discussed all of the options and what the meals should consist of. The chef understood what I wanted and told me he'd do what he could. I went to the opening ceremony hoping for the best.

We played the Canadians on December 28 in

our first game of the tournament. We knew it would be tough, because we'd just played them twice in Peterborough. The Russian spectators all seemed to support Team Canada, despite the fact we outplayed them for much of the game. Late in the third period, we were leading 4–3, but even the referees seemed to be against us. They awarded a penalty shot to the Canadians. Team Canada tied it, but we kept the pressure on, buzzing around their net. Then, with less than ten seconds to go in the game, a shot destined for the Canadian goal hit the crossbar instead and bounced right to a Canadian winger. He picked up the puck, streaked down the ice, and scored on a breakaway. The Canadians won 5–4. We looked at each other in disbelief.

Then we got even more bad news. Our captain and the best defenseman, Gary Sargent, had gotten a hard check to his thigh during the third period. He had a severe muscle bruise. It was so bad, in fact, that Gary missed almost the entire tournament. We returned to our hotel very disappointed and unhappy about the whole thing.

The next morning, after breakfast, Al and I planned to go to the arena early to get the drinking water ready for practice. We asked the receptionist to call us a taxi. She was nice and polite but said, "I can't do that from here. Please go to room 23 on the second floor. They must arrange all transportation."

I said, "Okay, fine, we'll go there," and we went to the second floor and found room 23. I told the man sitting there that I was the doctor from the American hockey team and needed to arrange a taxi to the arena.

The man said, "Oh, no. This is not the right place. You have to go downstairs and find Tatyana. She is the one who arranges all transportation. I am sorry."

We trudged back down the stairs to look for Tatyana. When we finally found her and told her our story, she said, "I'm sorry, but I can't do that. It's not in my line of duty. You have to go see Olga. She is at that counter."

So we went back to the reception desk and asked for Olga. As it turned out, Olga was the same girl that we'd asked to call a taxi in the first place. She smiled very politely and tried to send us to room 23 once again.

Wait a minute, I thought, *I lived in Latvia under a Communist government for a year in 1941. In some instances, there is only one kind of message these people understand.*

I pounded my fist on the desk and said, "You, *sabotashnics*! You are just trying to sabotage things for us Americans so we cannot purify our water and get sick. You give us the runaround! I am going to report you to the hockey administrators and tell them how you treat us! We will see what happens then!"

Immediately Olga said, "Oh, no! Please don't get excited! I'll get a taxi for you right away. Just wait here a moment. Please, please, don't get excited!"

Sure enough, three minutes later, a taxi magically appeared.

Every day after that, when we came into the lobby, they were nice and polite to us. Everybody said, "Good morning! How are you?"

Al just laughed and said, "Hey, Doc, that really

worked, didn't it?"

Well, yes, it did. Sometimes that is the only way to deal with these people. From then on, we got to the rink quickly and had plenty of time to prepare the drinking water before practice.

The next morning, after breakfast, we had a team meeting and a light skate. We played the Swedes that afternoon. It was a very hard game for us. We never expected them to be that good. It was obvious they had practiced together for quite a while because they worked so smoothly together. We lost 11–1.

The next day we had the afternoon off, and a group of us went downtown with Valery to look at some shops. By then the boys had noticed that there were certain places Valery couldn't take them. So, they were giving him a hard time, asking him all kinds of questions. "Valery," they teased, "can we go see the monastery?" Or, "Valery, will you take us to the flea market? We heard there are good things to buy there."

Finally, Valery exploded. He got up, turned to me, and said, "Doc, you know why we can't go to those places! Tell those idiots to stop bothering me!"

I thought, *Oh, Valery, now you need my help.*

I said, "Okay, boys, time to cut it out. If you have something special you want to see, don't bother Valery with it, come to me instead and we'll talk it over. Then I'll talk to Valery and we'll figure out the arrangements."

After that, the boys went easier on Valery and everyone got along better. He even took us shopping downtown on New Year's Eve.

At that time there were no Christmas celebrations in Soviet Russia, but New Year's Eve and New Year's Day were big events. Murray and Jim were invited to a special reception for all the dignitaries. When Murray got back, he was wiping his forehead and said, "Oh, Doc, it was really something. Jim and I were in trouble. After the speeches were over, the Soviets started toasting every two minutes for all kinds of reasons, and you had to empty your glass completely every time. There was no way we could keep drinking like that. I started throwing the contents of my glass over my shoulder. I think those guys were trying to get us really drunk!" Murray, of course, was shrewd enough to see that.

We had our New Year's Eve dinner at 6:00 p.m. It was much nicer than our previous meals. Afterward, most of the boys were hanging around in the hall because there was no place else to go. Soon enough it was midnight. I wished everybody Happy New Year and went to bed because, once again, Al and I had to get up early, go to the rink, and get the water ready.

I had just fallen asleep when the phone rang. It was Valery. He said, "Doc, I don't feel well. I want you to check my heart." Now, I don't know if he had noticed that I wasn't down at the party and wondered where I'd gone or if he was actually concerned about his health, but I said, "Sure, sure, Valery. Come up and I will listen to your heart and see what is going on."

He came up to my room and I checked his heart and pulse. There was nothing unusual, so I said, "Valery, I think maybe you got a little too excited about some of those toasts. Don't worry. Everything is fine. There's no problem with your heart at all."

He said, "I just wanted to check and make sure everything was all right."

I thought, *You were spying on me. You just wanted to check to make sure I was in my room.*

Not long after that, Andre returned. I told him about Valery's visit. We both had a good laugh and went to sleep.

On New Year's Day we had a light morning practice before our afternoon game against Finland. We were hoping for our first win. In the first period, everything went well, but later we made a few mistakes and the Finns made us pay. Meanwhile, we were unable to penetrate their defense and lost the game 4–1.

Later that afternoon, Murray said, "Doc, what do we have to do to win a game? Look at the Finns. They partied all night long. They were out with girls last night. Our boys behaved, they stayed in the hotel and got plenty of rest, but look at what happened on the ice!"

I said, "Murray, I don't know, but there's one thing I often wonder. In the States, we play our anthem before every game. Even a peewee game! I don't want to say that our boys disregard the anthem. No, no, they are good boys. They are proud when the anthem is played. But they hear that tune so often, it sometimes looks to me like they can't wait for it to be over. It's not that way in Europe. Here, they only play the national anthem at international competitions. Their anthem is sacred to them. Hearing their national anthem, the Finns disregarded their hangovers and played their hearts out for their country." It was difficult to find a good answer. We decided to stay positive and not get down on the boys.

On January 2, after a short morning practice, we took the boys to the famous Hermitage. Without a doubt, the Hermitage is one of the world's richest museums. The rooms are more ornate than any I have seen in any museum in the world. The surroundings are so lush and overwhelming—with all that marble, the big, beautiful malachite columns and golden frescoes everywhere—you can hardly look at the paintings. The boys were very impressed. They didn't know such a thing existed here in Russia.

After the tour, some of the boys wanted to go shopping. We were leaving in a few days, so there wasn't much time left. First, we went to a hat store, where I found a traditional Russian fur hat for my son-in-law. Next, we went to a shop full of amber jewelry that came from the Baltic Sea. I bought a necklace for my wife.

When we returned to the hotel, Valery was waiting for us. He said, "Gentlemen, I have made arrangements to go to the circus tonight. Let's have dinner quickly and get ready to go."

The circus was very good. The animal acts were superb, and the acrobats were amazing. Valery was happy to see how much we liked it. Everybody laughed at the clowns during the intermissions. We enjoyed the show very much and returned to the hotel in a jolly mood.

The next day, Paul Holmgren was horribly sick. Three days earlier, I had prepared the usual big container of drinking water in the equipment room. In came Paul. He walked right by the container and drank straight from the faucet.

I said, "Paul, what are you doing?"

He said, "Doc, I'm sorry. I completely forgot."

I said, "How can you do that? I've talked to you boys, day after day, about the bad water in Leningrad!"

He looked at me and said, "I'm sorry, I'm sorry."

I said, "Paul, it's your health, not mine."

Sure enough, three days later, Paul was terribly sick with cramps and diarrhea. The next day, a few more boys got diarrhea and couldn't practice. I thought, *Here we go. It's catching up with us now.* Then Paul developed a fever and more abdominal pain. I hoped he didn't have an infectious disease such as abdominal typhus. I had contracted that myself when I was sixteen by drinking straight from the faucet after a hockey game in Latvia. I knew how bad it could be. I thought, *My God, what can I do with him? I can't put him in a Russian hospital. We'll never get him out of there.* Luckily, I had some tetracycline and standard antidiarrheal medications. Those helped a little.

That day we played the Soviets. But with so many boys who'd contracted diarrhea, we couldn't compete. We lost the game 9–1.

That evening, when we got back to the hotel, Mike Radakovich asked me, "Doc, have you tried the white wine at the bar? It's really good."

I said, "I'm sure it is, Mike. They have good white wines over here, especially in Georgia and in some of the southern states. I haven't tried it yet, but I will."

Mike said, "Good, and if you ask them to, they'll even put in an ice cube for you."

I said, "Mike, you didn't really put an ice cube in your wine, did you?"

Mike got scared and asked, "Doc, do you think I'll get diarrhea from that?"

I said, "I don't know, Mike, you might. Ice cubes preserve *Giardia lamblia* organisms. Let's keep our fingers crossed."

On the last day of the tournament, we practiced early and started packing. In the afternoon we played the Czechoslovakians. This was the only time when the crowd cheered for Team USA. Czechoslovakia was their big rival, so the spectators rooted for us. It helped, and we won 4–3, our only victory. Czechoslovakia, though, didn't win a single game and finished last. We returned to the hotel in a better mood because we'd won at least the one game.

After dinner we took a bus to the train station, where we boarded the sleeper for Moscow. We were anxious to get home because several of the boys still had abdominal problems. We arrived in Moscow the next morning at 8:00 a.m. and were transferred to the airport. As soon as we boarded the plane, everybody felt relieved. When the plane took off, all the boys shouted and cheered, "Hooray! Here we go!" All of us gave a big round of applause for the pilots. We changed planes in London, and I went to check on Paul. He still wasn't feeling well.

Fortunately, the flight across the Atlantic was smooth. When we got to New York, we told the customs agents that we'd just come from Moscow. They laughed and said, "Well, there's nothing to buy over there. That makes it easy for us."

After New York, some of us continued home to Minneapolis, including Paul, who still had a fever. When we landed in Minneapolis, I talked to Paul and advised him to go to the hospital right away. That was not merely diarrhea, I told him, I was sure he had an infection. Later, I found out that Paul did have abdominal typhus and was in the hospital for a couple of weeks.

As we waited for our baggage, one of our players said, "Doc, after being in Russia for two weeks, oh boy, now I realize how much we take for granted here at home."

It was a lesson for them to see how people lived behind the Iron Curtain and how nice it was in the United States. It was nice to hear young people say how much they appreciated being back home again.

*US National Hockey Team at 1974 World Championship, Pool "B" in Ljubljana, Yugoslavia.
Front row (L-R): Assistant Coach Grant Standbrook, Captain Len Lilyholm, Doug Palazzari, Buzzy Schneider,
Mike Polich, Ed Walsh, Blaine Comstock, Steve Sertich, Steve Alley, Carl Lackey, Bob Krieger, Head Coach Bob
Johnson. Back row: Myself, General Manager Art Berglund, Mike Usitalo, Bob Goodenow, John Taft, Richie
Dunn, Bill Nyrop, Dean Talafous, Dave Arundel, Al Hangsleben, Gary Smith, Bob Lundeen, International
Chairman Bob Fleming, Trainer Al Mathieu.*

Yugoslavian Hospitality

1974 Group B World Championships, Ljubljana, Yugoslavia

Team Roster

In Goal: *Blaine Comstock, Ed Walsh*

Defense: *Dave Arundel, Richie Dunn, Al Hangsleben, Bob Lundeen, Bill Nyrop, John Taft*

Forwards: *Steve Alley, Bob Goodenow, Bob Krieger, Carl Lackey, Len Lilyholm, Doug Palazzari, Mike Polich, Guy Smith, Buzzy Schneider, Dean Talafous, Mike Usitalo*

Sunday, March 17, 1974, was a clear, brisk early spring morning in Boston. The NCAA Men's Ice Hockey Championship had concluded the night before with the University of Minnesota's 4–2 victory over Michigan Tech.

That morning I met five of the players who'd just competed in the tournament: Ed Walsh from Boston University; Bob Goodenow from Harvard; Mike Usitalo from Michigan Tech; and Mike Polich and Buzzy Schneider from University of Minnesota. All of them had been selected to play for the US National Team in the Group B World Championships in Ljubljana, Yugoslavia, and it was my job to get them organized and over to Europe. In fact, Coach Bob Johnson and the rest of the team were already in Sweden, where we were scheduled to play two exhibition games before traveling to Ljubljana. We met our general manager, Art Berglund, at the Boston airport and flew to Stockholm.

Before our arrival, the newly formed Team USA had already played a game in Strömstad, which they won 5–2. Two nights later, with the help of the five new players that I'd brought, we won the second exhibition game in Jönköping as well, 6–2. Both wins boosted the confidence of our freshly assembled team as its members were just learning each other's names.

On Tuesday, March 19, we took a bus to Gothenburg Airport for our scheduled flight to Ljubljana, Yugoslavia. However, at the airport we had a little complication. The airport official declared that we were considerably overweight and had to pay $900 before we could board the plane. Of course, we had a verbal agreement with the Swedish airline representative in New York that we would not have to pay overages, but we didn't have the letter on hand to prove it. Art tried very hard to convince the officer about our agreement, but the airport official insisted on written verification.

At that moment, one of Murray Williamson's old tricks flashed in my mind. I whispered in Art's ear about asking them to send the bill to our office in Colorado Springs. Then Executive Director Hal Trumble could fix it with the airline representative in New York. Art smiled. He pleasantly explained that we were at the beginning of an extended trip with a fairly tight budget. Would the airport official be so kind as to send the bill to our home office in Colorado Springs? The airport official accepted this proposal and took the name and address of our executive director, and we boarded the plane. With sparkling eyes, we looked at each other and said, "Let's have a beer!"

The flight was smooth and uncomplicated. After we landed in Ljubljana, a friendly young student named Andy greeted us warmly. He was going to be our host and translator. I felt immediately like this was going to be much different from the trip to Romania four years ago. We breezed through customs and took a bus to a nice, modern hotel in the center of downtown Ljubljana.

As always, one of my first jobs was to meet the chef to discuss our meals. He was very helpful in arranging and planning our menu the way our players preferred.

Later that first day we got our identification cards and practiced. While walking around the arena to get familiar with the building, I ran into a good friend of mine, Stane Aljančič. It turned out that Stane was the manager of this sports complex, which also featured a basketball court, a tennis court, and exercise rooms. Stane invited me to have a cup of coffee in his office, where I met some other building officials. It was a friendly visit.

After practice, we took the bus back to the hotel. On the way one of our players asked, "Andy, do Yugoslavs feel inclined to the East or to the West?"

Andy smiled broadly and said, "Let me tell you a story. There was an international conference near

Belgrade to which Marshal Tito had invited Russian and American delegations for lunch. After lunch was finished, they all drove back to Belgrade. On the way, there was a fork in the road. But no matter which road you took, you arrived at your destination.

"First to arrive at the fork was the Russian delegation. The driver asked, 'Comrade Chairman, which road should we take? The right or the left?' The chairman of the Russian delegation answered, 'Take the left one, of course!'

"Shortly after that, the American delegation arrived at the fork. The driver asked, 'Mr. Ambassador, which road should I take? The right or left one? The American ambassador answered, 'Take the right one.'

"Finally, the Yugoslavian delegation arrived. The driver asked, 'Marshal Tito, which road should we take? The right or the left one?' Marshal Tito said, 'Signal to the left, but take the right one.'"

Everybody on the bus burst out laughing, and there were no more questions about that point.

That afternoon there was a meeting of the Passport Control Committee. Art was busy with other duties and asked me to serve as the American representative. It was nice to see some old friends, including Ernst Gassler, the team manager for Austria; Freddy Schwiers, manager of Team Holland; and Mr. Luxa from Yugoslavia.

We all sat around a big conference table and compared lists of players to their respective passports. I was given the Dutch team. The players on the list all had Dutch passports, but their names sounded more English, French, or Canadian. Also, many of the

passports seemed new and freshly printed, like the ink had barely dried. Of course, everything was completely legal and correct, but I had the feeling that we'd see more Canadian players than Dutch players when we played against Team Holland in this tournament.

The next morning, Thursday, March 21, we had a team meeting after breakfast. Len Lilyholm was chosen captain. He did an outstanding job inspiring, disciplining, and holding the team together throughout the tournament.

Team Japan was our first opponent. Everyone on the team gave a solid effort, and we won, 7–4.

Friday, following a light morning practice, Buzzy Schneider and I decided to walk downtown before lunch. Andy came along and showed us all the best shops, restaurants, and banks. It was a nice spring day. The sun was shining, and the air was clear and crisp. Magnolia trees were blooming, and the tulips were still showing the splendor of their different colors. We worked up a good appetite, had a hearty lunch, and rested before the game against our hosts, the Yugoslavians.

We knew the game against Yugoslavia would be much harder than the one against Japan because of the spectators and home ice advantage. Therefore, our boys were determined to give it everything they had.

We clearly outskated the Yugoslavians, and by the end of the game Mike Polich's and Doug Palazzari's lines drew admiration from the Yugoslavian fans despite the fact we won the game 5–0.

The next morning, the Ljubljana newspapers predicted a smooth ride for the American team. The

Meeting enthusiastic hockey fans while visiting Bled, Yugoslavia (L-R): Mike Usitalo, Bill Nyrop, Mike Polich, John Taft.

speed of Bobby Krieger, Mike Polich, and Buzzy Schneider's line, in particular, was highly praised.

We had the next day off, so Andy organized a trip to Bled, a pretty little Alpine resort town on the shore of a lake by the same name. Across the lake from Bled sits an old castle on top of a hill. The bus dropped us off at the base of the hill, and we walked up the steep, winding road. At the top we crossed the drawbridge and entered the castle courtyard.

There was a beautiful view of the lake, which had an island in the middle. On the island was a small, white church that definitely added to the fairytale panorama. Andy noted that Marshal Tito had a summer place on this lake. We walked around the castle, sat in the warm spring sunshine, and took a lot of pictures. Then we walked around the lake to the village of

Bled. It was a nice, small town with many small shops and cafés. On the way back to the bus, our boys met a group of Yugoslavian girls who recognized them from the game. There was a lot of fun and laughter.

During the one-hour return trip through the countryside of what was then Yugoslavia and is now Slovenia, we saw many small houses and fields. Very frequently, horses worked the fields instead of tractors. People were dressed in simple, usually dark clothes, but their faces shone with happiness and contentment. Some of the younger people were even cracking jokes and laughing. It was all so different from Romania, where everybody we saw in the countryside was dressed very poorly. Even in Bucharest, people walked with sad expressions on their faces. There was a much happier mood here in Yugoslavia. We returned to Ljubljana in good spirits from an excellent outing.

On Sunday at 10:00 a.m., we played Norway. It wasn't an easy game for us, but we won 5–3.

The next day our opponent was Team Holland. As expected, most of the Dutch players spoke English and played Canadian-style hockey. We were prepared for that, and our consistent, well-organized plays gave us a 7–4 victory.

There were no games scheduled for Tuesday, March 26, so our Yugoslavian hosts organized a wine-tasting tour for all of the teams' administrative staffs. Since our head coach, Bob Johnson, had opted to stay back for morning practice with the team, Art Berglund invited me to join him. Naturally, I accepted and was quite happy to join the group.

All of us met in front of the hotel at 9:00 a.m. and boarded a nice, comfortable bus. It was another warm, sunny spring morning, and everybody was in a good mood. After thirty minutes or so, the bus stopped in a quaint little village for breakfast. As I stepped off the bus, I saw a very interesting post office that must have been a postal relay station for exchanging horses and carriages many years ago. In fact, four or five antique postal carriages were parked under the eaves of an old carriage house across the road.

Our hosts led us into the post office for breakfast. Inside, the ceiling was low and there wasn't much light coming through the little windows. In one corner, however, there was a large brick furnace and an L-shaped table decorated with bright spring flowers, which made the room quite cozy. We sat down on the long benches, and soon plates of sandwiches made with different kinds of sausage and cheese were served. Before we dug in, however, our glasses were filled with a strong, vodka-like drink called Slivovitz—the local plum brandy. With that, the head of the Yugoslavian organizing committee raised his glass and toasted to a good tournament and warm friendships among its participants. Of course, we had to empty our glasses to that! Oh, it went down my throat like fire—the first thing we'd had for breakfast!—and hit my empty stomach very hard. I saw Art practically dive for some sausage and bread. I felt a little better, knowing that I wasn't the only one who had such a hard time handling a drink so early.

After that, thankfully, coffee was served while more Silvovitz was poured in our glasses. As everyone ate and drank, they got more talkative. At one point, one of the German representatives asked Freddy Schwiers, head of the Dutch delegation, "Freddy, tell us, what does your team sing when they win a game?" He continued, mimicking the tune of "O Canada!" as he sang, "Is it 'O Hollanda, my home and native land?'"

Everybody laughed.

Then, my good Austrian friend Ernst Gassler, who was sitting next to me, stood up and said, "Oh, you guys are terrible, giving Freddy such a hard time. Don't you guys know? Freddy is a good friend of Austria! He knows the Olympic Winter Games will be held in Innsbruck in two years' time. Just think, if his boys on Team Holland can win some games and get into the A Group, Canadians could claim the gold *and* silver medals in the same Olympic Games!'" The table erupted with laughter, but Freddy just sat there in silence, puffing his big cigar, smiling at all the jokes.

A little after that, the president of the District of Slovenia arrived and joined us. Of course, we had another toast of Slivovitz to welcome him to our group. After that, everybody got back on the bus for the rest of the drive to the country winery.

After leaving the main highway, the bus took a country road through some beautiful rolling hills for about a mile or two. Then the road got very narrow, and we had to get out and walk the rest of the way. The proprietor, a stocky man with dark curly hair, wearing a white shirt and green apron, welcomed us cordially to his place, and soon we were all seated on a little terrace with a gorgeous view of the hilly countryside. After we'd settled in, we were served wine in special pottery jugs while everybody cut their own pieces of homemade sausage. Dark country bread added a special flavor.

After a couple glasses of wine, the Slovenian president suggested that we have a "song festival" in which everybody would sing a special song from his country. One of the Japanese delegates was especially enthusiastic, and he and the president didn't want to stop once they got going.

Another of the Japanese delegates was their coach, Hitoshi "Mel" Wakabayashi, with whom I'd celebrated during the Winter Olympics in Sapporo, Japan when he'd invited me to dinner with his parents. We talked about old times—college games in the WCHA from many years ago, when Mel played at Michigan, and the more recent Winter Olympics—and expressed our mutual delight with Yugoslavian hospitality.

The next day we played Austria at 10:00 a.m. It was an easy game for us. Our solid defense, with Bill Nyrop, John Taft, and Alan Hangsleben, gave the Austrians no chance to seriously threaten our goal. We won 6–0. Ernst Gassler was very impressed with our team and invited me to dinner.

That night, he wanted to talk about a European tournament to be held next summer. He explained to me that every summer during July or August, the Count of Füssen, a town in West Germany, would sponsor an international ice hockey tournament called the Thurn-and Taxis-Pokal (*pokal* means "cup"). It consisted of eight or nine teams: four West German club teams and four or five foreign clubs.

Ernst said that in a day or two, a couple of German representatives from the Füssen Organizing Committee would be in Ljubljana to look for potential teams to invite to the 1975 tournament. Ernst also knew that most of our players (sixteen out of twenty) were college students and was wondering if an American college would be interested in participating. I told him that the University of Minnesota, where Mike Polich and Buzzy Schneider were rostered, had just won the NCAA Championship ten days ago, and both of them would still be eligible to play for the University of Minnesota in summer 1975. I also told Ernst that as the team physician for the University of Minnesota, I would be glad to talk to the coach and the athletic director to help arrange our participation.

Ernst said he was sure the Germans would be very happy to invite the University of Minnesota team. He would arrange a meeting as soon as the Germans arrived. We toasted a glass of wine to a future game between the Innsbruck Hockey Club and the University of Minnesota. I expressed my appreciation for his thoughtfulness in regard to our American boys.

The next day, a day off for all of the teams, our hosts had arranged a trip to the stalagmite caves at Postojnska Jama. A bus picked us up after breakfast, and an hour later we were there. We took our seats in some small, open mine cars that ran on tracks to the interior of the cave, about two hundred yards away. Inside, we got out of the carts and walked down through larger and smaller caves illuminated by the electric lights. Here and there were wooden planks

straddling puddles of water. Suddenly, the lights went out. Shortly after they came back on, and our guide laughed and laughed. This, apparently, was a joke they always pulled on groups visiting the caves for the first time.

Early the next morning, as I was brushing my teeth, the telephone rang. It was Ernst. He told me to come down to the lobby immediately. The Germans of Füssen had arrived. So, without shaving, I dressed quickly and went down to the lobby, where Ernst introduced me to the business manager, Walter Richter, and other representatives from Füssen.

Ernst started praising the American team, particularly the speed of our forwards, and stressed the fact that most of our players were from college teams. I added some statistics about the college players on our national teams over the last ten years and also noted that the University of Minnesota, for which Polich and Schneider would still be playing the next year, had just won the NCAA Championship in Boston two weeks earlier.

I also told them that in December of 1970, the University of Minnesota had participated in an international tournament in Switzerland, taking second place against national teams from Switzerland, Austria, and Poland. Apparently, the Germans were sufficiently impressed. They became quite interested in the possibility of the University of Minnesota participating in the Thurn-and-Taxis-Pokal Tournament.

Ernst noticed this development and readied a glass of Slivovitz for each of us. Then he proposed a toast to the idea of an American college team playing in the Thurn-and Taxis-Pokal in 1975. I liked the toast, but I wasn't so crazy about pouring strong alcohol into my empty stomach again. Somehow I survived, and when I was able to catch my breath again, I invited the Germans to our last two games. Ernst had been trying to push the Germans for an immediate commitment, but I said that I would feel better if they made their decision after they had seen us play a game. The Germans were pleased with that proposition and suggested another toast. I thought, *Oh no! Not again!* and said, "Gentlemen, perhaps you have not yet eaten. Would you please join me for breakfast?" Everybody was agreeable to that proposition, and we moved to the cafeteria, where we finally got some food in our empty stomachs.

Our discussion soon turned to the beautiful Füssen countryside and the subject of skiing. I told them that during my years in medical school at the University of Tübingen, I went skiing at Christmas and Easter breaks in the village of Jungholz in Tyrole with my brother and sister and our friends. This Tyrolean village in Austria is just a short trip from Füssen. As soon as I mentioned that, we discovered some mutual friends, and it was like I was almost one of them. After this lovely, lengthy breakfast, I had to excuse myself to catch up with my team at practice.

At five o'clock that evening we were scheduled to play Romania. With that in mind, Coach Johnson had the boys out for an easy, light morning skate. Even I put on my skates, as I sometimes did in those days to get a little exercise and get my blood pumping.

While I was skating, Andy came up to me and asked what size my skates were. When I said size 8, he almost exploded with joy. His friend, one of the Yugoslavian players, was looking for size-8 skates to replace his old, worn-out pair. Mine were a nice pair of nearly new Super Tacks. While I was talking to Andy, his friend approached, and I could see that he wanted my skates very much. I told Andy I wouldn't mind selling, but they only had Yugoslavian money and I'd already bought all my souvenirs. I had no use for Yugoslavian money.

Seeing the sad expression on the player's face, I was about to give him my skates when I noticed a ring with a green stone on his finger. I'd always wanted a jade ring, so I asked him if it was jade. He said, yes it was. I told him, if you can find me a jade ring like that, I will trade you my skates and even kick in some money on top. Andy and his friend were happy and promised to find me a ring that night or the following morning.

At five o'clock we played Romania. By this time our team had played and practiced together enough that our playmaking was getting better from game to game. We were also a much faster team. The Romanians didn't prove much of a test, and we beat them 5–1.

After the game, Mr. Richter and the other Germans congratulated me on our victory and extended an official invitation to the University of Minnesota hockey team to participate at the Thurn-and Taxis-Pokal Tournament in the summer of 1975.

On Saturday, March 30, we played West Germany in our last game of the tournament. That morning

The "Fast Line" (L-R): Bob Krieger, Mike Polich, Buzzy Schneider

After winning the tournament. In the center-front, the US Ambassador to Yugoslavia, Mr. Malcolm Toon.

we had a short practice, and then everybody packed. Andy and his friend came over with a nice jade ring for me. The piece of jade was even larger than the one on the player's ring. I told them how much I liked it and asked how much I should pay on top of trading my skates. The player asked for forty American dollars, but I gave him fifty. A big smile spread across his face. Both of us were happy with the deal. I wouldn't have even turned down a glass of Slivovitz at that moment, because I had finally gotten the jade ring I'd always wanted. The Yugoslavian player was thrilled with his skates, and we happily shook hands.

We were all dressed up for our last game because the awards ceremony and banquet immediately followed the game. The West Germans were our toughest test, but we managed to win 5–2.

We had won all seven games and would return to Group A next spring. The US ambassador, Mr. Malcolm Toon, had arrived from Zagreb to watch our last game and personally congratulated us after the game.

Outstanding defenseman honors of the tournament went to Alan Hangsleben. Mike Polich was also recognized as the most successful forward, with seven goals and five assists. Bill Nyrop and John Taft were chosen as defensemen of the All-Tournament team.

I had a glass of wine, first with our team management, and then our players, and then with Stane Aljančič, Ernst Gassler, Freddy Schwiers, Mel Wakabayashi, Dr. Ignaz from Romania, and many other friends from different countries.

I will always remember this tournament as one of the most pleasant in my twenty-four years with the United States National Hockey team.

1975 World Championship Games in Munich and Dusseldorf, West Germany. Front row (L-R): Jim Warner, Tom Ross, Assistant Coach Grant Standbrook, Head Coach Bob Johnson, Blaine Comstock, Jim Warden, Manager Art Berglund, myself, Mike Polich, Ron Wilson. Back row: Trainer Tom Ryan, Herb Boxer, Richie Smith, Bob Goodenow, Bob Lundeen, Steve Jensen, Clark Hamilton, Jack Brownschidle, John Taft, Steve Alley, Buzzy Schneider, Jeff Rotsch, Mike Eruzione.
Not pictured: Steve Sertich, Peter Brown, Wally Olds.

10

The Longest Five Weeks

World Championships, Munich and Düsseldorf, West Germany, 1975

Team Roster

In Goal: *Blaine Comstock, Jim Warden*

Defense: *Jack Brownschidle, Clark Hamilton, Bob Lundeen, Bill Nyrop, Wally Olds, John Taft, Ron Wilson*

Forwards: *Steve Alley, Herb Boxer, Peter Brown, Mike Eruzione, Bob Goodenow, Steve Jensen, Mike Polich, Tom Ross, Jeff Rotsch, Buzzy Schneider, Steve Sertich, Rich Smith, Jim Warner*

Following the United States' victory at the Group B World Championships in Ljubljana, General Manager Art Berglund and Coach Bob Johnson were reappointed. The Group A World Championships were scheduled for Munich and Düsseldorf, West Germany, from April 3 to 19, 1975.

The team was assembled just one day prior to leaving for Europe, with fifteen out of its twenty players coming from the college hockey ranks. On Monday, March 17, we left New York for Oslo, Norway, to begin a series of seven exhibition games in Norway, Finland, Sweden, and Czechoslovakia before continuing on to

West Germany.

After a day of rest on Tuesday and visits to the famous Norwegian ski jumping area of Holmenkollen and Frogner Park in Oslo on Wednesday afternoon, we played our first exhibition game on Wednesday night against Norway. It was an easy game, and we won 5–2.

The next morning we flew to Helsinki for a game against a Finnish team that night. It was a much tougher contest, and we lost 4–3.

On that Friday, March 21, we flew to Stockholm and took a bus to Gävle, where we faced a very fast-skating Swedish team that night, losing badly 10–2.

The next morning we took a bus to Södertälje, near Stockholm, where we had the afternoon off. On March 23, Palm Sunday, we lost the game in Södertälje to another Swedish team, the Vikings, 9–5. On Monday morning we traveled by bus to Örebro, where we played the Swedish National Team and lost that game 7–4.

Tuesday, March 25, was a day of rest. After three losses in a row, the mood was sour. The next morning we took a bus to Karlskoga to play our last exhibition game in Sweden. That night we played the Swedish National Team again. This time, we played better and managed to win 6–5. The boys' mood quickly improved.

On Thursday, March 27, we took a bus to Stockholm, where we boarded a plane for Prague, Czechoslovakia. Friday was a day off, and almost everybody went shopping for crystal in Prague. Of course, I fulfilled my obligation by visiting the Moser Shop that afternoon.

The next day we played the Czechoslovakian National B Team. The game was unusually rough. Bob Goodenow was crosschecked in the mouth and needed four stitches in his upper lip. Steve Sertich got a high stick to the nose, and that also needed suturing. It was a completely different style than the games we'd played in Sweden, and we lost 7–1.

On Easter Sunday, March 30, we played the Czechoslovakian National A Team, composed of highly skilled players. The game was not rough at all, but we were badly outplayed. Some of the Czechoslovakian players were such good skaters and puck handlers that we had a hard time ever getting the puck from them. We lost 15–1. Mike Polich summed up the boys' feelings when he said, "Doc, we don't belong in this league."

On Monday, March 31, we practiced after breakfast and toured Prague that afternoon. As was now the custom, Jiri was our host and guide.

The next day we traveled by bus to Munich, West Germany. On the way we stopped in Pilsen, Czechoslovakia, where we visited the famous Pilsner brewery and ate lunch after a tour.

When we got to the Czechoslovakia–West Germany border, we were in for a big surprise. The Czechoslovakian border guards ordered us out of the bus and collected our passports. Then they held us outside the bus while they conducted an extensive search. After that, they called us to board the bus one at a time, carefully inspecting each passport before

*With Jiri Holik after the game vs. the Czech "A" team (L-R): Buzzy Schneider, myself,
Art Berglund, and Jiri Holik.*

returning it to its owner. The boarding procedure alone took about an hour, which meant that it was late in the evening when we finally arrived in Munich.

On Wednesday, April 2, we practiced in the morning at the Munich Olympic Arena and got our tournament ID tags that afternoon.

On Thursday we played our first game, against the mighty Soviet juggernaut. We lost 10–5, but Buzzy Schneider scored a hat trick against Vladislav Tretiak, who was widely acknowledged to be the best goalie in the world at that time. It was sensational, and the next morning the Munich papers were filled with pictures and stories about Buzzy and his amazing feat. He was only the second player to score a hat trick against Tretiak in international competition. Some newspapers even tried to claim a Bavarian heritage for him and wrote that Buzzy's grandfather might have had a farm near Munich.

Sadly, this was the only bright spot for us in the whole tournament. The next day we played Finland and lost 7–4.

On Saturday, April 5, we enjoyed a day off and went sightseeing after practice. The day after that, we played the very talented Czechoslovakian team again. We gave them a bit more competition this time, but we still lost 8–3.

On Monday, April 7, the fast-skating Swedes didn't give us a chance and shut us out 7–0. Tuesday was a day for rest, and I regretted that we had not organized a tour of Munich for the team.

We played our last game of the first leg on Wednesday, April 9, against Poland. We had high hopes for a win, but the puck didn't bounce our way and we lost 5–3. It was our fifth consecutive loss. We hoped for better luck in the second round at Düsseldorf.

The bus ride to Düsseldorf, in the northwestern part of West Germany, was very quiet. Nobody laughed or told a funny story. The mood was somber, and team spirit flagged.

To make matters worse, we started the second round against the dominant Russian and Finnish teams, to whom we lost 13–1 and 9–1, respectively. Following another shutout loss on Tuesday, April 15—this time 8–0 to the Czechoslovakians—I had my hands full trying to keep the team in good spirits and convincing some players not to leave. We were not functioning well at all and lost to the Swedes 12–1.

Thursday, April 17, was our last free day in Düsseldorf, the richest and most fashionable city in the northwestern part of West Germany, but nobody wanted to shop or go sightseeing.

On Friday, April 18, our last game of the tournament, we lost to Poland again, this time by a score of 5–2. It was not surprising that our spirits were incredibly low.

Saturday was set aside for packing and a boat trip on the Rhine River organized by our hosts, but few players were willing to go.

On Sunday, April 20, we flew back to the USA. It was a long, long silent flight.

11

Vienna in Spring with John Mariucci

World Championships, Vienna, Austria, 1977

Team Roster

In Goal: *Mike Curran, Dave Reece*

Defense: *Russ Anderson, Jim McElmurry, Joe Micheletti, Lou Nanne, Wally Olds, Bob Paradise*

Forwards: *Dave Debol, Mark Heaslip, Dave Hynes, Steve Jensen, Bob Krieger, Bob Miller, Warren Miller, Tom Rowe, Buzzy Schneider, Tom Vannelli, Warren Williams, Tom Younghans*

In 1976, I was unable to travel with the US Olympic or National teams to their respective tournaments because two doctors at the clinic where I worked had left suddenly and unexpectedly, leaving us short staffed. In 1977, however, I once again became the United States Team Physician for the World Championships in Vienna, Austria, in April of that year. John Mariucci and Frank Gallagher were assigned as coach and general manager, respectively.

It was a special time for me because things had come full circle. My USA

US National Hockey Team at 1977 World Championship in Vienna, Austria.
Front row (L-R): Dave Reece, Bob Paradise, Assistant Coach Jack McCartan, Head Coach John Mariucci,
Captain Lou Nanne, General Manager Frank Gallagher, myself, Russ Anderson, Mike Curran.
Middle row: Trainer Al Mathieu, Tom Younghans, Jim McElmurry, Wally Olds, Bob Sheehan, Bob Krieger, Buzzy
Schneider. Upper row: Tom Vannelli, Warren Miller, Joe Micheletti, Dave Debol, Warren Williams, Bob Miller,
Mark Heaslip, Dave Hynes.

Hockey travels had started when John Mariucci invited me to join him on a trip to Vienna ten years ago. Because John had resigned his position, however, we'd never traveled together. Finally, I got the chance to go to Vienna with John.

The team was composed of players of varying abilities. During the exhibition portion we had mostly college and semipro players. Later, in Vienna, some higher-level pros were set to join the team when their seasons were over. It was not surprising, then, that we

At the ice arena in Vienna, with my Latvian hockey friends (L-R): myself, Leonid Vedejs, and Erik Konecki.

lost our opening exhibition games in Prague by scores of 7–1 to the Czechoslovakian National A Team and 7–2 to the Czechoslovakian National B team.

On Saturday, April 16, we took the long bus ride from Prague to Munich. Again, we waited an hour at the Czechoslovakian border, enduring the same basic procedure as the year before. This time they even opened some of our bags and trunks. Oddly, after the inspection, the customs officers smiled and wished us a good trip.

We arrived in Munich late that afternoon, and everybody was anxious to get out and walk around in a free country again. We played the West German National team at the Olympic Stadium that night and lost 7–4. On top of that, Bobby Sheehan was sent home with a fractured left forearm, a tough loss for

My daughter Brigita at the Viennese Opera House.

our team. Ironically, while rushing to get Bobby to the airport in New York, Bobby's wife had fallen down the stairs and fractured her leg. Bobby had taken her to a doctor to get a cast and almost missed the flight out. Now he was going home with a broken left forearm to a wife with a broken leg and a little baby to care for.

On Monday, April 8, to boost team morale, Frank Gallagher and John Mariucci planned a bus tour of Berchtesgaden National Park in the Bavarian Alps. Along the way we drove through some quaint and picturesque villages such as Reit-im-Winkl and Ramsau.

We spent a lovely day admiring nature's beauty, especially the Königssee, a stunning natural lake completely surrounded by mountains, including the majestic Watzmann peaks on the west. We returned to Munich just in time for dinner. Afterward, everybody packed for the trip to Vienna the next morning.

On Tuesday, April 19, we took a bus to Vienna via Salzburg and Linz, arriving at the Schönbrunn Park Hotel late in the afternoon. Our hotel was across the street from Schönbrunn Palace Garden, and some of us took an evening walk through the beautiful park after dinner. The IIHF Hockey World Championships were scheduled to start in two days, on Thursday, April 21.

The next day, after practice, trainer Al Mathieu discovered that our newly arrived game jerseys had the wrong numbers and names on them. Poor Alan

worked late into the night until everything was corrected. I was unable to help because I had to attend a conference of team doctors explaining new rules and regulations and doping control procedures.

Later that afternoon, some of our team members' wives arrived. With them was my daughter, Brigita, who had just graduated from the School of

My sister, Dr. Aina Abols, with Brigita (right) after lunch in Grinzing.

Dental Hygiene at the University of Minnesota and had accepted a position in a dentist's office in Davos, Switzerland, set to begin on May 1. Brigita had never been to Vienna, and my wife, Velta, who was always so unselfish, suggested that Brigita join me and have a nice vacation before starting her new job.

With Helmut Balderis at Schönbrunn Palace in Vienna.

On Thursday, April 21, we practiced early, followed on the ice by the Russian team. By then I knew that the Soviets had an outstanding Latvian player named Helmut Balderis. Buzzy Schneider had seen him play in the 1976 World Championships in Katowice, Poland. He told me, "Doc, the Soviets have a new star with incredible speed. He's not just quick going forward, he accelerates going sideways." When I asked Buzzy who it was, he replied, "I think his last name is Balderis." Sure enough, I had heard of Balderis before and was glad he'd been given a chance to play for the Russian National Team.

As I was watching our boys practice that morning, a player in a Russian uniform approached me and said in Latvian, "You must be Dr. Nagobads."

I said, "And you must be Helmut Balderis."

I was very happy to meet him. We shook hands, and I told him that our players were impressed with his play and skating skills.

Helmut, just like me, was born in Riga, the capital city of Latvia. The main difference was that while I enjoyed my youth in a free country with high living standards, Helmut was born at a time when the Soviets occupied Latvia. His blazing skating speed and superb technical skills came from his figure skating days. In his early school years, his parents had tried to develop him into a figure skating champion, but Helmut liked hockey too much and was becoming quite good at it. Soon he was a dominant player and leading scorer for the Riga Dinamo team. In the 1976–1977 season he was the top scorer in the Soviet Union's upper league and was invited to play on the national team.

After our nice little chat, we decided to meet one morning after breakfast.

That afternoon, the IIHF held the opening ceremonies. Our first game, against Canada, followed. We started the tournament poorly with a 4–1 loss.

The next morning, Friday, April 22, Brigita and I visited downtown Vienna after breakfast. It was an early spring day, with the magnolia trees still blooming. We walked around the Ringstrasse, or "Ring Street," and I told her a little story about the beautiful buildings and monuments. We stopped at the Vienna Opera House and saw that the ballet *Romeo and Juliet* was scheduled for that evening. Knowing how much Brigita liked ballet, I bought two tickets. Then we hurried back to the hotel to get ready for the two o'clock game against Romania. It was an easier game for us, and we won 7–2. However, Tommy Rowe injured his right knee, and we lost him for the tournament, which

put a definite damper on the win.

After I got Tommy into bed with ice packs on his knee, it was time for dinner. Then Brigita and I grabbed a taxi for the Vienna Opera House, which was beautifully illuminated. Because it was a major performance, with a dancer from Great Britain's Royal Ballet Company performing the part of Romeo, people were very well dressed. It was a magical setting. Brigita enjoyed the evening very much, which gave me deep satisfaction.

The next morning I met my sister, Aina Abols, and her husband, Guntar, who had just arrived from Paris. For lunch we all went to Grinzing, the pretty little suburb of Vienna well known for its *Gemütlichkeit,* feelings of great health and happiness. We chose a rustic, cozy wine restaurant where we enjoyed our lunch very much, another interesting experience for my daughter.

After lunch I hurried back to the hotel to check on Tommy's knee. It was even more swollen and stiff. I was now convinced that there was serious ligament damage. Bad news.

I had made reservations for that evening at my favorite Viennese restaurant, the Czardasfürstin. I'd asked for a nice corner table for the Mariuccis, the Gallaghers, Brigita, and myself, and as soon as we entered, the musicians greeted us with a powerful Hungarian melody. We all enjoyed our favorite meal of Wiener schnitzel and paprika schnitzel and good glasses of white wine. Later, while the band was entertaining us, John taught them how to play "I Lost My Heart in San Francisco." They played it very well, and we ordered a round of drinks for the performers in appreciation of their wonderful music.

On Sunday, April 24, we had an early practice. Tommy's knee was still quite stiff and swollen. He was hobbling around on crutches and had to spend most of the time in bed with his right leg elevated. We played West Germany at 5:00 p.m. It was a close game, as expected, that ended in a 3–3 tie.

On Tuesday, April 26, I met Helmut Balderis for our promised breakfast, and we went for a walk in the park across the street from the hotel. We talked about our hockey experiences. I asked him about the eventual possibility of him playing in the NHL. Helmut smiled and said, "No, I would have to defect, and that would be very bad for my parents and my wife." He was very happy in Riga because he was a hero there. He also enjoyed many privileges and better living conditions than most and was frequently able to go on trips to foreign countries. We walked around Schönbrunn Palace Park quite a while and then went back to our hotel. The KGB guys were waiting and lectured Helmut about his behavior.

After an early afternoon practice, we got ready for our game against the good Finnish team. We played hard, but lost 3–2.

On Wednesday, April 27, we had the day off. It was Brigita's last day in Vienna, so we went downtown for one last stroll along Kärntner Street and the Graben, where the most exclusive Viennese shops are located. We took pictures at the Opera House, in front of the Hofburg Palace, at the Parliament, and in front of the Rathaus, the city hall.

Later that evening, John Mariucci, Frank Gallagher, and their wives decided to take Brigita to a cozy neighborhood restaurant for her last dinner in Vienna. It was one that we'd been to before, and the proprietor greeted us like old friends. We ate delicious Viennese food and drank the good house wine. John and Frank told interesting stories, and the time went by very quickly.

At one point we watched a large group of men with only one lady enter the restaurant and sit down at the table next to ours. Soon they started singing some Viennese songs. Of course, then John had to sing "I Lost My Heart in San Francisco." It was a hit, and our new friends applauded.

After another round of wine, we started chatting more with our neighbors and found out that they were a Viennese men's choir who'd stopped by for a glass of wine after their performance at the Musikverein concert hall. The lady was the wife of the chairman and an opera singer herself. We asked her to sing one of her favorite songs, and she gave an amazing performance. It was an unforgettable experience. They even invited us to their next concert a few days later. Unfortunately, we had a game that night and were unable to attend.

It was getting quite late when we finally left the restaurant, which was supposed to close an hour earlier. However, the proprietor enjoyed the evening so much himself that he brought out more wine—on the house—and we kept on singing.

The next morning, Brigita left for Davos. I took her to the railroad station, and we said our good-byes.

When I returned to the hotel, I got a telephone call from my jolly old hockey friend, Erik Konecki. He was calling from Dortmund, West Germany, to ask if Helmut Balderis was playing for the Russian team. I said, "Yes, he is. In fact, I've already met him." Erik was a star hockey player in his younger days in Riga and one of the top West German players in the late 1940s and early 1950s. He was quite interested in meeting Helmut and watching him play, but he was concerned about hotel reservations. I told him not to worry, I would take care of it, and he promptly got on the train to Vienna.

That afternoon we played a very strong Swedish team that had already beaten the Soviets 3–1. Between periods, my dear friend Dr. Ignaz, the Romanian team physician, came to me and expressed his concern that the Swedish team was possibly using some kind of performance enhancement drugs. He wanted me to see a group of Swedish players all standing in line for the men's room. I told him that Dr. Reen, the Swedish team physician, was a member of the doping committee and that I was sure he wouldn't let his players take any illegal drugs. At that moment, the Czechoslovakian team physician, Dr. Otto Trefny, walked by, and I told him about Dr. Ignaz's concern. Otto just laughed and said, "Sure, they're taking that new Swedish electrolyte drink called Plus-9 to help them feel less fatigued. We have a similar drink. It makes you use the bathroom more frequently, but it's not illegal." That explanation satisfied Dr. Ignaz, but it couldn't help me understand why we lost the game 9–0!

The next morning, after breakfast, Helmut asked me to whom I'd been speaking in Latvian the day before. His room was just below mine, and he'd heard me on the phone. I told him it was Erik Konecki and then told him all about Erik's hockey career. When the two of them met later, they had a lot to talk about.

That afternoon we took a trip along the Danube River from Melk to Krems through the beautiful Wachau Valley. It was the perfect time of year, when all the fruit trees were in bloom. In Melk we visited one of the world's finest baroque abbeys and then continued our trip along the left bank of the Danube to Dürnstein, where the ruins of old Dürnstein Castle could still be seen high up on the mountain. We explored the romantic little town with its narrow, curbed streets and sat on a restaurant terrace that overlooked the river as it flowed peacefully through the lush green hills.

After resting for a while, we took the bus to Krems, where we toured a small, private winery. Everyone enjoyed this stop the most. The proprietor invited us to see his large wine cellar, which was cut into the mountainside. After our eyes adjusted to the dim lighting, he offered us a taste of his wines. In the end, almost everyone bought some bottles of their favorite wine, heartily encouraged by our wine enthusiasts, John Mariucci and Lou Nanne.

Saturday, April 30, was a difficult day for us. First we had to play the mighty Soviets. We held up pretty well for the first two periods but eventually lost 8–3. There was a bigger problem, though. Bobby Krieger was selected by doping control again. He'd had trouble producing the first time, and sure enough, it was worse this time. It took almost two full hours before we were allowed to leave. By then, of course, we'd missed dinner at the hotel.

Two days later we played the talented Czechoslovakian team in our last game of the first round. With Jiří Holeček in goal, team captain František Pospíšil on defense, and a stellar forward line of Jiří Holik, Vladimír Martinec, and Ivan Hlinka, it was a very tough game for us and we lost 6–3.

We finished outside of the top four teams in the first round, which meant that we had to start our second round of games the next day. First we played West Germany. It was a better game for us, and we won 5–2.

Wednesday, May 4, was our day off. Just before morning practice, Wally Olds and Assistant Coach Jack McCartan came to me and said, "Doc, that Russian doctor is going through your bag!" I wasn't too happy about that. I followed them into the dressing room. My dear old friend Dr. Oleg Belokovski had found some suppositories and was curious as to their use. I tried to explain to him how they were applied, which resulted in peals of laughter from the players.

That evening, the Mariuccis, the Gallaghers, and I attended Emmerich Kálmán's operetta *Countess Maritza*. Like all Kálmán operettas, it was filled with beautiful melodies and exciting Hungarian dances. I particularly enjoyed the performance of Marika Rökk, a famous Hungarian actress who'd starred in several German movies back when I was a student. It was wonderful to see her live on stage. All of us were delighted to see a true Viennese operetta and

hummed several of the more memorable tunes as we walked back to our hotel.

The next day we played Romania. We had beaten them 7–2 in the first round and were perhaps a bit overconfident. At one point, Coach Mariucci turned to me and said, "Doc, every goal the Romanians score is against our NHL defenseman!"

I said, "I don't think they're taking the Romanians seriously."

A bit later, one of our defensemen got a two-minute penalty for holding. As soon as the penalty expired, John called him to the bench. But the player stayed on the ice and was called for another penalty. John was furious. Some of our other players had to restrain him from physically confronting the guy. It was all very unpleasant, and we lost the game 5–4.

Friday, May 6, was our last day for shopping. It was good to be downtown, away from the rink, because nobody wanted to talk about our loss to the Romanians.

Later, my Latvian friend Erik Konecki wanted to watch some of the other games, so we went to the arena. There we met another Latvian player, Leonids Vedejs, who for many years had been the captain of the Latvian National Team. Now he lived in Grand Rapids, Michigan, near his son, Dainis, who played for Michigan State. We talked and reminisced about the good old hockey days in Riga and were amazed by how much the game had changed.

We played Finland on Saturday, May 7, our last game of the tournament. This time our team was ready to play, and we won 3–2. Everyone was happy to end the tournament on a winning note and excited to see who would win the championship.

On Sunday morning, right after breakfast, Helmut and I took our now-usual walk in the park across the street. I had just seen an article in the morning paper with Helmut's picture. The headline said, "The fastest player on the Russian team is the Latvian, Balderis." I asked Helmut if he had been interviewed for the piece. He said, "Yes, in the presence of our political advisors, so I didn't say anything bad about anybody or anything."

Helmut didn't know German well, so I translated the article for him. It was true, he hadn't said one bad word, but he was praised so highly that I was concerned he would be transferred from Riga to a club in Moscow. I expressed my concern, but Helmut doubted it would happen. I wished him good luck in staying at home.

That afternoon, the Swedes beat the Soviets. So the Czechoslovakians ended the tournament with fifteen points, the Swedes and the Soviets both had fourteen, and Canada had thirteen. Czechoslovakia was the champion, the Swedes took second, and the Soviets finished third.

On Monday morning, May 9, everybody else left for home and I went to visit Brigita in Davos for a few days.

This will always be one of my favorite trips with the US National Team. First, I got to enjoy the company of John Mariucci and Frank Gallagher in Vienna, absolutely my favorite city in the world. Second, Brigita was there for most of the time. On top of that, I was able to spend time with my sister and her husband, and also met some Latvian hockey friends, old and new. There are so many songs written about May in Vienna, and they are all true! It was just wonderful!

US National Hockey Team at 1978 World Championship in Prague, Czechoslovakia.
Front row (L-R): Jim Warden, Curt Bennett, General Manager Frank Gallagher, Head Coach John Mariucci,
Assistant Coach Andre Beaulieu, myself, Pat Westrum, Pete LoPresti.
Middle row: Czech volunteer masseur Harry Martinek, Mark Johnson, Craig Norwich, Tom Younghans, Jim
Warner, Mike Eaves, Bob Collyard, Czech host Jiri Trnka, Trainer Bud Kessel.
Upper row: Dave Debol, Bill Gilligan, Dick Lamby, Harvey Bennett, Don Jackson, Steve Jensen, Mike Fidler.

12

The First IIHF Medical Conference
Prague, Czechoslovakia, 1978

Team Roster

In Goal: *Pete LoPresti, Jim Warden*

Defense: *Don Jackson, Dick Lamby, Ken Morrow, Craig Norwich, Glen Patrick, Pat Westrum*

Forwards: *Steve Alley, Curt Bennett, Harvey Bennett, Bob Collyard, Dave Debol, Mike Eaves, Mike Fidler, Bill Gilligan, Steve Jensen, Mark Johnson, Jim Warner, Tom Younghans*

The 1978 IIHF World Championships took place from April 22 to May 14, 1978, in Prague, Czechoslovakia. Once again, Frank Gallagher was the general manager of the US National Team, and John Mariucci was coach. Bud Kessel was the trainer. I served as team physician. Our team, which consisted of fourteen professionals and six college players, had almost no preparation before leaving for Europe on April 16, 1978.

Because of my heavy workload, I flew separately to Prague and caught up with the team on Friday, April 21. By that time they'd already played two exhibition games in Finland, on April 18 and 19, which they'd lost 7–1 and 10–3, respectively.

In Prague, my old friend Jiri Trnka greeted me with a happy smile and introduced me and our team to our sponsors, representatives from a ceramics company. We were all happy to meet them and promised to visit their factory on our day off.

Before starting the World Championships, we were scheduled to play two exhibition games against the Czechoslovakian National A and B teams. We played the B team first, on Saturday, April 22. After having played just two exhibition games in Finland, our team had yet to develop adequate communication and team play, as evidenced by our 6–4 loss to the B team. The next day we faced the A team. It was an even tougher game, and we lost 8–2. Thankfully, we had two days off before the World Championships began.

Monday, April 24, and Tuesday, April 25, were beautiful, sunny spring days. On Monday morning I met my Czechoslovakian friend Dr. Marian Kartusek and Coach Stanislav Nevesely. They were happy to see me again and suggested we play some tennis at the local club, where they had connections. Andre Beaulieu, assistant coach of the US National Team, joined us for two fun-filled afternoons on the tennis courts of Prague.

We played our first game of the tournament on Wednesday, April 26. After a short morning practice, our boys rested and prepared to play Russia at 6:00 p.m. As always, it was a very tough game for us. Somehow, we managed to score five goals, but we still lost 9–5.

The next day we played a very fast-skating Swedish team. Our legs were still tired from the Russian game, and we had a difficult time keeping up. We lost 5–1.

Saturday was another beautiful spring day. After practice, Jiri suggested a walking tour of Prague. We started, of course, at the famous Charles Bridge, lined on both sides with its famous baroque-style statues. Then we crossed the Vltava River to an area called Gold Lane, where in the time of Emperor Rudolf II, alchemists tried to turn lead into gold. Next we climbed the hill to Hradčany, the Castle District, former home of Bohemian kings and site of Prague Castle, said to be the biggest castle in the world. After a tour of Hradčany Square and Prague Castle, we entered the very impressive Saint Vitus's Cathedral, the largest church in Prague. We finished by walking down the hill to a simple but well-known restaurant where Jiri had arranged our lunch. Everybody had worked up a good appetite, and we enjoyed a typical Czechoslovakian meal with a cold bottle of Pilsner. Back at the hotel, everyone stretched out and rested.

After a light morning practice on Sunday, April 30, we played the Canadians that evening. It was another difficult game, and we lost 7–2.

There was no game on Monday, May 1, so Jiri arranged for a bus to take us to the ceramic factory. After a friendly reception, our sponsors told us about their products and gave us a tour. In one of the exhibition rooms, Gretchen Mariucci spotted some dishes that featured the Ming Dynasty–inspired Zwiebelmuster pattern, a cobalt blue "onion" design first made famous by the Meissen porcelain factory in 1740. We both liked them very much and bought several pieces. Our sponsors were pleased.

On Tuesday, May 2, we played Czechoslovakia on their home ice. They easily outplayed us and beat us 8–3, another loss.

The next day we faced West Germany. We played well but missed some scoring chances. The West Germans, on the other hand, scored a few lucky goals and beat us 7–4.

After practice on Thursday, May 4, our sponsors arranged for a bus to take us to Konopiště Castle, a picturesque hunting retreat thirty miles southeast of Prague in the city of Benešov. Long a favorite of wealthy royals and their guests, it was the last residence of Archduke Franz Ferdinand, heir to the Austro-Hungarian throne, whose assassination in 1914 sparked World War I. The bullet that killed him in Sarajevo is on display in the castle's museum.

After a tour of the castle and grounds, we ate lunch at a cozy restaurant. Most of us had pork roast with sauerkraut and a bottle of good Czechoslovakian beer. It was all very relaxing, and everybody returned to our hotel in a good mood.

Friday, May 5, was the start of the three-day IIHF Medical Conference for team physicians, trainers, and coaches. That evening, Dr. Thomas Pashby, from Canada, presented a paper on eye injuries. He reported that, of the 287 eye injuries in the 1972–1973 season, 20 resulted in blindness. High sticks had caused 75 percent of those injuries, which were predominantly suffered by junior players.

The Czechoslovakian team physician, Dr. Otto Trefny, was sitting next to me, and I noticed that he was drawing a portrait of a team doctor across the aisle instead of paying attention to Dr. Pashby's lecture. I elbowed him and asked why he wasn't interested. He said, "George, that is only your problem in North America. Our coaches are very strict about no sticks above the shoulder. We don't have that problem." A few years later I understood why Czechoslovakia was so late in adopting full-face protective cages for junior players.

On Friday evening we played East Germany. I warned our players about the East Germans' dirty tricks, and our boys didn't take any retaliation penalties. We won 7–3, our first victory of the tournament. Everybody was very happy.

Saturday morning I presented my paper, "Treatment of Face Lacerations in Ice Hockey." Before the advent of face masks in the college and junior ranks, face lacerations used to be one of the most frequent injuries in ice hockey. In my positions with the University of Minnesota Golden Gophers and St. Paul Fighting Saints, I had a great many opportunities to practice my skills, learned from plastic surgeon Dr. Sam Balkin during my surgical residency at the Swedish Hospital in Minneapolis. I was well qualified to speak on the subject.

On Saturday evening we had no games scheduled, so I accepted an invitation from the Mariuccis

John Mariucci (left) and Frank Gallagher signing the membership book at the Moser Club.

and Gallaghers to join them for a promenade along the beautiful boulevard of Wenceslas Square. After our walk we enjoyed dinner at a classy Czech restaurant while I briefed the Mariuccis and Gallaghers about the induction ceremony for the Moser Club, scheduled for next Wednesday. They were very excited about it and couldn't wait for the day to come.

Sunday, May 7, was the last day of the medical conference. No further papers were presented, but summaries, conclusions, and proposals were discussed and resolutions adopted.

In the evening we played Finland in our final game of the first round. It was a competitive game, and we were happy to finish with a 3–3 tie.

Monday, May 8, was a day off. After practice, I went shopping downtown with Buddy and Harry

Martinek, trainer for the Czech National Team. Buddy looked for more souvenirs, while I tried to find a wrought iron lantern for the entrance hall of my house in Edina. The streets of downtown Prague were teeming with happy, smiling Czechoslovakian fans. Their team had beaten the Soviets 6–4 on Saturday and was in first place heading into the second round.

The Most Valuable Player trophy—a big, beautiful crystal vase—stood in the window of one of the shops. As the locals wandered by, they pointed to the vase and said, "That's Hlinka's vase." For them, there was no question that Ivan Hlinka, the best Czechoslovakian player of the tournament, would win the award.

After the first round, the teams were divided into two brackets: Czechoslovakia, Russia, Canada, and Sweden in the upper, medal tier, and West Germany, USA, Finland, and East Germany in the lower, consolation tier. We were set to play three more games in the lower tier.

On Tuesday, May 9, we played East Germany. This time, the East Germans were more careful and stayed out of the penalty box. The game ended in a 5–5 tie.

Wednesday, May 10, was a day of rest. Jiri had made arrangements for the Mariuccis and Gallaghers to be inducted into the Moser Club. I'd recently picked up a bottle of French cognac for the occasion, so after lunch we met Jiri and walked to the Moser Shop, where Mr. Slama was waiting. Jiri introduced the Mariuccis and Gallaghers, I presented the bottle of the French cognac, and Mr. Slama guided us through the shop,

where we admired the beautiful crystal and china displays. Mr. Slama excused himself, and moments later, he slid open the door and the heavy, dark red velvet draperies, inviting us into the Moser Club room.

Immediately, I noticed something different. In a specially illuminated china cabinet there were cocktail glasses of different colors and six huge cognac snifters of slightly different sizes, which created an elegant setting for the induction ceremony. Mr. Slama gave each of the Mariuccis and Gallaghers a different snifter. Then, as the giant snifters slowly spun around table, he said, "To pass the test, you must pour cognac into the traveling glass without touching its rim." I was glad to see that the ladies were given snifters with large openings and passed the test without too much difficulty. John and Frank also passed without spilling too much cognac on the table. After the initiation, we toasted to a long-lasting friendship and the new inductees signed the membership book.

Afterward, we bought some beautiful Bohemian crystal glasses to commemorate the occasion and invited Jiri to dinner. The Mariuccis and Gallaghers loved it. Gretchen Mariucci and Marjorie Gallagher, in particular, couldn't stop raving about the unique and gorgeous pieces at the Moser Shop.

On Thursday, May 11, we played Finland. Bill Gilligan and Mike Fidler played exceptionally well, and we won 4–3. Now, we felt much more comfortable heading into our final game, against West Germany. Even if we lost, we wouldn't finish lower than sixth.

Saturday, May 13, was the last day of play in the lower tier. In the early game, Finland beat the East

Germans. We played West Germany, then one point ahead of us in the standings, later that evening. With a victory, we'd win the lower tier and place fifth overall. The game started well for us, but after a while, the puck didn't bounce our way. The West Germans won 8–4, and we finished sixth in the 1978 World Championships.

Sunday, May 14, was the last day of the tournament, featuring two games in the upper tier. In the early afternoon Canada beat Sweden for the bronze medal. The gold-medal game between Czechoslovakia and Russia was later that evening. The Czechoslovakian fans were hoping for a victory and the third consecutive World Championship. Since they'd beaten the Soviets 6–4 in the first round, even a one-goal loss would earn the Czechs the gold medal.

At the arena, I met my Canadian friend Marshall Johnston, assistant general manager of the Canadian team, and we found a nice place to watch the game. In the first period both teams played cautiously. A few minutes before the end of the period, however, Helmut Balderis, playing forward for the Soviets, jumped over the block of two Czechoslovakian defensemen, picked up the puck, and scored. Marshall slammed his hand on my side and said, "That's all I had to see. Doc, I'm going home."

The second and third periods were also very even, but the game ended 3–1 in favor of the Soviets. Both teams ended the tournament with eighteen points. The head-to-head two-game goal total was also tied, at seven goals apiece. The Soviet team, however, had a better total goal differential for all tournament games

Myself on entrance to Charles Bridge in Prague.

and became the 1978 IIHF World Champions.

Before the teams got their medals, individual awards were presented. The MVP trophy—that big, beautiful Bohemian crystal vase—went to Helmut Balderis. After the medal ceremony, I went to the Russian locker room and congratulated Helmut on his award. It was the first time I ever saw Soviet Coach Viktor Tikhonov smile.

Monday, May 15, was not a happy morning. The Czechoslovakians were sad about losing to the Soviets in the decisive game. On top of that, we had to say good-bye to our friends Jiri and Harry. Soon after breakfast, the bus arrived and we left "The Golden City" for Frankfurt, West Germany. Before leaving Czechoslovakia, however, we stopped once more in Pilsen. Our friends at the Pilsner brewery were very friendly and happy to see us again. We had an excellent lunch and more good, cold Pilsner beer. All of the boys were laughing and having a good time.

As we approached the Czechoslovakia–West Germany border, I told everyone what to expect. But this time the Czechoslovakian border guards were much friendlier. Passport control didn't take long at all, and we got to Frankfurt in time for dinner.

The next morning we boarded a plane for Copenhagen, where the players and staff continued on to their respective American cities. We spent our last few hours together as a team in the Copenhagen Airport. I had lunch with the Mariuccis and Gallaghers before we boarded our flights for home. It was another wonderful World Championship trip with John Mariucci and Frank Gallagher. I will never forget it.

After congratulating Helmut Balderis on the MVP award.

1979 US National Hockey team in Moscow, USSR. Front row (L-R): Jim Craig, Asst. Captain Craig Bennett, Head Coach Herb Brooks, Captain Craig Patrick, Manager John Carlton, Asst. Captain Dan Bolduc, Jim Warden. Middle row (L-R): Goalie Coach Warren Strelow, Eric Strobel, Craig Sarner, Les Auge, Steve Christoff, Jim Korn, Phil Verchota, Jack Brownschidle, Rob McClanahan, Bobby Collyard, Asst. Manager Ken Johannson. Back row: Equipment Bob Webster, Trainer Tom Woodcock, Mark Johnson, Joe Mullen, Bill Baker, Don Jackson, Wally Olds, Ralph Cox, Jack O'Callahan, myself.

13

IIHF World Championships

Moscow, USSR, 1979

Team Roster

In Goal: *Jim Craig, Jim Warden*

Defense: *Les Auge, Bill Baker, Jack Brownschidle, Don Jackson, James Korn, Jack O'Callahan, Wally Olds*

Forwards: *Curt Bennett, Dan Bolduc, Steve Christoff, Robert Collyard, Ralph Cox, Mark Johnson, Rob McClanahan, Joe Mullen, Craig Patrick, Craig Sarner, Eric Strobel, Phil Verchota*

The 1979 IIHF World Championships were played in Moscow, USSR, from April 14 to 27. John Carlton was general manager for the US National Team, Ken Johannson was assistant general manager, and Herb Brooks was head coach. Warren Strelow coached the goalies, Tom Woodcock was trainer, and Bob Webster was equipment manager. Dr. Bertram Zarins, team physician for the Boston Bruins, joined me on the Team USA medical staff as our orthopedic specialist.

Prior to the 1979 World Championships, Herb Brooks had been selected to coach the US men's hockey team in the 1980 Olympics in Lake Placid, New York. The World Championships in Moscow, then, were something of a tryout for

*Rob McClanahan (left) and Bill Baker at the Pavo Nurmi Statue by
the Olympic Stadium in Helsinki, Finland.*

several young, talented college players Herb wanted to test in international competition. Older, more experienced players, such as team captain Craig Patrick and assistant captains Curt Bennett and Dan Bolduc, were expected to lead the team both on the ice and off.

After the team assembled in New York, we left for Europe on the evening of Monday, April 9, 1979. We arrived in Helsinki on Tuesday morning and were quartered in the elegant Hesperia Hotel, across the street from a city park and the Olympic arena.

On April 11 and 12 we played two exhibition games against Finland. We lost both games but were not discouraged. The players and coaches were still getting to know each other and had yet to gel as a team.

On the evening of Friday, April 13, we boarded a train for Moscow, arriving at nine o'clock the next morning.

The eight-team field was divided into two groups. Group A was made up of Canada, Czechoslovakia, Finland, and the United States; Group B was West Germany, Poland, Sweden, and the Soviet Union.

On Saturday, April 14, we played Canada in our first game of the tournament. We were still somewhat tired from the overnight train ride and running around, taking care of logistics upon our arrival. As a result, we didn't play very well and lost the game 6–3.

On Sunday morning we had a light practice and rested before our game against Finland that night. It was a good, hard-fought game. Our defense played

well, and we tied the Finns 1–1.

We enjoyed some much-needed rest after practice the next day, in preparation for our game against the very strong Czechoslovakian team on Tuesday. I

Tom Woodcock and Herb Brooks by the entrance gate to the Kremlin.

called my Russian friend, Dr. Igor Silin, at the Central Red Army Hockey Club dispensary, and we decided to get together on Thursday morning. After lunch, Coach Brooks, Tommy Woodcock, and I walked over to Red Square to see Saint Basil's Cathedral and the Kremlin Wall.

By the morning of Tuesday, April 17, the boys were starting to feel better acclimated and we had a good practice. In the evening we played the Czechoslovakians in what turned out be one of our best games of the whole tournament. Our boys played very well, and Jim Craig was outstanding in goal. The Czechoslovakians outshot us badly, but we eked out a 2–2 tie. It was our last game of the preliminary round-robin series. With two ties and one loss, we joined Finland, Germany, and Poland for the relegation round.

On Wednesday, April 18, we played Poland. Our game against Czechoslovakia the night before had taken a lot of energy out of the boys. The game ended in a 5–5 tie.

Thursday morning, as promised, Dr. Silin picked me up from the hotel in his car. He asked if I'd like to see the Russian National Team's training facility on the banks of the Moscow River. I said that sounded interesting, but I was a little concerned about leaving the city limits. Igor assured me that the police knew his car very well and there wouldn't be any trouble. About ten miles outside of Moscow, as we were driving through a small village lined with old, run-down houses, Igor said, "Look, George, this is the hometown of Vladimir Petrov," who was the top center on the Russian National Team, as well as starting center on his Moscow club team. I thought, *Ah, now I understand why Petrov plays so well. He doesn't want to be sent back to this place!*

After another ten miles we arrived at a large, well-kept estate surrounded by park-like grounds. Nobody was there, so Igor led me around to the special installations for strength training and conditioning.

At one point, Igor said, "Let's go to Ludmilla's grave." I asked who Ludmilla was and why her grave was so special. Igor told me that Ludmilla was the darling daughter of the count who'd previously owned the estate. She died at an early age from tuberculosis and was buried right by the chapel, in the prettiest part of the park, where the Moscow River bends sharply back on itself. As we arrived at the chapel, Igor gestured toward the high, steep bank of the river said, "How do you like it here?"

I said, "It's a very nice view of the water."

Igor said, "No, not the river. I mean the steep bank of the river."

I guessed what he meant and said, "Igor, do you mean to tell me that Viktor Tikhonov makes his players run up and down this steep bank?"

"Yes," he replied with a little chuckle. "Tikhonov stands here, stopwatch in hand, barking at his players as they sprint up and down the hill. Helmut doesn't like it one bit, though he always makes the best time."

I said, "What if somebody slips and falls into the river?"

Igor brushed it off, saying, "That seldom happens. It's not a big deal."

On the way home, I thought about Vladimir Petrov and the other Russian players, who likely came from similar situations. I thought, *They accept this kind of vigorous training and harsh conditioning or they get sent back to their crummy old villages.* Still, I was definitely impressed by the Russian training facilities and the methods used by the Russian coaches to get their players in the best possible shape.

On Friday, April 20, Dr. Zarins arrived. He'd been unable to join us earlier because of a prior

Moscow 1979 with Helmut Balderis, Dr. Boris Sapronenkov, Vladislav Tretiak, and myself.

commitment to lead a teaching seminar on orthopedic surgery in Bahrain and Kuwait. I was happy to have him join me because in a place like Moscow, it's comforting to be able to discuss an injury or illness with someone you know and trust.

That evening we played West Germany. We did not play poorly, but we couldn't seem to score and lost the game 6–3.

We didn't play on Saturday, so after practice,

Dr. Zarins and I went to the main arena where the Soviets were practicing. Dr. Zarins was Latvian too, so naturally he wanted to meet our fellow countryman Helmut Balderis. When we got to the arena, practice was just ending. My old friend Dr. Boris Sapronenkov was there, and we were happy to see each other again. I asked if it would be possible for us to visit with Helmut, and Boris said, "Sure, he's probably taking a shower. I'll tell the trainer to let him know you're here. Meanwhile, why don't we say hello to Coach Tikhonov? I'm sure he'd enjoy seeing you again."

We walked to the other end of the rink and shook hands with Coach Tikhonov, who remembered me from Prague the year before. We took a few pictures with him, and then Boris and I went back to the locker room to find Helmut.

When Helmut finally came out, I introduced him to Dr. Zarins. They were happy to meet each other. Dr. Zarins told Helmut that he'd heard a lot about him since Helmut had joined the Central Red Army Hockey Club in Moscow. Helmut played on the top line with Viktor Zhluktov and Sergei Kapustin. We also talked about Riga and that steep bank on the Moscow River. Helmut shook his head and explained that if you wanted to play at the Winter Olympics in Lake Placid, you had to play on the Red Army team for at least a year—that was the only way to make the Soviet Olympic team. We had little time to talk because Helmut had to leave with his teammates, so we made arrangements to meet again on Monday afternoon, when neither Russia nor the United States had a game.

After our morning practice on Sunday, we held a team meeting to talk about our game that night versus Finland. After a full week of practice, the boys had gained more confidence and were functioning well as a unit. The game against the Finns was difficult, but this time we won 6–2. Everybody was happy, and I could see that Herb was especially pleased by the performance of our younger players.

On Monday afternoon, Dr. Zarins and I met Helmut and his wife, Anita, at the Lenin Sports Complex in Luzhniki. We walked across a bridge over the Moscow River to Moscow University and into a small park filled with young birch trees near the main building. We enjoyed the pleasant surroundings and took some pictures while we listened to Helmut's stories about playing in the Soviet League.

The next day we played Poland. The boys played well, and Jim Craig was especially good in the net. We won 5–1.

We didn't have a game on Wednesday, April 25, so most of the players went souvenir shopping. Our Russian guide wasn't very helpful in suggesting places to find good deals, but we did manage to get tickets to the Bolshoi Ballet's performance of Tchaikovsky's *Swan Lake*. Embarrassingly—though perhaps predictably—some of the guys fell asleep, and many left the theater at the first intermission.

Thursday was our last day in Moscow. Dr. Zarins and I went for a stroll and checked out the state-run department store, GUM. As expected, the store featured a large inventory of low-quality shoes and clothing for the working people of Moscow, whose budgets were quite limited. We walked around the store for a while, but couldn't find anything we wanted to take home, not even for a souvenir.

Later that evening we played West Germany in our last game of the tournament. I don't know why, but we frequently had trouble playing against the West Germans. This was no exception, and we lost 5–2. Nonetheless, Herb was pleased that he'd found some good young players for the 1980 Olympic team.

Herb directs the strategy of the game. In front, far left: Trainer Tom Woodcock. Players on the bench (R-L): Eric Strobel, Jim Korn, and Bob Collyard. Behind the bench: Herb Brooks, Ken Johannson, myself, and Dr. Bert Zarins.

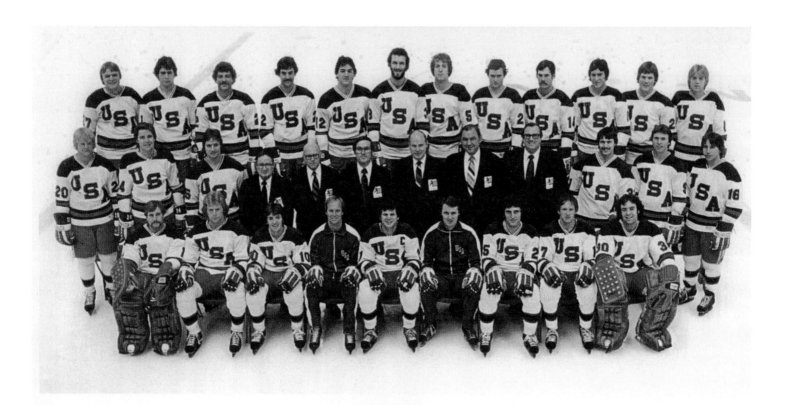

1980
UNITED STATES OLYMPIC HOCKEY TEAM
XIII WINTER OLYMPICS
GOLD MEDALIST

Front Row (L-R) Steve Janaszak, Bill Baker, Mark Johnson, Craig Patrick (Ass't Coach/Ass't GM), Mike Eruzione (Captain), Herb Brooks (Head Coach), Buzz Schneider, Jack O'Callahan, Jim Craig

Middle Row (L-R) Bob Suter, Rob McClanahan, Mark Wells, Bud Kessel (Equipment Manager), V. George Nagobads (Physician), Gary Smith (Trainer), Robert Fleming (Chairman), Ralph Jasinski (General Manager), Warren Strelow (Goalkeeping Coach), Bruce Horsch, Neal Broten, Mark Pavelich

Back Row (L-R) Phil Verchota, Steve Christoff, Les Auge, Dave Delich, Jack Hughes, Ken Morrow, Mike Ramsey, Dave Christian, Ralph Cox, Dave Silk, John Harrington, Eric Strobel

14

Preparation for the Olympic Games

Lake Placid, New York, 1979–1980

Team Roster

In Goal: *Jim Craig, Steve Janasek*

Defense: *Bill Baker, Dave Christian, Ken Morrow, Jack O'Callahan, Mike Ramsey, Bob Suter*

Forwards: *Neal Broten, Steve Christoff, Mike Eruzione, John Harrington, Mark Johnson, Rob McClanahan, Mark Pavelich, Buzzy Schneider, Dave Silk, Eric Strobel, Phil Verchota, Mark Wells*

In August 1979—after the Olympic Summer Sports Festival in Colorado Springs, Colorado—Herb Brooks and the United States Olympic Hockey Selection Committee nominated a core group of twenty-six players. Ken Johannson was general manager, Herb Brooks was head coach, and Craig Patrick was assistant coach and assistant general manager. Warren Strelow was goalie coach, Gary Smith was trainer, Bud Kessel was equipment manager, and I was team physician.

On Sunday, August 26, the management group and sixteen players left

Minneapolis for Albany, New York. There, ten more players from Eastern and Midwestern colleges joined us, and we boarded a bus for Lake Placid, where we arrived in the late afternoon. After dinner we had a team meeting in which Ken and Herb made introductions and gave us general information about our upcoming schedule: five days in Lake Placid, followed by three weeks in Europe.

Monday morning's practice session ran for two hours. Afterward, we ate lunch at a nearby restaurant. There was only one sandwich per player, which was not exactly what we had expected. The afternoon practice was also two hours long and included more skating. We ate dinner at 8:00 p.m., and then everybody went to bed. I was happy to see that nobody had pulled a groin, a frequent occurrence after a hard first day's practice.

The next morning, Herb skated them even harder, with two additional runs of a nearby hill. For better or worse, the hockey rink was located downtown on the main street, and our hotel was on the other end of town, at the top of the hill. Needless to say, the boys got to know that run quite well.

After lunch, Herb added a thirty-minute weightlifting session. The afternoon practice was spent primarily on strategy and positioning.

Later, Mike Ramsey complained about right shoulder discomfort and Gary Ross had developed slight tendon inflammation in his right foot. One of our goalies had a tension headache, but mainly our players just asked for more food.

On Wednesday, August 29, there was a heavy fog over the ice, so the morning practice was light. Then, instead of weightlifting after lunch, the boys practiced outside with a soccer ball for a change of pace. After a hard afternoon skate, Les Auge complained about pain in his wrist. I ordered x-rays, which were negative. My main concern at that point was keeping the boys well fed. I talked to the hotel and made arrangements to get more food at lunchtime.

Practice on Thursday morning was light because we had a scrimmage that afternoon. There were no injuries in the game except for our goalie, who took a shot to the testicle and had to miss practice the next day.

Friday, August 31, was our last day of practice in Lake Placid. The morning session featured a heavy skate, but the afternoon practice was light—sweats only. After that we started packing for our trip to Europe.

The next morning, after an early breakfast, we boarded the bus for Albany, where we caught a flight to New York City and then another to Copenhagen. The flight across the Atlantic was rough. Several players needed Dramamine to settle their stomachs, and very few of us slept. We landed in Copenhagen on Sunday morning at 6:30, only to fly to Amsterdam at 9:55 a.m. From there we took a two-hour bus ride to Tilburg, where we had lunch and finally rested before a full-gear practice that evening. It had been a long, grueling two days, and the players were exhausted. Everybody went to bed early.

The next morning, at breakfast, everyone but me felt more energetic after a good night's sleep. I, on the

Herb Brooks and Warren Strelow in front of Olympic Arena.

With Herb Brooks at the Training Camp of Lake Placid.

other hand, had been unable to sleep because of Ken Johannson's constant snoring. Craig Patrick was in charge of assigning roommates and had stuck me with Johannson. I told Craig about Ken's snoring and asked him to please make a change. The others all laughed and said, "Oh, yes, everybody knows about *that*."

Meanwhile, Eric Strobel had developed an ear infection and had a perforated eardrum, so I started antibiotics immediately. Fortunately, he responded well to treatment and didn't miss a beat. I don't even think he missed practice.

After lunch and a good rest, we played the Dutch

Mark Pavelich (left) and Buzzy Schneider by the lake in Savonlinna, Finland.

In Savolinna at the campfire with Finnish visitors.

National Team. It was an easy game for us, and we won 8–1.

Tuesday, September 4, was the first sunny morning since our arrival. After a late breakfast, we practiced for two hours straight, working on skating drills and our penalty kill. After lunch we toured a wooden shoe factory, which everyone enjoyed.

On Wednesday morning, the boys practiced in sweats. After lunch we took a bus to The Hague. On the way we stopped in Delft, famous for its high-quality blue-glazed Delftware china and pottery. Many of the boys bought souvenirs at the factory shop, which made us late for our game against the Dutch National Team that evening. Luckily, it was another easy game and we won 11–4.

Unfortunately, our postgame dinner was served very late, and we didn't get to bed until almost 1:00 a.m. To make matters worse, we had to get up at 6:00 a.m. the following morning to catch a bus to the Amsterdam airport. Then our flight was delayed. Everyone got even more tired and cranky sitting around the airport. Finally, at about 10:30 a.m., the plane took off for Helsinki. Thankfully, the flight was smooth.

After landing in Helsinki, we took a bus to Lahti, where we arrived at about 3:30 p.m. After unpacking at the Hotel Lahti, we ate lunch and went straight to the rink for our 6:30 game against Reipas Lahti, the local club team. It was a good, hard game, but our players were exhausted and we lost 2–1. Mark Pavelich, one of our best forwards, kept blinking and crossing his eyes. He'd barely slept the night before and was fighting to stay awake on the bench. After the game, he said, "Doc, I was so tired I couldn't tell which goal was ours!"

Needless to say, everybody slept in the next morning. After a late breakfast, we took a bus to Lappeenranta, close to the Russian border, where we were quartered in a quaint hotel on the shores of a large, beautiful lake. After unpacking, we had a light practice, ate lunch, and rested. Craig Patrick and I walked down to the lake and sat on the dock. We were enjoying the peaceful stillness when we saw two men come out of a nearby farmhouse and go into a sauna at the edge of the water. After a few minutes, the two men ran out of the sauna—stark naked—and jumped into the lake, hooting and hollering at the top of their lungs. Craig and I looked at each other and laughed. I thought, *I guess that really is how Finns take a sauna.*

That evening we played Saimaan Pallo, known as SaiPa, from the Finnish Elite League. It was a good, fast game, which we won 4–1, but we suffered a few injuries. Buzzy Schneider reinjured his left thumb, Rob McClanahan was slashed on the elbow, and the puck hit a defenseman in the testicle while he was blocking a shot.

The next morning, right after breakfast, I took Buzzy to the hospital for x-rays. Unfortunately, his thumb was fractured, so I ordered a plaster splint. When we got back to the hotel, the bus was waiting to take us to Savonlinna.

We all enjoyed the scenic two-hour bus ride through the Finnish countryside. The clear, sparkling lakes and big, beautiful birch trees were reminiscent of northern Minnesota and made some of the guys a bit homesick. Craig sensed the boys' wistful mood, so when we got to our destination, he found a campsite down by the lake among some small cabins and built a campfire. It was a beautiful, tranquil spot. Later, when the fire was roaring, some pretty female Finnish students joined us. They spoke excellent English and were very hospitable. We spent the evening relaxing by the fire and telling stories. It was perfect.

I got up early the next morning, went down to the lake, and sat on the dock. As the sun climbed into the sky, the fog began to burn off the water. Everything was so quiet, the only thing I heard was the distant, rhythmic sound of two oars: *plack, plack, plack.* The call of a moose broke the silence as a boat emerged from the last thin wisps of fog. At first I thought it was a fisherman placing his lines, but as the boat got closer, I recognized Mark Pavelich. I said, "Mark, what are you doing up so early? This is a big lake. Be careful, you could get lost in the fog."

He just laughed and said, "Doc, I'm from northern Minnesota. This is just like home. I could never get lost on a lake." He glided toward the dock. "It's so beautiful out here," he said. "I even saw a moose taking a drink in the shallow water."

"Yes, yes," I said, "I heard him saying good morning to you."

Just then, Buzzy Schneider came down to the dock with another Minnesota boy. All of them were happy.

In the spirit of our surroundings, Herb added a run through the woods after morning practice. Some of the boys were not used to that kind of trail running, and Mark Wells sprained his ankle badly. I took him to the local hospital and ordered x-rays. Luckily, there wasn't a fracture.

That evening we played Savonlinnan Pallokerho, or SaPKo, one of the best teams in Finland's second-tier league. We shut them out 6–0.

The next morning, the boys stretched and ran. Then, soon after lunch, we boarded a bus for Oulu, six hours away on northern shore of the Gulf of Bothnia, a mere 150 miles south of the Arctic Circle. As we traveled further north, there were fewer and fewer lakes and the birch trees got smaller and smaller. To me, it looked just like the tundra. We arrived in the late afternoon and ate dinner. The boys were given the evening off for rest and relaxation.

Morning practice was light in preparation for our afternoon game against Oulun Kärpät, from the Finnish Elite League, which we won 5–4. After dinner we walked to the train station and boarded a sleeper to Tampere.

The train arrived in Tampere at 7:45 a.m., but everybody slept until 8:30. Everybody, that is, except our Finnish guide, Rauli Virtanen, who'd shared a sleeping car with Ken Johannson. Conveniently, we'd neglected to tell Rauli about Kenny's horrible, nonstop snoring. Rauli got off the train looking shaken and pale. "Guys," he said, "why didn't you warn me?" Everybody laughed, but we all felt sorry for Rauli because he was such a gracious host and a very nice man.

We ate breakfast at a nice little restaurant across from the train station and took yet another bus two hours west to Rauma, a busy port city on the west coast of Finland. After arriving, we had a light practice in sweats and rested after lunch. That evening we played Rauman Lukko, another team from the Finnish Elite League, and beat them 5–3.

The next day, after our breakfast and practice, we went to visit the Koho hockey stick factory in Forsa. As I was leaving my hotel room, I noticed a wedding ring sitting on the back of the sink. My roommate, Kenny Morrow, must have forgotten it there. I put the ring in my pocket and decided to have some fun.

As I boarded the bus I looked for Kenny, and I sat down next to him. For the first half hour or so I didn't mention the ring or say anything suspicious. Then, when we were good and far from the hotel, I pretended to notice his bare hand and said, "Ah, Kenny, I see on your day off you want to impress some of these pretty Finnish girls by not wearing your wedding ring."

Kenny immediately got flustered, nearly leaping from his seat and stopping the bus right there. "Oh my God, Doc!" he said. "Oh no! We have to go back right away!"

Unfazed, I continued the prank, calmly telling him, "Kenny, not to worry, these things happen. I'm sure your wife will understand."

"No, Doc, no," he pleaded, "we have to go back and get it!"

"You know," I reassured him, "when I was a young surgical resident, I used to take off my ring all the time when I scrubbed up for surgery. After forgetting it a few times, leaving it on the sink, I decided to go to Woolworth's and buy half a dozen cheap imitation wedding rings and always keep one in my pocket. I kept my real wedding ring at home and wore an inexpensive one at work. You know, I might still have one with me . . ." At that point, I dug around in my pocket and pulled out Kenny's ring. "Here's one," I said, holding it up for him to see. "You can have this old thing."

Of course, he recognized his ring right away and said, "Oh my God, Doc, thank you!" He took it out of my hand and quickly slipped it on, thankful the crisis was over. After a moment, he said, "Doc, don't do that to me! You know you had it all along." Everybody laughed, and we all had a good time lightheartedly kidding Kenny, who took it all in stride, knowing he'd have his chance to dish it back before too long. But that wasn't even the end of it! A couple of days after that, Kenny forgot his ring again on the sink in our room. This time, however, he remembered it before the bus left and came running back to the room in a panic. I smiled and gave him the ring, and he never forgot it again.

After the Koho factory tour, we ate lunch and rested at the Cumulus hotel in Forssa, where we were quartered for the night. During the last few days, it had become colder and quite windy. Several players caught colds and had sore throats. I spent the afternoon checking up on sick players and dispensing throat lozenges and nasal spray. We didn't have a game that evening, so after dinner everyone stayed at the hotel. Most of the boys just rested or played cards, but some tried their luck on the slot machines in the hotel casino.

On Friday, September 14, we got up at 7:30 a.m. and took the bus to Helsinki after breakfast. We checked into the Intercontinental Hotel and practiced soon after that. During practice, Bill Baker strained his lower back and developed spasms. I gave him some medication and ordered physiotherapy and an ultrasound, but I was sure that he would be unable to play for the next two or three days.

We ate our pregame meal after practice, and the boys rested briefly before our evening game. That night, we played Jokerit Helsinki—the Helsinki Jokers—a club team known for their nonphysical style of play. It was a very unusual game.

Over the last eight days we had played five games in Finland and thought we knew very well what the Finnish referees would allow and what they wouldn't. That night in Helsinki, however, we were penalized every time one of our boys even touched a Jokerit player. The home team, on the other hand, was never penalized. Herb got very upset and almost pulled our players off the ice. After we'd lost 4–1, Rauli told us a secret: since Reipas Lahti had beaten us first, Jokerit absolutely had to win too, or Reipas would give Jokerit such a hard time that they'd never hear the end of it. Herb said, "Why didn't you tell me that before the game? I wouldn't have gotten so upset." When we told the boys the story, they laughed and understood.

Two days later, on Sunday, we took a bus to Helsinki Airport, where we boarded a plane for Stockholm. In Stockholm, Sweden, we changed planes for Oslo, Norway. We arrived in Oslo at 11:30 a.m., unloaded at our hotel, had lunch, and rested. Instead of practice that afternoon, a scrimmage was arranged against a local club team. We gave them two of our defensemen, Mike Ramsey and Bob Suter, but still beat them handily, 7–0. It was a low-key game on soft ice without any injuries.

On Monday, September 17, we ate breakfast at 8:30 a.m. and practiced from 10:00 to 12:00. After lunch, the boys relaxed at the hotel before our game against the Norwegian National Team at 7:30 p.m.

During the last ten days in Finland we'd competed against high-quality teams from the top Finnish leagues. Our boys had adapted well to the less physical, high-finesse European style of play, winning four games and losing just two. That night, against the Norwegians—widely regarded as less skilled than the Finns—the boys expected an easy win.

They began the game at a much lower tempo than normal, but this was an entirely different style of play. The Norwegians speared and slashed and roughed up our boys in the corners. As is frequently the case, however, the referees only noticed our retaliations and called penalties on us. Our tempo slowed even more. Unlike our games against the Finnish teams, this game turned into a grind, ending in a 3–3 tie. Herb was quite unhappy. He thought the boys hadn't skated hard enough. After the Norwegian players had shaken our hands and left, Herb kept his team on the ice and said, "You guys didn't want to skate *during* the game, so we'll skate *after* the game."

Herb blew his whistle, and the boys started skating. The Norwegian spectators were filing out.

They looked confused. Perhaps this was the typical American postgame cooldown? Some of them watched for a while, but they quickly grew bored and left. The arena was empty. Craig Patrick and I stood behind the players' bench. After watching several minutes of hard skating, I turned to Craig and said, "I'm going to go tell Herb to take it easy. They have a game tomorrow."

Craig said, "That's a good idea, why don't you do that."

So I went down on the ice and said, "Herb, come on, we have a game tomorrow. . . ."

Herb turned to me and said, "Doc, I know what I am doing."

The next morning, after breakfast, the boys skated in silence for thirty minutes. Around noon, the weather finally cleared and everybody went shopping. At seven o'clock that night we played the Norwegian National B Team. The boys came out flying, and we were dominant right from the start. It was never even close. We shut them out 9–0.

After the game, Craig said, "Maybe Herb knew what he was doing."

The next morning we got up early, ate breakfast, and took a bus to the airport. The European leg of our exhibition schedule was over. We'd played ten games in sixteen days, going 7–2–1, proving we could skate with some of the best teams in Europe. It was a nice sunny day, and the boys were happy and hopeful, glad to be heading home. The flight back across the Atlantic was smooth, and we arrived in Minneapolis upbeat and well rested. The guys were all laughing and joking as we got off the plane and gathered our luggage. Then I noticed one player who wasn't so happy. In fact, he wasn't smiling at all.

Goaltender Jimmy Craig was born and raised on the East Coast. He grew up in North Easton, Massachusetts, and played for Boston University. He'd never lived far from home. Before he arrived in Minnesota for Olympic training camp, he'd asked to live with a local family instead of the team apartments with the other out-of-state players. Unfortunately for Jimmy, a host family was never found and he was very, very unhappy. Watching the other boys light up, thrilled to be back home, I felt sorry for Jimmy and went to talk to my wife, Velta, who'd come to pick me up. Both of our daughters had moved into a sorority house at the University of Minnesota, so we had plenty of room. Velta agreed that we should invite Jimmy to stay with us. We thought Jimmy should see the place first, but he was already sold. "Thank you, Doc, thank you!" he said. "I don't have to see it. I know I'll like it." He grabbed his bag from the carousel and happily went home with us. From that day until the Winter Olympics started, our house was Jim Craig's second home.

With a four-day break in the schedule, everyone parted ways for some much-needed downtime. The team reassembled on Monday, September 24. Herb held two practices daily, from 1:30 to 3:30 p.m. and again from 7:00 to 8:30 p.m., to get ready for the remainder of our grueling pre-Olympic exhibition schedule.

The first four exhibition games of the fifty-two we played in North America were against NHL teams. The play was rough and hard-hitting, as if the pros were bent on showing their physical superiority. On Saturday, September 29, we played the Minnesota North Stars at Met Center. It was an extremely bittersweet welcome home. In the first minute of the game, one of our strongest forwards, Phil Verchota, lost two front teeth. I was lucky to have a friend who happened to be an oral surgeon with me at the game. He wired Phil's teeth back in his mouth. Needless to say, from that moment forward, our boys were quite concerned about not getting seriously injured. Everybody wanted to stay healthy for the Olympic Games in February. We lost the game 4–2, but more importantly, nobody else got hurt.

We lost the next three games as well: 9–1 to the St. Louis Blues, 6–1 to the Atlanta Flames, and 5–4 to the Washington Capitals. It was a tough stretch for us. Thankfully, we beat the Maine Mariners, a minor league pro team, 4–2 on October 8. After that, we had another four-day break to rest and recuperate from the countless minor bruises, strains, and contusions suffered in the last ten days.

We played the Canadian National Team twice on the weekend of October 13 and 14, beating them in the first game 7–2 and shutting them out in the sequel, 6–0. It was a real mood lifter for boys. Our fighting spirit was back, and we won the next seven games—against minor league pro teams and college teams—by impressive margins, including a 15–0 rout of the Flint Generals on October 30. We didn't lose again, in fact, until November 7, when we lost to the Houston Apollos 4–3 in a tightly contested game. We rebounded quickly, though, and won the next five games, outscoring our opponents 29–13.

We flew to Calgary on November 21 for a three-game series against the Canadian Olympic team. We played well north of the border, but we lost all three games, by scores of 7–6, 6–2, and 4–3.

We returned home to Minnesota during the first week of December for a well-timed break. We enjoyed several days' rest and practice on our home ice before winning our next four games in convincing fashion.

Feeling back on track, we left for Lake Placid on December 11 for a five-team pre-Olympic tourney with the Canadian Olympic team, the Swedish National B Team, the Czechoslovakian National B Team, and the Russian Junior All-Star Team. On the way there we stopped in Glen Falls, New York, for a game against the Adirondack Red Wings. It was a very physical game, which we lost 1–0, picking up a few minor injuries in the process. Luckily, we had four days to rest and practice before the competition began.

We played our first tournament game, against the Swedish B Team, on Sunday, December 16. The pace was very fast, but we won the game 4–2. The next day we played the Canadian Olympic team. It was another close, hard-fought game, but we pulled out a 3–1 win.

After a two-day break, we played the Czechoslovakian B Team on Thursday, December 20. Exactly as expected, the Czechoslovakians were in no mood for a hard, physical game and that was just fine with us. Both teams played very fast, skating and passing well, but we shut them out 3–0. On the last day of the tournament, December 22, we beat the Russian Junior All-Star Team 5–3 and took the gold medal.

Winning all four tournament games was huge for our morale. Our confidence was sky-high. Now, there was no question we could skate and compete with the top European teams.

On Sunday, December 23, we flew to Minneapolis, where everyone had two days off for Christmas.

By then, Jimmy Craig was like part of the family. In fact, before we'd left for Lake Placid, he and Velta had talked and decided to invite the other boys on the team who were far from home, away from their friends and family, to Christmas Eve dinner. Jimmy had even agreed to help prepare the meal. I couldn't have been happier.

I'll never forget when Jimmy and I were driving home after our light morning practice on December 24. I said, "Jimmy, we should stop and pick up a couple quarts of milk for dinner tonight."

Jimmy laughed and said, "Doc, we'll need at least two or three *gallons*."

Once we got to the house, each of us fell into our Christmas Eve dinner role: Jimmy was the organizer, Velta was the cook, and I was the deliveryman. Herb Brooks and Craig Patrick were also there, so we had about ten people at the dinner table. After dinner,

Herb extended his compliments to Velta for such a wonderful meal, but said that it was time for him to get home to his own family. The boys went outside and had a snowball fight while Craig, Velta, and I enjoyed a glass of wine. It was a wonderful evening, enjoyed by all.

As the calendar turned to 1980, we suffered a bit of a letdown. On January 3, in our first post-holiday game, we tied the minor league Indianapolis Checkers 2–2. Two days later, in Rochester, Minnesota, we lost 3–2 to the Gorki Torpedo, a team from the Soviet Union. We bounced back quickly, however, and won our next four road games, against minor league pro teams, in Oklahoma City and Tulsa, Oklahoma, and Wichita, Kansas.

On January 15 we beat the University of Wisconsin 6–2 at home at Met Center. The next day we traveled to Texas, where we lost 4–3 in overtime to the Fort Worth Texans. Two days later, the score was reversed in Dallas when we beat the Dallas Black Hawks 4–3 in another overtime game. On January 21, we played the International Hockey League All-Stars in Milwaukee, skating to a 4–4 tie.

The next two road games brought nasty injuries. First, Mark Johnson suffered a hyperextended right hand and bruised ribs in Madison against his former team, the University of Wisconsin Badgers. Then Bill Baker was slashed across the chest in a particularly rough game on our return trip to Fort Worth. Bill skated back to the bench spitting blood, the sign of a possible lung injury. Needless to say, Herb and

the rest of the players were scared. Mark was our top scorer, and Bill was one of our best defensemen. We didn't want anyone getting hurt just four weeks before the Olympics, least of all those two. Herb had told me once that Mark was the spark plug. If he played well, the team played well. Understandably, Herb was very concerned about Mark's health. Fortunately, they both recovered quickly.

On January 31 we won our last home game at Met Center, beating Dallas 10–6. We were happy to finish our home schedule with an impressive victory.

After our morning practice on Friday, February 1, we packed our bags for Warroad, Minnesota, the legendary hockey town a mere eleven miles from the Canadian border that is the birthplace of former Olympians Gordon Christian, from the 1956 silver-medal team, and his brothers Roger and Bill Christian, from the 1960 team that won the gold medal in Squaw Valley, California.

The next morning, the boys took a twin-engine puddle-jumper to Warroad for a game against the Warroad Lakers, who'd famously beaten the 1960 US Olympic team 6–4 just weeks before Team USA struck gold by going undefeated in the Olympic tournament that year. With twenty-one-year-old defenseman Dave Christian on the team—Bill Christian's son and the fourth member of the Christian family to play hockey for a US Olympic team—playing the Warroad Lakers before heading to Lake Placid was a rite of passage. Unlike the 1960 team, however, we beat the Lakers 10–0.

I didn't travel with the team, but as Rob McClanahan told it to me, they'd had some excitement on the way home. While taxiing onto the runway, the plane bumped into a light pole. Luckily, nothing was damaged, but all of the players had to get out and push the plane back so the pilot could start a new approach to the runway. Eventually, everything worked out and the team returned safe and sound from its last road exhibition game in that famous little hockey town on the shores of magnificent Lake of the Woods.

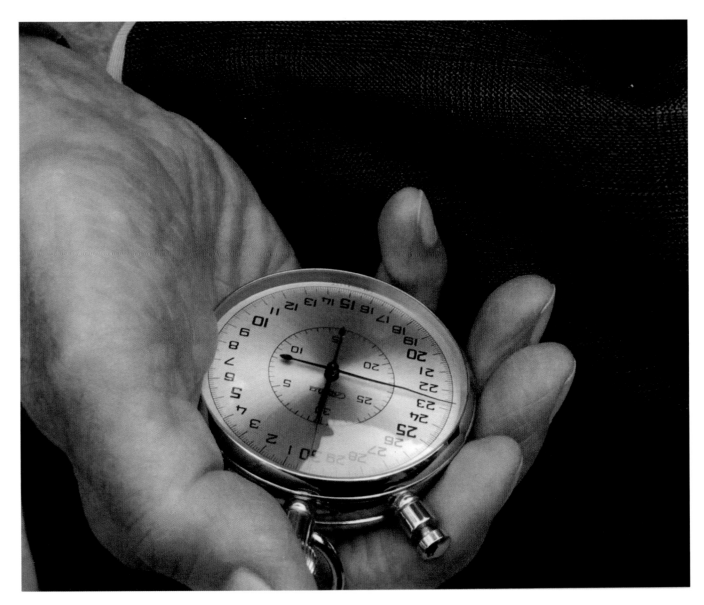

That "magic" stopwatch!

15

The Magic Stopwatch

Winning the Olympic Gold Medal, Lake Placid, New York, 1980

On Monday, February 4, 1980, the US Olympic hockey team boarded a plane for Detroit. The boys had been invited to attend the NHL All-Star dinner that evening.

On Tuesday, before the NHL All-Star Game at Joe Louis Arena, we played a twenty-minute exhibition period against the Canadian Olympic team. We lost 1–0.

We flew to Albany on Wednesday and took a bus to Lake Placid. For some reason, our equipment didn't get on the plane, so our trainer, Gary Smith, and our equipment manager, Bud Kessel, stayed with our gear to make sure it got to Lake Placid. They arrived at the Olympic Village late in the afternoon. Meanwhile, the players settled into their rooms and got their credentials. We practiced at 7:00 p.m., ate a late dinner, and went to bed.

Over the next two days, our practices were tough, but the media was all over us and it was difficult to focus. Herb told the reporters, as he always did when they asked him to comment on specific players or forward lines, "We aren't a team of stars, but we have a mission to fulfill." He said they could talk to him or Craig Patrick, but there would be no players available for media interviews.

On Saturday, February 9, we played the Soviets at Madison Square Garden in our final exhibition game. The 1980 Olympic Winter Games were set to begin

The opening ceremony of the 1980 Olympic Winter Games in Lake Placid.

just three days later. The game itself was inconsequential, nothing more than a final tune-up and a showcase for the fans. Herb didn't want the boys to lose their legs before the real tournament got underway, so he held them back. Our fans—and the sports commentators—didn't know this, so when we lost 10–3, everyone agreed we were no match for the Soviets. Only the Russian coach, Viktor Tikhonov,

had noticed our intentional lack of intensity and cautious style of play. In the press conference after the game, he said, "We showed them everything, but they didn't show us a thing."

The loss itself was unimportant, but one of our best defensemen, Jack O'Callahan, injured his left knee. Herb was upset and worried about losing Jack for the tournament. I examined Jack's knee after the

In Lake Placid with silver medalist Linda Fratianne and Bud Kessel.

game and was sure that there was no tearing, but there had been considerable strain to his medial collateral ligament. Nonetheless, I was confident that Gary Smith and our other trainer, Bruce Kola, would do a great job in physical therapy and get Jack back on the ice in about a week. I also consulted with my friend Dr. Bert Zarins, who'd been our orthopedist in Moscow the year before. He already knew Jack and agreed with

my treatment plan. He also agreed to come to Lake Placid in a few days' time to examine Jack's knee personally. Herb was relieved by the diagnosis, and Jack was very happy that he could stay with team.

There were twelve men's hockey teams at the 1980 Olympic Winter Games. The Blue Division featured Sweden, the United States, Czechoslovakia, West Germany, Norway, and Romania. The Red Division consisted of the Soviet Union, Finland, Canada, Poland, the Netherlands, and Japan.

After the preliminary round-robin games, the top two teams from each division advanced to the medal round. Each of those four teams then crossed over to play its final two games against the two teams in the other division. Points from head-to-head games in the divisional round carried over into the final point tally. Teams earned two points for a win, one point for a tie, and zero points for a loss. Technically there wasn't a championship gold-medal game. The highest point total won. Every game was important.

On Tuesday, February 12, we played Sweden in our first game. We knew that the Swedes were very fast. Our defense, especially, would have to be careful not to let anyone get behind them. We started the game well enough, played hard, and skated stride-for-stride with the Swedes. Early in the first period, however, Rob McClanahan was checked hard into the boards, severely bruising his right thigh. Then, a few minutes later, Buzzy Schneider seemed to score, but the goal was disallowed because the linesman ruled him offside. That slowed us down a bit, and the Swedes struck first, midway through the period, which ended 1–0 in their favor.

Once we got to the dressing room, I told Rob to take off his gear because I was pulling him from the game. Moments later, as I left the locker room, I ran into Herb in the hallway. He stopped me to ask how bad McClanahan's injury was and if he could skate at all. I told Herb that it wasn't so bad that Robbie wouldn't be able to skate, but the bruise was pretty severe. I'd told him to get undressed and sit out for the rest of the game.

A little grin spread across Herb's face. He patted me on the shoulder and told me not to get excited. Nothing against my judgment, he said, but he needed to fire up the team, and Rob's case would help him do that. He thought the boys were playing too cautiously and wanted to challenge them to raise their intensity level. He went into the dressing room and accused McClanahan of being too soft, unable to play a tough game against one of the best teams in the world. It became quite ugly, but Herb got what he wanted. Rob returned to the ice.

The boys came out in the second period with much more intensity, playing for the most part in the Swedish end. The Swedish goalie and defense played well, turning back our scoring chances, but with just twenty-eight seconds to go in the middle period, Dave Silk finally scored, assisted by Mike Ramsey and Mark Johnson. It was our first goal of the Olympics. The game was tied 1–1. The boys had risen to the challenge.

The third period started with fast-paced, end-to-end action. Both teams skated well, but Sweden pulled ahead at the 4:45 mark on a goal from Thomas Eriksson. They led 2–1 and seemed to be in control. Despite our frequent attacks, we were unable to put the puck past Swedish goalie, Pelle Lindbergh. Then, with less than a minute left in the game and face-off deep in the Swedish end, Herb pulled goalie Jim Craig and sent an extra attacker onto the ice.

Mark Johnson won the draw back to defenseman

Mike Ramsey. Ramsey unloaded a shot from the point, but it was blocked by a sliding Swede and skittered across to Bill Baker. Baker dumped it into the corner, where it was nudged along the boards, behind the Swedish goal, into the other corner. Mark Pavelich gained possession and slid the puck to Bill Baker, moving in from the point. Baker one-timed a slapshot from the top of the circle, beating the Swedish goaltender cleanly to tie it up 2–2 with twenty-seven seconds left. Our fans went crazy as the boys flew off the bench, mobbing Baker in celebration.

Moments later, with the game back underway, the panicked Swedes iced the puck, setting up yet another face-off deep in their end with nine seconds left in the game. This time, however, we failed to win the draw cleanly. The Swedes gained control of the puck and cleared the zone, ending the game in a tie. We'd earned a very important point against one of the top seeds in our division.

It is hard to overstate the importance of Bill Baker's game-tying goal. It was not just a bonding moment that brought the boys closer together; it gave our players confidence that they could play with the best teams in the world.

Wednesday, February 13, was a day of rest. I checked with trainer Gary Smith about Jack O'Callahan's left knee, and he told me that it was improving very well.

The next day we played Czechoslovakia, the silver-medal team at the 1979 World Championships. At that tournament, we'd battled to a 2–2 tie, thanks to Jim Craig's brilliant goaltending. We knew we could skate with them, but we'd have to play a nearly perfect game. There was no room for mistakes.

We started the game a bit nervously, and Czechoslovakia scored first. We regained our composure, however, and completely surprised them with our speed and playmaking ability, with Mike Eruzione and Mark Pavelich scoring a goal each, just over a minute apart, to take a 2–1 lead. The Czechs tied it up on a goal from Peter Stastny about six minutes later, and the first period ended 2–2.

We came out strong in the second period and got the go-ahead goal from Buzzy Schneider to make it 3–2. From then on, we never looked back. We won the game 7–3, but in the final minutes a Czechoslovakian defenseman crosschecked Mark Johnson hard on the left arm. Mark grimaced in pain and grabbed his shoulder. We were all worried about his condition. Herb was especially mad about such a cheap shot at the end of the game and unleashed a string of extremely angry words at the Czechoslovakian player and coaches.

After such an impressive victory against Czechoslovakia, we were quite confident about advancing to the medal round. We still had to play Norway, Romania, and West Germany, but those teams were nowhere near as strong as Sweden and Czechoslovakia. With one win and one tie against the top two teams in our division, we'd earned three of four possible points and were in the driver's seat.

We didn't have a game on Friday, February 15, so I went to watch Eric Heiden skate the men's 500-meter race. He won his first gold medal, beating Yevgeny

Kulikov from Russia and Lieuwe de Boer from the Netherlands.

The men's 5000-meter speed-skating event was scheduled for the next day, but I knew I couldn't go because we were set to play Norway. This time, the Norwegians couldn't play the slashing and spearing style that they had used in Oslo back in September. It proved to be an easy win for us: we beat them 5–1 on goals from Eruzione, Johnson, Silk, Wells, and Morrow. It was a total team effort. Later, I got news that Eric Heiden had won his second gold medal of the Olympics, beating two Norwegians, Kay Stenshjemmet and Tom Erik Oxholm, in the 5000-meter race.

Sunday, February 17, was a day of rest. Jack's injured knee had improved enough that he took a light skate at the morning practice. He said his knee felt fine, which made us all very happy. After practice Buddy and I went into town, relaxed, and had a beer.

On Monday, after practice, I got a telephone call from Boston. It was Dr. Zarins. He told me that he would be there to check Jack's injured knee the following morning. I told him that Jack's left knee was responding well to treatment, but I looked forward to his opinion. That afternoon we played Romania. As expected, it was our easiest game. Buzzy Schneider scored twice as we cruised to a 7–2 win.

When Dr. Zarins arrived the next day, Gary and I gave him a full report, noting that Jack's knee had made such remarkable progress that he'd been permitted to practice the last three days. Dr. Zarins examined the knee and agreed that it would be safe to let Jack play against West Germany on Wednesday.

Herb and Jack were very happy about that decision.

Meanwhile, there was more good news. Eric Heiden had won his third consecutive gold medal. This time he'd beaten Canadian skater Gaétan Boucher and Russia's Vladimir Lobanov in the 1000-meter event. Mark Johnson, who like Eric was from Madison, Wisconsin, was particularly happy, as the two had been good friends for years.

On Wednesday, February 20, we played West Germany in our last game of the preliminary round. The first period did not start well for us. Just under two minutes into the game, Horst-Peter Kretschmer surprised Jimmy Craig with a long shot to take a 1–0 lead. We became a little disorganized and gave up our second goal when Udo Kiessling scored on a power play with just fifteen seconds to go in the first period. The period ended 2–0 in favor of the West Germans.

We started the second period much more intensely and tied the score on goals by McClanahan and Broten. The period ended 2–2.

In the third period we took complete control of the game, scoring our third and fourth unanswered goals. McClanahan scored his second of the game, assisted by Johnson and Christian, and Phil Verchota added his first, with assists from Christian and Wells. We won the game 4–2 and advanced to the medal round, undefeated in divisional play.

Sweden, also undefeated but with a better point differential, was the top seed in the Blue Division. The United States was second. In the Red Division, the Soviets finished first with a 5–0 record, while Finland finished second at 3–2. Our first game of the medal round was to be against the Soviet Union on Friday, February 22. Our second game, against Finland, was set for two days later. Everyone was happy about not losing a single game in the preliminary round, but facing the mighty Soviets—who'd scored a whopping fifty-one goals while surrendering just eleven thus far in the tournament—was a different story.

After morning practice on Thursday, February 21, Herb told me to come see him after lunch. Herb was always thinking, so I wondered what he had in mind. I knew it was something special. When I walked into his office, Herb said that he'd been thinking a lot about the upcoming game against the Soviets. They were an excellent team, he observed, but our team was also in top condition. He thought if we could skate with them—or even outskate them—with a little bit of luck, we might be able to beat them.

The most important thing, he noted, was that our players needed to have fresh legs. That meant shorter shifts, no longer than thirty-five to forty seconds each. He showed me his stopwatch and said, "Doc, I want you to clock the shifts. Stand right next to me and tell me when the boys hit thirty, thirty-five, and forty seconds. If by forty seconds I haven't changed the shift, grab me by the sleeve. And Doc, those thirty-five or forty seconds are playing time. When the whistle blows, you stop the stopwatch. As soon they drop the puck, you start the stopwatch again."

I said, "Okay, Herb, I'm sure I can do it."

Herb handed me the stopwatch, and I practiced my new assignment all afternoon. I even forgot to go watch Eric Heiden win the 1500-meter race for his fourth gold medal.

On the morning of Friday, February 22, everyone was quiet, but you could sense their determination. Everyone was ready to play their best game of the tournament. Herb gave his famous speech before the game in the dressing room. "Tonight, we are the greatest hockey team. You were born to be hockey players, each one of you. You are meant to be here tonight. This is your time, not theirs! Now go out and do it!"

We started the game a little tight, seemingly unable to clear our own zone, but eventually overcame our first-period jitters and started playing better. The Soviets scored first, when Vladimir Krutov deflected Alexei Kasatonov's slapshot from the point past Jim Craig, but about four minutes later we tied it. Mark Pavelich picked up the puck at our blue line, carried it through center, and hit Buzzy Schneider with a pinpoint pass. Schneider raced up the left wing and fired a slapshot that beat Tretiak cleanly in the upper right corner, Schneider's fifth goal of the Olympics.

With the score now tied 1–1, our fans started chanting, "USA, USA, USA," giving our team more courage. The boys skated even harder and wouldn't let the Soviets play their smooth passing game. Late in the first period, however, the Soviets scored again to take a 2–1 lead. Aleksandr Golikov carried it into the zone and dropped it back to Sergei Makarov. Makarov tried to return the pass to Golikov as he streaked to the net. Instead, the puck deflected off our defense, right back onto Makarov's stick. Jim had played the pass and was moving toward Golikov as Makarov launched an unexpected shot. It went in on the high glove side.

The boys were undaunted, however, as Craig bounced back with a string of brilliant saves that rallied the team. Then, with just five seconds to go in the first period, Dave Christian launched a desperation slapshot from the US side of the red line. Tretiak made the save, but failed to control the rebound. The puck deflected to Mark Johnson, breaking hard for the net. He skated around the Soviet goalie and easily slipped the puck into the open net.

Coach Tikhonov was furious with his goaltender and benched him for the rest of game. In fact, the Soviets—thinking time had expired—had retreated to their dressing room in disbelief. The referee, however, determined that one second remained. After a minute or two of confusion, the Soviet backup goalie, Vladimir Myshkin, and just three Soviet skaters returned to the ice for the face-off, clearly stunned.

Meanwhile, our boys were ecstatic, still celebrating our last-second goal as we went into the locker room. Tied 2–2 after one period, we knew we could skate with the Soviets.

After the intermission we came out flying. Our short shifts confused the Soviet players. At one point Vladimir Petrov, the leading scorer in four previous World Championship tournaments, took three consecutive face-offs against three different US players in a single shift. Knowing that I'm Latvian, Petrov skated close to our bench and said to me in Russian, "What is this?" I answered him, also in Russian, "Why don't you ask your own coach!" He looked at Tikhonov, who gestured vaguely with his hands as if to say, *I don't know either. Stay out there, stay out there!*

Unfortunately, the Soviets managed to score a bit more than two minutes into the second period on their first power play of the game. We were killing the penalty well when Aleksander Maltsev sprang loose for a breakaway and beat Jim low on the stick side. We killed off another penalty later, and the period ended 3–2 in favor of the Soviets.

We came out with even more intensity in the third period, but I almost didn't see the game because I was so busy watching the stopwatch and saying to Herb, "Thirty seconds . . . thirty-five seconds . . . *forty seconds!*" and grabbing him by the sleeve.

By now we were completely outskating the Soviets. They were shocked by our speed at this late stage of the game and were getting frustrated. Then, as is often the case, their frustration boiled over. Krutov slashed Broten and was called for high-sticking. The two-minute man advantage boosted our morale and gave us a burst of energy. We mounted a ferocious attack on the Russian goal, now tended by Myshkin, but the Soviets kept turning us back. Then, with our power play about to expire, the puck found Mark Johnson's stick again, deep in the Soviet zone. He ripped out a shot and scored. Everyone went wild. The game was tied 3–3!

Now we were really buzzing, but Herb kept yelling, "Short shifts, short shifts, short shifts!"

Two minutes later, Buzzy Schneider skated by the bench and said, "I'm tired." Herb immediately pulled him off and sent Mike Eruzione to take his place. The puck was deep in the Soviet end, where John Harrington was fighting for it. Harrington slid the puck along the boards to Pavelich, who quickly got it back to Eruzione, streaking into the slot. A Soviet defender went down to block Mike's shot, but Eruzione let loose a low, hard wristshot that whipped past Myshkin, screened by his own defenseman.

Everybody in the arena went crazy!

We were beating the Soviets 4–3, but there were still ten minutes left. In the preliminary round, the Soviets had been losing to the Canadians, at one point by two goals, and had trailed the Finns by a goal with just five minutes left in the game. They'd gone on to win both games. This contest was far from over.

It was, by far, the longest ten minutes of the Olympics. To me, it seemed like the stopwatch was losing power because those thirty-five-to forty-second intervals were coming so slow.

Herb said to the boys, "Play your game, play your game," so they wouldn't go into a defensive shell, and they didn't. Their fighting spirit and determination was unbelievable. Craig was outstanding in goal, but our defensemen and forwards courageously blocked shots as well. Every player expended his last drop of energy keeping the puck away from the Soviet team.

Finally, the fans started counting down, "Five, four, three, two, one!" Sticks and gloves flew into the air. The boys leaped over the boards and skated toward Jim Craig, hugging him and each other in an outpouring of emotion.

At the other end, Soviet players stared in disbelief, leaning on their sticks, silently watching our players celebrate victory.

After congratulating Herb, I also jumped the boards and ran to hug the boys, especially Jim.

Once the initial rush of excitement died down, the two teams lined up for the official handshake. The Soviets were gracious in defeat, while our boys beamed with joy.

I noticed that Helmut Balderis hadn't returned to his own bench, but instead was gliding toward ours. I knew immediately that he was coming to congratulate Herb. I also knew that Coach Tikhonov wouldn't like it at all. I said to Balderis in Latvian, "Helmut, why do you have to do this?"

Helmut responded, also in Latvian, referring to Tikhonov, "He can go to hell!" Then he said to Herb, in English, "Congratulations, Coach. Very good job."

The two men shook hands, and Balderis skated slowly back to his bench. Herb turned to me and said, "Doc, he wasn't sore about losing the game."

I said, "Herbie, you know, he would much rather play for us than the Soviets."

The fact that we'd just beaten the mighty Soviets was hard to comprehend in those first moments. Herb's hard work and creativity, combined with the boys' tremendous fighting spirit, determination, and courageous play—and that magic stopwatch—resulted in an unforgettable 4–3 American victory.

Outside, the whole Olympic Village was in a celebratory mood. Mike Eruzione, who'd scored the winning goal, was the big hero, of course. But it was John Harrington's and Mark Pavelich's tenacity in Soviet end, their hard work in the corners and along the boards, that first won the puck and led to the play where Mark passed to Mike for the winning goal.

Harrington and Pavelich should not be forgotten for their incredible efforts.

Thankfully, Saturday, February 23, was a day of rest. From early morning to afternoon, the medical dispensary at the Olympic Village was full of US hockey players. Many had contusions from blocking shots. Others had bumps and bruises from throwing checks and scrapping for pucks. I was especially concerned, however, about Kenny Morrow, who'd blocked several very hard shots destined for the US goal. When I asked him about his contusions, he told me repeatedly, "I'm fine, Doc, I'm fine," but I knew that he must have been in considerable pain.

Meanwhile, both of our trainers, Gary Smith and Bruce Kola, had their hands full. I'd listed fifteen separate injuries in my report, five or six of which were severe. And yet, not a single one of those injured players was willing to miss the next game. They all were determined to play against Finland in the finals. That was the spirit that characterized the team.

While I was tending to our players in the dispensary, Eric Heiden skated in his last event, the 10,000-meter race. It was his favorite distance, and he won the contest easily, setting a new world record of 14:28.13. Eric had won an incredible and unprecedented five Olympic gold medals. We were all so proud of him.

That afternoon I saw the Soviet hockey team doctor, Boris Sapronenkov. He said, "You Americans have two Supermen: one is on TV and the other is on the speed-skating track!"

We both laughed, and I said, "Yes, he is quite a skater!"

On Sunday morning, February 24, the boys were in a serious mood. No one cracked a joke at the breakfast table. Everybody knew that our work was far from over. Our surprising upset of the Soviet juggernaut, incredible as it was, did not guarantee the gold medal. In fact, if we lost to the Finns by two goals or more and the Swedes tied the Soviets, we wouldn't win a medal at all. The final game was decisive. It all came down to this. No encouraging pregame speeches were necessary. The boys knew very well what they had to do.

The game started with intense skating by both teams. Finland forechecked hard and played a strong physical game. Then, in the fourth minute of play. Finland took a penalty and we went on the power play. We had several scoring chances, but couldn't get the puck past Jorma Valtonen, who made one incredible save after another.

After surviving our onslaught and killing off the penalty, the Finns rallied and scored on a slapshot by Jukka Porvari, who wound up near the blue line and ripped it past Jim Craig. For the sixth time in seven games, we'd given up the first goal and fallen behind 1–0.

In the second period the boys played more aggressively, with better passing and puck movement. Then, about two and a half minutes into the period, defenseman Mike Ramsey took a penalty, leaving us shorthanded. As soon as we'd killed off the penalty, however, Steve Christoff scored an unassisted goal to tie the game 1–1. It felt like the tide was turning. We were playing well and clearly outskating Finland, but less than two minutes later, Buzzy Schneider was

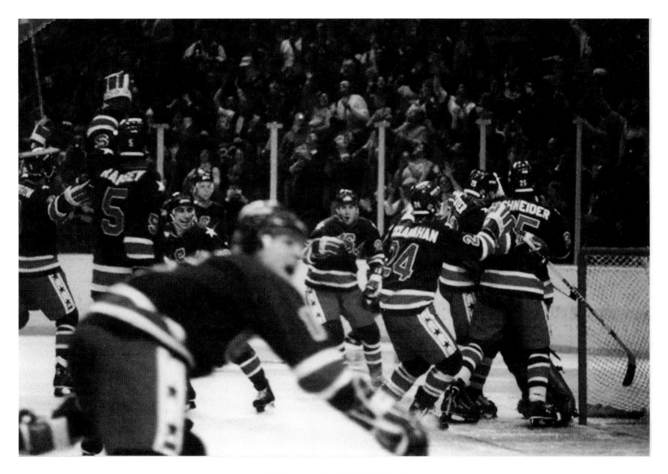

We won the Gold Medal!

called for slashing and the Finns scored a power-play goal. The momentum had shifted again. Suddenly the Finns were on top 2–1, despite the fact that we were outplaying them and had doubled their shots on goal, 14–7. Valtonen continued playing well in the goal, and the second period ended 2–1.

At the intermission, Herb was clearly disappointed as he silently entered the dressing room. At first he didn't say anything—he just looked around the room at each of the boys. Everybody sat quietly, not daring to say a word. Finally, Herb broke the silence and said, "If you lose this game, you will take it to your fucking grave!" He walked to the door, turned around, and repeated, "*To your fucking grave,*" and left.

The boys came out charging like lions, clearly outplaying Finland, constantly swarming their net, trapping them in their zone. Then, less than three minutes into the final frame, Phil Verchota—a good

The "Locker Room Staff" celebrates (L-R): Bruce Kola, Gary Smith, Bud Kessel, and myself.

Finnish boy from Duluth—took a pass from Dave Christian and scored, tying it 2–2.

The boys' emotions ran sky-high. They attacked the Finnish goal in wave after wave. Four minutes later, Valtonen steered away a backhand shot from Christian and Johnson scooped up the loose puck in the corner. He battled along the boards, blanketed by two Finnish players, spun suddenly, and passed the puck to McClanahan, standing on the doorstep.

McClanahan calmly took the pass, waited for Valtonen to commit, and buried it for the go-ahead goal. The fans went wild, cheering and chanting "USA! USA! USA!" at the top of their lungs.

The gold medal was within our reach.

Just forty-three seconds later, however, things took a sudden, dramatic turn for the worse when Broten was called for hooking, the first of two consecutive US penalties in a span of four minutes and six

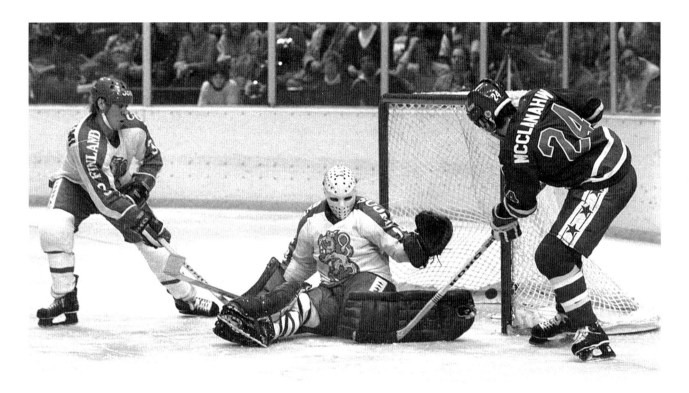

Rob McClanahan scoring the gold medal-winning goal!

seconds. We successfully killed off the first penalty, but as soon as Broten stepped out of the box, Christian was called for tripping. From that point forward, however, our superior conditioning proved to be the difference. Finland was running out of gas—even with the man advantage—while Christoff, Eruzione, and the others were still buzzing, effectively killing off our two back-to-back penalties. Finally back at full strength, we thought we'd survived the worst.

Then, with 4:35 left to play, Phil Verchota was penalized two minutes for roughing. But even while killing penalties, our forecheck was relentless. Time

and time again, the boys beat the Finns to the puck, bottling them up in their end, creating scoring chances. With less than four minutes left, still on the penalty kill, Ken Morrow iced the puck deep into the Finnish zone. Christoff flew in after it, wrestled it free from a Finnish defender, and slid it back to Johnson, cruising in from the blue line. Johnson drove hard to the net and shot a backhand. Valtonen kicked it out, but Johnson fought for the rebound and banged it home.

We were winning the gold-medal game with just 3:35 left to go.

I turned to Herb and said, "Herb, is it really

going to happen?"

Herb said, "Don't talk, Doc, don't talk!"

In the last minute of play, Herb sent Eruzione, Schneider, and Pavelich onto the ice. They almost scored our fifth goal when Mike's shot hit the post, but the puck bounced across the goal mouth, hit the other post, and skittered away. Shortly after that, the final buzzer sounded. We all had tears in our eyes.

Craig Patrick and I congratulated Herb, who quietly left the bench and went into the dressing room. Craig and I ran onto the ice to congratulate the boys. The fans were going wild. Some of them even managed to get onto the ice to give superstar goalie Jim Craig the American flag. He draped it over his shoulders and skated around the rink, looking for his father.

It was almost too hard to believe that we'd really won the gold medal. But, yes, it was true! I was so happy for Herb and all of the boys, who'd shown the world what young, intelligent hockey players can do when in peak condition.

The award ceremony was much later, after the Soviets had beaten Sweden 9–2. With five total points in the medal round, we won the gold medal. The Soviets took the silver with four points. Sweden earned the bronze with two points. The Finns went home emptyhanded.

After the medals were presented to each team, Mike Eruzione called all of our players to join him on the podium as the US national anthem played. It was a wonderful sight. Every one of us was so very, very happy!

Once the official ceremony ended, I went to the medical office to write the injury report. I'd just started to get my notes together when Helmut Balderis came in with two other Russian players, Viktor Zhluktov and Valeri Vasiliev. Helmut said, "Doc, we need your help. Viktor and Valeri would like to buy some moon boots for their wives, but we have difficulty communicating with the people at the store."

I said, "Helmut, I have to work on my injury report—otherwise I will forget."

Helmut said, "Doc, they will be closing the shops at the Olympic Village in thirty minutes. Please come and help us."

I said, "Okay, let's go!"

After we'd finished our shopping, Valeri pulled a champagne bottle out of his leather jacket. He placed the bottle on top of the counter and said, in his thick Russian accent, "American people, good people. Let's have a champagne toast to their gold medal."

The store clerks were very surprised and said, "Oh, my, these Russian boys are not so bad."

I said, "Sure, sure, they are good boys. Otherwise, I wouldn't be here with them."

After we'd had a few sips of champagne, Valeri turned to me and said, in his broken English, "Doctor, we know each other for a while."

I said, "Yes, Valeri, it's true. We have known each other a while."

He continued, "So now, you can tell me, what did you give your players to eat and drink that they could skate like that in the last period? The last period has always been ours. There has never been a team who could skate with us in the last period. When we were ahead three to two, after the second period, we were celebrating already. But in the last period, your boys were skating so hard that we were grabbing our heads and saying, '*Horror! Horror! Horror!*'"

I said, "Well, Valeri, that was our fountain of youth."

Helmut interrupted and said, "Valeri, didn't you see? They changed lines three times for every one of ours."

I said, "Oh, Helmut, you did notice that!"

Helmut replied, "Yes, it was so obvious!"

The store clerks said it was time for them to close up shop. It was time for us to go. Viktor and Valeri had their moon boots, and I could return to my injury report.

Earlier that afternoon we'd received an invitation from President Carter to come to the White House for lunch the following afternoon. On Monday, February 25, our team boarded an Air Force plane for the flight to Washington, D.C.

It was a very nice reception, with the military band playing in the front hall. Everybody enjoyed lunch, but it was also bittersweet, because it was the end of our journey together. During those seven months of grueling training, practices, and exhibition games, the team had experienced bitter defeats and wonderful victories. All of it had molded the boys into a close-knit family. Lifelong friendships had developed between them. In the first days of training camp, there was frequent teasing and competition between the eastern and western players, but in the end, we

At the White House reception with Buzzy Schneider.

were united. In particular, Jack O'Callahan and Mike Ramsey became close friends.

Twelve players went on to sign professional contracts: Bill Baker (Montreal Canadiens), Neal Broten (Minnesota North Stars), Dave Christian (Winnipeg Jets), Steve Christoff (Minnesota North Stars), Jim Craig (Atlanta Flames), Mark Johnson (Pittsburgh Penguins), Rob McClanahan (Buffalo Sabres), Ken Morrow (New York Islanders), Jack O'Callahan (Chicago Blackhawks), Mark Pavelich (New York Rangers), Mike Ramsey (Buffalo Sabres), and Dave Silk (Boston Bruins).

Only Broten and Christoff (both of them North Stars) and Ramsey and McClanahan (both Buffalo Sabres) ever played together again. The rest of the players were all on different teams, competing against each other.

1984 United States Hockey Team. Front row (L-R): Bob Mason, Mark Kumpel, Rich Costello, Phil Verchota, Coach Lou Vairo, Chairman Walter L. Bush, Jr., General Manager Larry Johnson, John Harrington, Pat LaFontaine, Mark Fusco, Marc Behrend. Middle row: Assistant Coach Bob O'Connor, Assistant Coach Dave Peterson, Assistant Coach Doug Woog, Assistant Coach Tim Taylor, Gary Sampson, Scott Fusco, Scott Bjugstad, Corey Millen, Tim Thomas, myself, Team Physician Dr. Sheldon Burns, Trainer Dennis Helwig, Equipment Manager Bud Kessel. Back row: Steve Griffith, David H. Jensen, Chris Chelios, Bob Brooke, Kurt Kleinendorst, Tom Hirsch, Al Iafrate, David A. Jensen, Ed Olczyk, Paul Guay, Gary Haight, Assistant Equipment Manager Gene Barcikoski.

16

14th Olympic Winter Games

Sarajevo, Yugoslavia, 1984

Team Roster

In Goal: *Marc Behrend, Bob Mason*

Defense: *Chris Chelios, Mark Fusco, Tom Hirsch, Al Iafrate, David H. Jensen, Tim Thomas*

Forwards: *Scott Bjugstad, Bob Brooke, Scott Fusco, Steve Griffith, Paul Guay, John Harrington, David A. Jensen, Mark Kumpel, Pat LaFontaine, Corey Millen, Ed Olczyk, Gary Sampson, Phil Verchota*

The 1984 Winter Olympics took place in Sarajevo, Yugoslavia from February 7 through 19. USA Hockey appointed Larry Johnson as general manager, Lou Vairo as as head coach, and Tim Taylor as assistant general manager and assistant coach. Bob O'Connor and Dave Peterson were also assistant coaches. Dennis Helwig was team trainer, Bud Kessel and Gene Barcikoski served as equipment managers, and Dr. Sheldon Burns and I were team physicians.

In 1981, one year removed from the famous Miracle on Ice, Team USA had finished a respectable, but disappointing fifth place at the IIHF World Championships in Gothenberg, Sweden, amid picketing by the Swedes against the "unnecessary brutality" of hockey. That was also the last tournament I'd attended. During 1982 and the winter of 1983 I was unable to travel with the team because I was recovering from a heart attack I'd suffered in December 1981. By the summer of 1983, however, I was back and ready for duty, feeling as good as ever and looking forward to rejoining the boys.

Training camp began on Sunday, August 7, 1983, in Colorado Springs. The core group of players consisted of talented young standouts Chris Chelios, Tom Hirsch, and Al Iafrate on defense, and Pat LaFontaine, Ed Olczyk, David A. Jensen, Scott Bjugstad, and Corey Millen on the forward lines. Good as these young players were, however, they lacked international experience and needed leadership. Thus, Phil Verchota and John Harrington, veterans of the 1980 team, were named captain and alternate captain, respectively.

After two weeks of training camp, the boys departed for Anchorage, Alaska, on Saturday, August 20, to play a four-game series against Krylya Sovetov—the Soviet Wings—a top professional team from Moscow. Dr. Burns served as team physician on the trip. The boys lost the first game 4–1 on August 22, tied the second game 3–3 on August 24, won the third game 4–1 on August 26, and lost the finale 5–3 on August 28. Our exhibition record stood at 1–2–1.

The boys returned to Colorado Springs, only to turn around and leave again three days later for a two-week training camp in Vierumäki, Finland. This time, I traveled with the team.

We arrived in Helsinki on Thursday, September 1, and took a bus to Vierumäki, our home base for the next ten days. Located seventy miles north of Helsinki, Vierumäki is an idyllic, quiet village that looks almost exactly like the northwoods of Minnesota. It is also home to one of the finest athletic training facilities in the world. We spent the next three days resting, practicing, and getting acclimated.

On Sunday, September 4, shortly after breakfast, we took a bus to Mikkeli for our first game. That night we played the Finnish Olympic team. It was a good, tough game, but we lost 5–2. After the dinner in Mikkeli, we took the bus back to Vierumäki.

The next day we had a late breakfast and took another two-hour bus ride to Lappeenranta. Again, we played the Finnish Olympic team. This time, however, we skated to a 3–3 tie. After dinner we returned to Vierumäki by bus.

On Tuesday, September 6, everybody slept late. We spent the afternoon on dry-land training and practice, then packed our gear and rested. Wednesday, after an early breakfast, we took a bus to Helsinki Airport for our flight to Oulu, almost four hundred miles due north. That night we played Oulun Kärpät, the local team in the Finnish Elite League, SM-liiga. We shut them out 2–0. After dinner we took an overnight train to Riihimäki and from there a bus back to Vierumäki, arriving the next morning at 7:30 a.m.

Thankfully, Thursday, September 8, was a day of rest. In the last three days we'd traveled nearly eight hundred miles, getting to bed quite late and getting up again early. A good rest was very much needed and well deserved.

On Friday afternoon we took a bus to Lahti for

Dry land training at Vierumaki, Finland.

a game against the Finnish Elite team Reipas. We blanked them 5–0 and returned to Vierumäki after dinner.

Saturday, September 10—our last day in Vierumäki—was a day of rest. After some light dryland exercises in the morning, the boys finally had a chance to enjoy their beautiful surroundings and the Vierumäki campgrounds.

The next day, after an early breakfast, we boarded a bus for Pori at 8:00 a.m. We arrived three hours later and went straight to the rink for practice. Afterwards, we checked into the beautiful Hotelli Karhun Kruunu, or "Bear's Crown Hotel." After lunch, the boys took a break and prepared for our game against Ässät Pori, winners of two Finnish Elite League championships in the 1970s. It was a good, tough game that ended in a 4–4 tie. After the game we returned to our hotel for dinner and a good night's rest.

On Monday, September 12, we ate breakfast and then practiced at 10:00 a.m. After lunch we took a bus to Turku, where we checked into the Rantasipi Hotel. We practiced again at 4:30 p.m., but there wasn't a game that night.

On Tuesday we practiced after breakfast and ate an early lunch in preparation for our 6:30 p.m. game against Turun Palloseura (usually abbreviated to TPS), our final game in Finland. We won 7–3, which was a great way to close out the trip. After dinner we boarded a bus for the Dipoli Hotel, near Helsinki Airport. We arrived at midnight, checked in, and went to sleep.

On Wednesday, September 14, we ate a relaxing breakfast and took the bus to Helsinki Airport for our long flight back to the United States. It had been a very enjoyable training camp at a world-class facility in a truly idyllic setting. Even so, we'd played six games in ten days, traveling hundreds of miles on buses, airplanes, and trains. Everyone was happy to be heading home, especially with a record of three wins, two ties, and one loss.

After returning from Finland, the boys rested and practiced in Minneapolis for a week. Then we began the toughest leg of our pre-Olympic schedule. Over the next four months we played fifty games in dozens of cities all over the US and Canada against NCAA Division 1 college teams, minor league professional

teams, NHL teams, and international teams.

On the first leg we played seven games against six different NHL teams between September 21 and October 2. We finished at exactly .500, with three wins, three losses, and one tie. We beat the Hartford Whalers 8–4, the New York Rangers 7–3, and the Washington Capitals 2–1. On the other side of the ledger, we lost to the Pittsburgh Penguins 4–3, the Detroit Red Wings 7–5, and the Minnesota North Stars 5–3. We tied the North Stars 3–3 in Minot, North Dakota, in our second straight game against them.

Five days later, we played three games against minor league pro and college teams before starting a five-game series against the Canadian Olympic team. We tied the Canadians 3–3 in each of the first two games, played first in Duluth and then in Minneapolis. We dropped the next game 4–1, in Edmonton, before tying them for the third time 3–3 and beating them in Calgary 6–4 in the finale. The series ended inclusively, with each team winning one game and tying the other three.

Over the next twenty-five days, we played thirteen games against minor league pro and college teams before playing a second five-game series against the Canadian Olympic team in late November and early December. This time the Canadians came out on top, beating us 5–4 in Montreal, 6–4 in Battle Creek, Michigan, and 5–3 in Cleveland, Ohio. We won just two of the five games, outscoring them in Toronto 4–1 and 2–1 in Moncton, New Brunswick.

Four days later, on December 7, we traveled to Lake Placid, New York, where the boys went through

After practice with Corey Millen.

doping control the following day.

On Friday, December 9, we kicked off a six-game, six-city tour against the Soviet Selects, essentially the national B team, at the Olympic Arena in Lake Placid in front of an overflow crowd of 9,110 fans. Late in the third period, it felt like the old magic was back when Phil Verchota sprang loose for a breakaway and scored, giving us a 5–4 lead with just 1:18 left to play.

The familiar chants of "USA! USA! USA!" rang out as the final seconds ticked off and we hung on to win, completing the "storybook game," as Chris Chelios later called it.

Over the next seven days, we played the Soviets five times. We beat them two more times, in Cleveland and St. Louis, lost to them twice, in Minneapolis and Indianapolis, and tied them once, in Cincinnati, ending the series in our favor.

After the Christmas break we played ten games against minor league pro and college teams between December 28, 1983, and January 17, 1984.

Then, before leaving for Europe, we played two more games against the Canadian Olympic team. We beat them 5–3 in Minneapolis on January 19 and again two nights later in Milwaukee by a score of 8–2.

On Tuesday, January 24, the team assembled in New York. General Manager Larry Johnson had arranged for the team to spend a week in Austria to adjust their body clocks and play two final exhibition games against the Austrian Olympic team, and thus, on Wednesday, they boarded the plane for Vienna. They arrived on Thursday morning, January 26, and boarded a bus to Graz for a five-day training camp. I was unable join the team because of a prior commitment to present some papers about sports injuries and illnesses at the 1984 Winter Olympics Sports Medical Conference in Dubrovnik, Yugoslavia, in the first week of February.

The team played its first exhibition game against the Austrians in Graz on February 1 and won 9–3. The next morning they returned to Vienna by bus and played the second exhibition game, beating the Austrians 9–2. At 5:00 p.m. on Friday, February 3, the team boarded a train for Sarajevo and the 1984 Winter Olympic Games.

Twelve teams participated in the Olympic hockey tournament, divided into two groups. The Blue Division consisted of Canada, Czechoslovakia, Finland, the United States, Austria, and Norway. The Red Division featured the Soviet Union, Sweden, West Germany, Poland, Italy, and Yugoslavia.

Once in Sarajevo, our team was quartered at the Europa Hotel. We had three days to practice and get familiar with our new surroundings. Our first game of the Olympic tournament was scheduled for 1:30 p.m. on Tuesday, February 7—before the opening ceremonies—against the now very familiar Canadian team.

I arrived from Dubrovnik just in time for the game, but I didn't bring any good luck to our boys. We lost the game 4–2. Everybody was disappointed. It was not how we'd wanted to start. I didn't know it at the time, but during the previous week some of our better players had suffered injuries and illnesses. Pat LaFontaine had contracted a bad upper respiratory infection, Chris Chelios had injured his knee, and David A. Jensen had injured his leg. Those lingering medical problems clearly reduced the boys' energy and effectiveness. We had the next day off and tried to rekindle our spirits before our upcoming game against Czechoslovakia on Thursday, February 9.

Our young, very talented team, however, was overmatched by the more experienced, highly skilled Czechoslovakian team. Their goalie and defense played exceptionally well, and we simply couldn't score. We lost 4–1. Two games into the tournament, and we were already deep in the hole. It would be very difficult to advance to the medal round with two losses. It now seemed all but certain that one of the top teams in our division, either the Canadians or the Czechs, would go undefeated, and the other would lose just once, relegating us to the consolation bracket.

Ironically, early the next morning I had to fly back to the sports medicine conference in Dubrovnik to present a paper about upper respiratory tract infections. I returned to Sarajevo on Saturday, February 11, in time to help Dr. Burns cover our game against Norway at 5:00 p.m. We clearly outplayed the Norwegians, but only managed a 3–3 tie. After playing three games in the preliminary round, we'd only earned one point. Even with two more wins, to earn a total of five points, it would be nearly impossible to advance to the medal round.

Our fourth game was scheduled for Monday, February 13, against Austria. Meanwhile, my daughter Brigita and the wives of some of the staff had arrived. Needless to say, they all attended the game, as did Dr. Zarins, who was serving as chief medical officer for the US Olympic team. Perhaps the wives' presence lifted our mood. Perhaps it was the knowledge that we'd already beaten the Austrians twice in a row in our last two exhibition games. In any case, we won 7–3. Dr. Zarins and I were glad to see the boys playing better and hoped for a good finish to the remainder of the tournament.

Tuesday was a day of rest. Brigita and I went for a walk in town after the morning practice. It was snowing quite hard, but we shopped at the local markets and some ethnic jewelry shops where we bought some copper teakettles and a fondue pot.

Our last game of the preliminary round was against Finland on Wednesday, February 15. It was a crucial game for us. If we won, we would qualify for the medal round. If not, we'd be knocked from contention. With a record of 2–2–0, Finland had earned four points, while our record of 1–2–1 gave us just three points. With a win we'd earn two points and move ahead of Finland. Plus, we'd hold the head-to-head tiebreaker. A loss or a tie would do nothing. We needed those two points.

Like every game against Finland, it was tough. The game ended in a 3–3 tie, with each team earning one point, and we finished fourth in our division, a major disappointment, given everybody's high hopes and expectations. The highest we could finish was seventh place.

We played our final game of the 1984 Winter Olympics at 8:30 p.m. on Friday, February 17, against Poland. Thankfully, we won 7–4, but the game was far from easy. In fact, the score was tied 2–2 after the first period. Then, to start the second period, Chris Chelios picked up the puck at center ice, drove to the net, and fired a shot. Włodzimierz Olszewski, the Polish goaltender, made the first save, but Pat LaFontaine gathered the rebound and banged it home for a 3–2 lead just fifteen seconds into the period.

We were in control and thought we could breathe easy, but nothing came easy for us. Every time we scored, Poland immediately answered. It was a wild second period of breakaways, goals, and crazy end-to-end action.

Moments later, in fact, Tom Hirsch held in the puck at the blue line and sent it low to Scott Fusco. Fusco made a beautiful pass, threading the puck between a Polish defender's legs to Scott Bjugstad at the side of the net. Bjugstad stickhandled once and

Behind the bench with Dr. Bert Zarins during February 14th game versus Austria. We won 7-3!

scored on a backhander for his second goal of the game. But just twenty-six seconds later, Wiesław Jobczyk, playing in his third Olympics, broke loose and fired a wrist shot past Bob Mason to cut our lead to 4–3.

We went up by two goals once again when Pat LaFontaine split two Polish defenders and slid the puck to David A. Jensen, who was crashing the net. Jensen flipped it home, and we led 5–3. But just nineteen seconds later, Poland sprang loose for a three-on-one break and made it 5–4.

Almost immediately after that, Gary Sampson picked up the puck at the blue line and set up a two-on-one. He deked the Polish defender, who slid to block the pass as he patiently held the puck. Then, with the defender well out of position, he slid a pass to Phil Verchota, who was wide open on the back side and blasted it into the net.

An incredible five goals had been scored in just two and a half minutes of play, three for Team USA and two for Poland. The period had started 2–2 but ended 6–4, luckily, in our favor.

Ironically, the third period was largely uneventful. The only goal was scored when Phil Verchota intercepted a pass deep in the Polish zone and quickly shot. Olszewski made the save, but the rebound bounced to Sampson, who barely got his stick on the puck—but it slowly trickled in, giving us a three-goal lead with just over three minutes left. We hung on from there and came away with the win, 7–4.

In the end, the Soviets won the gold medal, shutting out Czechoslovakia 2–0 in Tretiak's final Olympic game. The Czechoslovakians took silver, and Sweden blanked Canada 2–0 for the bronze. West Germany finished fifth, beating the Finns 7–4 and knocking them into sixth place. Team USA, defending gold medalists, finished in the bottom half of the pack, a disappointing seventh place. As Coach Lou Vairo later told reporters, "You won't see me at the souvenir stands. I don't want any other memories of Sarajevo and the 1984 Olympics."

Early on Saturday morning, February 18, Brigita and I left Sarajevo by car for Dubrovnik, where I presented one more paper on unnecessary brutality in hockey. The winter roads were a little rough and the countryside somewhat ragged, but we arrived in the early afternoon and had time to walk around that interesting old town on the shores of the Adriatic Sea. That evening we enjoyed a nice dinner with some of my friends from the American College of Sports Medicine.

On Sunday morning we visited the old church and the harbor. Right after lunch we boarded our flight home. It was a nice, clear day, and we could see the Dalmatian coast very well. The flight was smooth and uneventful. We arrived back in Minnesota late in the evening, a little tired from the long flight, but happy to have seen another very interesting city of mosques and minarets.

USA Hockey Team 1984 Canada Cup Tournament. Row 1 (L-R): Glenn Resch, John Vanbiesbrouck, Rod Langway, Head Coach Bob Johnson, General Manager Lou Nanne, International Chairman Walter L. Bush, Jr., Byran Trottier, Dave Christian, Tom Barrasso.
Row 2: Mark Fusco, Bryan Erickson, Mark Johnson, Administrative Assistant Art Berglund, Assistant General Manager Craig Patrick, Business Manager Larry Johnson, Joe Mullen, Aaron Broten, Neal Broten. Row 3: Gordie Roberts, Mike Ramsey, David A. Jensen, myself, Honorary General Manager Thomas N. Ivan, Brian Lawton, Phil Housley, Chris Chelios.
Row 4: Bob Carpenter, Ed Olczyk, Tom Hirsch, Trainer Skip Thayer, Assistant Coach Lou Vairo, Assistant Coach Ted Sator, Trainer Larry Ness, Bob Brooke, Brian Mullen.

17

The 1984 Canada Cup

Team Roster

In Goal: *Tom Barrasso, John Vanbiesbrouck, Glenn "Chico" Resch*

Defense: *Chris Chelios, Mark Fusco, Tom Hirsch, Phil Housley, Rod Langway, Mike Ramsey, Gordie Roberts*

Forwards: *Bob Brooke, Aaron Broten, Neal Broten, Bob Carpenter, Dave Christian, Bryan Erickson, David A. Jensen, Mark Johnson, Brian Lawton, Brian Mullen, Joe Mullen, Ed Olczyk, Bryan Trottier*

The 1984 Canada Cup was played in the first three weeks of September in five different cities: Halifax, Nova Scotia; Montreal, Quebec; Buffalo, New York; Calgary, Alberta; and Edmonton, Alberta. The final medal round games were scheduled at Calgary and Edmonton. Six teams participated in the tournament: Canada, Czechoslovakia, Russia, Sweden, United States, and West Germany.

The Team USA administrative group consisted of International Chairman Walter L. Bush Jr.; Honorary General Manager Thomas Ivan; General Manager Lou Nanne; Assistant General Manager Craig Patrick; Head Coach Bob Johnson;

Assistant Coaches Lou Vairo and Ted Sator; and Team Trainers Skip Thayer and Larry Ness. I served as team physician.

Unlike the Winter Olympics or other officially sanctioned IIHF championships, the 1984 Canada Cup was an invitational tournament, played under NHL rules. Both amateurs and professionals were allowed and expected to compete, regardless of amateur status. Consequently, our roster was almost entirely different from the team that had competed in the Winter Olympics just seven months earlier. Older, more experienced NHL players such as Rod Langway, Bryan Trottier, Glenn "Chico" Resch, Phil Housley, and Joe Mullen made up the core of the team. Younger, rising NHL stars like goalie John Vanbiesbrouck and forward Aaron Broten, as well 1980 gold-medal team members Mike Ramsey, Neal Broten, Dave Christian, and Mark Johnson, rounded things out. Only six players returned from the 1984 Olympic team: Bob Brooke, Chris Chelios, Mark Fusco, Tom Hirsh, David H. Jensen, and Ed Olczyk.

Team USA assembled in Colorado Springs on Sunday, August 5, with physical examinations the next day. We practiced there for five consecutive days before returning to Minneapolis on Sunday, August 12. After two days of practice there, we flew to Edmonton, Alberta, on Tuesday, August 14, for the first of four exhibition games. The next night, we played Team Canada. It was a tough, tightly contested game, but we won 5–4.

On the morning of Thursday, August 16, we returned to Minneapolis for a rematch against Team

Canada that night at Met Center. It didn't go very well for us, and we lost 9–3.

We practiced in Minneapolis for the next two days and then traveled to Montreal, where we played our third consecutive game against Team Canada on Monday evening. We lost 4–1.

Our fourth exhibition game was also against Team Canada, played in Halifax, Nova Scotia, on Thursday, August 23. This time we managed to play them to a 2–2 tie. We returned to Minneapolis for two days of rest.

Our last exhibition game was against Team Sweden in Minneapolis on Monday, August 27. It was a good, fast-skating, high-scoring game that we won 9–7. We started tournament play two days later.

In the early afternoon of Thursday, August 30, we flew to Halifax. We checked into our hotel, and I went to get my medical bag. By then, all of our equipment had been unloaded and piled in a small storage room. The floor was covered with hockey sticks. My medical bag was in back. As I stepped over the loose hockey sticks, my foot slipped and I twisted my back. Our trainers, Skip and Larry, had to help me get my bag. I was quite stiff for several days.

We played Sweden on Saturday, September 1, in our first game in the tournament. Tom Barrasso, who'd just won the Vezina Trophy in his rookie NHL season, played great in goal, and six different players scored to give us a 7–1 win. Everybody was thrilled with our start to the tournament.

On Sunday morning we flew to Montreal for a Monday-night game against Team Canada. It was

In Buffalo (L-R): Myself, Glenn Resch, Bob Carpenter, Bob Brooke, and Neal Broten.

a tough, physical game that ended in a 4–4 tie. We were trailing 4–2 going into the third period, but Joe Mullen scored to close the gap and Dave Christian tied it up with less than five minutes left, so we felt good about the comeback. After just two games, we'd earned three out of four possible points.

On Tuesday, September 4, we traveled to Buffalo for two days of practice before playing Team Czechoslovakia on Thursday. It was possibly our best game of the Cup. Everyone gave a good effort. The Broten brothers started things off when Neil scored on a pass from Aaron just over five minutes into the game, Brian Lawton kept it going, scoring twice in the second, and Barrasso was stellar once again in the net. We won 3–2.

The next morning we flew to Edmonton, Alberta, to play against the USSR on Saturday, September 8. After Sergei Makarov scored just twenty-two seconds into the game, it looked like the Soviets might blow us out, but the first period ended with the Soviets up just 1–0 and we matched them the rest of the way. Both teams traded goals in the second, no one scored in the third, and we lost 2–1.

On Sunday, after breakfast, we took a bus to Calgary. On Monday night we played the West Germans in our last game in the preliminary round. Mark Johnson and Neil Broten each scored twice, Dave Christian and Brian Lawton added a goal apiece, and we finished the preliminary round with a 6–4 victory.

That evening we were all in a celebratory mood. With a record of 3–1–1 in the preliminary round,

we'd earned seven points and stood in second place. Meanwhile, the Soviets topped the standings with ten points, having gone undefeated at 5–0–0. Team Sweden had earned six points, with a record of 3–2–0, putting them in third place. Canada, the host country, finished in fourth place with five points, at 2–2–1. Czechoslovakia and West Germany, with only one point each, were eliminated.

The semifinals pitted the top-seeded Soviet Union against the fourth-place Canadians, while second-place Team USA took on the third-place Swedes. The two winners would then play a best-of-three championship series for the gold medal.

We played Sweden on Wednesday, September 12, in Edmonton. The game started terribly when Tom Barrasso, who'd played a string of brilliant games in the preliminary round, gave up four first-period goals and was pulled in favor of backup Chico Resch just under twelve minutes into the game. The second and third periods were barely better as Team Sweden scored five more times, while we netted only two. Incredibly, we'd been knocked out of the tournament by a 9–2 loss to the very team that we'd thumped 7–1 in the opening game.

The following night, Thursday, September 13, Team Canada topped the Soviets 3–2 in Calgary, setting up the gold medal series between Canada and Sweden. On Sunday, September 16, Canada won the first game 5–2. The second game, in Edmonton, Canada, they won 6–5, sweeping the series two games to none.

In the final standings, points carried over from

the preliminary round. Canada won it all with eleven points and a record of 5–2–1. The Soviets, despite failing to advance to the gold medal series, placed second with ten points at 5–1–0. The Swedes hung onto third place with eight points and a record of 4–4–0. Team USA finished fourth with seven points and a record of 3–2–1. Winless Czechoslovakia and West Germany placed fifth and sixth, respectively.

The 1984 Canada Cup was a strenuous event, with six games played in five cities over a span of just eleven days. We'd played very well in the preliminary round, but obviously failed to build on that success in our semifinal game. Nonetheless, it gave the boys some great international tournament experience, especially the younger players.

1985 United States National Junior Hockey Team. Row 1 (L-R): Alan Perry, David Espe, Scott Young, Assistant Coach Dave Peterson, Head Coach Doug Woog, Captain Brian Johnson, General Manager Keith Blasé, Assistant Coach Ben Smith, Bill Kopecky, Steve Leach, Mike Richter.
Row 2: Equipment Manager Gene Barcikoski, Craig Janney, Doug Wieck, Eric Weinrich, Chris Biotti, Scott Schneider, Jeff Rohlicek, Brian Leetch, myself, Trainer Dennis Kovach.
Row 3: Greg Dornbach, Clark Donatelli, Allen Bourbeau, Jay Octeau, Brian Hannon, Perry Florio.

18

IJHF World Junior Championships

Finland, 1985

Team Roster

In Goal: *Mike Richter, Alan Perry*

Defense: *Chris Biotti, David Espe, Brian Johnson, Brian Leetch, Jay Octeau, Eric Weinrich*

Forwards: *Allen Bourbeau, Clark Donatelli, Greg Dornbach, Perry Florio, Brian Hannon, Craig Janney, Bill Kopecky, Steve Leach, Jeff Rohlicek, Scott Schneider, Doug Wieck, Scott Young*

The 1985 IIHF World Junior Championships were held in Finland from December 23, 1984 through January 1, 1985. Eight teams participated: Canada, Czechoslovakia, Finland, Poland, Russia, Sweden, the United States, and West Germany.

Keith Blase served as general manager of the US National Junior Team, with Doug Woog as head coach and Dave Peterson and Ben Smith as assistant coaches. Dennis Kovach was trainer, Gene Barcikoski was equipment manager, and I was team physician.

The team assembled in New York City on Sunday, December 16, and flew to Helsinki, Finland, that evening. We landed on Monday, December 17, and took a bus to Vierumäki for a five-day training camp. As we practiced and got acclimated, everybody enjoyed the setting and facilities very much. Unfortunately, the boys didn't care for the unusual food, which was mainly seafood with very little meat. After a few days they were getting hungry for an American home-cooked meal. Assistant Coach Ben Smith suggested driving to Tampere for McDonald's. Everyone expressed enthusiasm for this great idea.

Thus, on our last day in Vierumäki, Saturday, December 22, we took a bus straight to McDonald's, where everyone enjoyed hamburgers with fries and milk or Coke. On the way back we stopped at a glass factory, where we watched a glass-blowing demonstration and some players bought souvenirs.

The next morning we left for Turku, where we played Czechoslovakia in our first game of the tournament. They were very good and easily beat us 9–1.

The next day was Christmas Eve. After practice, we went downtown for Christmas shopping, followed by a nice dinner at our hotel.

On Christmas Day we played the host team, Finland. The large, supportive home crowd helped the Finns win 7–4. Without a day of rest, we faced the Soviets the next night. The spectators rooted for us, but the smooth-playing Soviets gave us a lot of trouble and we lost 4–2.

Thursday, December 27, was a much-needed day of rest and relaxation. We'd played two hard-skating games back-to-back and needed a break.

We played Canada on Friday, December 28, our last day in Turku. We played well and scored five goals, but we lost 7–5.

The next morning we traveled to Helsinki for two games there. First, on Saturday, December 29, we played the West Germans. Everyone was on edge because we'd lost our first four games and desperately needed a win to avoid getting relegated to the B pool. Our nervousness increased when we fell behind 1–0 in the first period, but we scored two unanswered goals and came away with a 2–1 victory. When the final buzzer sounded, we breathed deep sighs of relief.

On Sunday, December 30, we rested and prepared for our game against Poland, our last game in Helsinki, to be played on New Year's Eve.

The Polish team was considered to be the weakest team in the tournament, but we didn't start the game strong. In fact, Poland scored first and maintained the lead throughout first period. Once again, we were fighting to avoid the B pool. Fortunately, we played much better in the second and third periods and went on to win by a score of 6–2. Now we could relax. By beating West Germany and Poland, we assured our place in the A pool. Also, our victory over Poland gave us a reason for a New Year's celebration. Everyone was happy, and we had a very good time.

On New Year's Day, 1985, we traveled to Vantaa for a game against Sweden, our last of the tournament. The boys were relaxed, which worked in our favor. In the last period, however, we were leading comfortably when a big brawl broke out. Luckily, there were no injuries and we won 7–3.

We finished the 1985 IIHF World Junior Championships in sixth place and returned to the United States the following morning. Overall, it was an interesting experience. We knew that many younger players from this team, such as Mike Richter, Alan Perry, Brian Leetch, Scott Young, Craig Janney, Eric Weinrich, Steve Leach, and Greg Dornbach, would be back for the World Junior Championships in Canada the next year.

US National Hockey Team at 1985 World Championship Games in Prague, Czechoslovakia.
Front row (L-R): John Vanbiesbrouch, Mark Johnson, myself, Assistant Coach Jeff Sauer,
General Manager Art Berglund, Head Coach Dave Peterson, Administrative Assistant Dave McNab,
Moe Mantha, Chris Terreri. Middle row: Trainer Tom Woodcock, Tom Fergus, Bob Brooke, Joel Otto,
Bob Miller, Neil Sheehy, Kelly Miller, Jim Johnson, Paul Fenton, Gary Suter, Dan Dorion,
Equipment Manager Skip Cunningham. Top row: Corey Millen, Tim Thomas, Mark Fusco, Clark Donatelli,
Tony Granato, Aaron Broten, Mike O'Connell. Not pictured: Gary Haight.

19

Meeting US Ambassador Shirley Temple

IIHF World Championships, Prague, Czechoslovakia, 1985

Team Roster

In Goal: *John Vanbiesbrouck, Chris Terreri*

Defense: *Mark Fusco, Jim Johnson, Moe Mantha, Mike O'Connell, Neil Sheehy, Gary Suter, Tim Thomas*

Forwards: *Rob Brooke, Aaron Broten, Clark Donatelli, Dan Dorion, Paul Fenton, Tom Fergus, Tony Granato, Mark Johnson, Corey Millen, Bob Miller, Kelly Miller, Joel Otto*

The 1985 IIHF World Championships were held in Prague, Czechoslovakia, from April 17 to May 3. Eight teams participated: Canada, Czechoslovakia, East Germany, Finland, Russia, Sweden, United States, and West Germany.

USA Hockey assigned Art Berglund as general manager, Dave Peterson as head coach, Jeff Sauer as assistant coach, Dave McNab as administrative assistant, Tom Woodcock as trainer, Skip Cunningham as equipment manager, and myself as team physician.

*At the Moser Club, spinning of the cognac snifter
(L-R): Mr. Emil Slama, Jeff Sauer, Dave McNab,
George Gund, Dave Peterson, and Jiri Trnka.*

On Monday, April 8, the team assembled in New York City and flew to Helsinki, Finland. We landed the next morning, changed planes, and flew to Frankfurt, West Germany, where we then boarded a bus and drove to Augsburg, in the German state of Bavaria. By the time we got to our final destination, everyone was tired from traveling, so we ate dinner and went straight to bed. We practiced and relaxed for the next two days, preparing for our game on Friday, April 12, against a local club team. We lost that game 7–6. The next day we traveled by bus to Kaufbeuren, about thirty miles south of Augsburg, where we beat the local team 8–3. We returned to Augsburg after dinner.

On Sunday we practiced and rested before our long bus ride to Prague the following morning. We arrived in Prague in the late afternoon of Monday, April 15. I was very glad to see our perennial guide and translator, Jiri Trnka, once again. The next day, Jiri helped us get our credentials before a light practice in the afternoon. He and I also talked about the Moser Shop, and Jiri said he would make arrangements with Mr. Slama to have our new coaches and administrators inducted into the illustrious club.

We played the mighty Soviets on Wednesday, April 17, the first day of the 1985 IIHF World Championships, and lost 11–1. We played much better the next day and rebounded with a 4–2 win over Sweden.

Friday, April 19, was a day of rest. My good friend Harry Martinek came to our practice, and I introduced him to our trainer, Tommy Woodcock, and our equipment manager, Skip Cunningham. I told them all about Harry's experience as trainer for the Czech National Team and his skills as a masseuse. Everybody agreed he would be a great addition to our staff. Tommy got permission from Coach Dave Peterson and General Manager Art Berglund to add Harry as a volunteer member of our staff, and Harry happily accepted. Skip even found an extra USA Hockey jacket for Harry so he looked like the rest of us. From that moment on, Tom, Skip, and Harry were together all the time. Many of the players enjoyed Harry's massages, and he was happy in his new role.

On Saturday, April 20, we played Canada. It was another tough game, but we won 4–3. It was a great win for us, but we held off celebrating and rested for our game against Czechoslovakia the next day.

Sunday, April 21, was our big game against the home team. Team spirit was high. Everybody felt good and relaxed. We played very well and beat them 3–1.

The next morning, after practice, everyone went crystal shopping downtown.

On Tuesday, April 23, we played West Germany. We won 4–3, giving us a total of eight points. We were quite confident that we would advance to the medal round.

On Wednesday, we didn't skate hard enough against the East Germans, and the game ended in a 5–5 tie.

Thursday, April 25, was a day of rest. After lunch, most of the boys went shopping downtown. Meanwhile, I bought the customary bottle of French cognac in preparation for our trip to the Moser Shop. Soon after, Jiri and I took Art Berglund, Dave Peterson, Jeff Sauer, Dave McNab, and George Gund (one of the owners of the Minnesota North Stars and a member of the USA Hockey International Council), who had just arrived in Prague, to meet Mr. Slama and be inducted into the Moser Club. Mr. Slama greeted us all and gave us the tour. Then the now-familiar initiation ritual began.

Things proceeded as always until, while pouring cognac into the swirling glass, one of our staff members touched the rim of his glass with the cognac bottle. Suddenly, the big, crystal cognac snifter broke in several pieces. The room fell silent. Everyone held his breath. Mr. Slama started laughing and said,

By the Astronomical Clock in the Old Town Square (L-R): Tom Woodcock, Skip Cunningham, and Harry Martinek.

"Don't worry, sir! This is not the first time, nor will it be the last. I'll get you a new glass, but you must try not to touch the rim." All of us breathed easy again, and everything went smoothly thereafter. After passing the initiation and signing the guestbook, many of us bought crystal glasses or porcelain figurines.

On Friday, April 26, we played Finland in our last game of the preliminary round. Since we already

With the US Ambassador, Mrs. Shirley Temple-Black, and Mark Fusco (right).

had nine points and a guaranteed place in the medal round, the outcome was unimportant. Our goal was simply to avoid injuries and stay healthy, so we didn't play very intensely and Finland won 8–3. Still, everybody was happy with our results thus far.

At the end of the preliminary round, the Soviets had won all seven games, earning fourteen points and finishing in first place. The United States, Canada, and Czechoslovakia had earned nine points each to join the Soviets in the medal round. Unlike in most international tournaments, there were no carryover points. Only points earned in the final round-robin games would

count toward the final standings. Everybody started with zero points. It was like a whole new tournament.

Saturday, April 27, was a free day. After practice, we visited the United States Embassy in Prague, on a hill overlooking the Vltava River. As we entered the building, Mark Fusco and I admired the beautiful decor of the reception room. The American ambassador, a very good-looking lady, approached. We complimented her on the elegant setting, and I said, "Madame Ambassador, we are so thankful to you for allowing us the opportunity to visit our embassy in Prague."

Madame Ambassador said, "Thank you very

much. We are happy to have you here. By the way, my name is Shirley Black, but I'm better known as Shirley Temple."

Oh, my God! It was the famous child movie star! What a wonderful surprise! Mark and I gasped for air and told her how honored we were to meet her. I had seen several of her movies and mentioned this to her. Then, we had the honor of having our pictures taken with her—still one of my favorites to this day. In fact, for me, meeting Shirley Temple in person and having a nice conversation with her was the highlight of that trip to Prague.

On Monday, April 29, we played Canada in our first game of the medal round. It was another close one and a very tough game, which Canada won 3–2. After a day of rest, we played the Czechoslovakian team on Wednesday, May 1. They played very well, and we lost badly, 11–2.

On Friday, May 3, we faced the Soviets in a game that turned out to be for the bronze medal, since the Soviets, like us, were winless in the medal round. It was a very difficult game. The Soviets were angry about not winning and played unusually rough. At the very end of the game, Soviet defenseman Viacheslav "Slava" Fetisov crosschecked Jimmy Johnson in the face, opening a cut above Jimmy's upper lip and drawing blood from his nose. Several fights broke out, which triggered a bench-clearing brawl that lasted for many, many minutes. In the end, we lost 10–3. Ironically, after the game, Jimmy was selected to be tested by doping control.

We sat in the doping control room for quite some time, but Jimmy was so dehydrated that he couldn't produce any urine. The problem was, the rest of our team had to wait for the two of us before they could return to the hotel to change, pack, and leave for Frankfurt that evening. After a while, when Jimmy still couldn't produce any urine, I explained our situation to the doping control officials, and they finally let us go.

After some fast packing and a quick little meal, we boarded the bus for Frankfurt. Luckily, the border guards were in a good mood because Czechoslovakia had won the World Championship, so the border procedure was brief. We arrived in Frankfurt after midnight and checked into our hotel near the airport. The next morning we flew to Helsinki, changed planes, and continued on to New York. We stayed overnight at the Marriott Inn LaGuardia and returned to Minneapolis on Sunday, May 5.

We'd finished in fourth place. Czechoslovakia won the gold medal, Canada took the silver, and the Soviets won the bronze. Everyone was quite pleased with our team's performance in Prague. Therefore, management rewarded the players with a golfing vacation in St. Thomas, US Virgin Islands, from May 12 to 18, spouses included. Those who couldn't make it received a $2,000 bonus to cover the cost of a different vacation of their choice.

Down in St. Thomas, almost everyone played golf. I'm a lousy golfer, but enjoyed the free time, which I spent with my wife. We sat on the sunny beach, and I told her all about my interesting adventures in Prague. It was a very pleasant finale of the 1985 IIHF World Championship tournament.

1986 United States National Junior Hockey Team:
World Junior Championships in Hamilton, Ontario. Bronze medalists.
Row 1, L-R: Mike Richter, Greg Dornbach, myself, Assistant Coach Ben Smith, General Manager Art Berglund,
Head Coach Dave Peterson, Assistant Coach Terry Christensen, Captain Steve Leach, Alan Perry.
Row 2: Trainer Denny Kovach, Mike Kelfer, Tom Chorske, Mike Wolak, David Quinn, Lane MacDonald,
Paul Ranheim, Scott Paluch, Dan Shea, Equipment Manager Gene Barcikoski.
Row 3: Public Relations Representative Mike Schroeder, Chris Biotti, Greg Brown, Scott Young, Jim Carson,
Brian Leetch, Craig Janney, Eric Weinrich, Max Middendo

20

A Bronze Medal for the Juniors

Ontario, Canada, 1986

Team Roster

In Goal: *Mike Richter, Alan Perry*

Defense: *Chris Biotti, Greg Brown, Brian Leetch, Scott Paluch,*
David Quinn, Eric Weinrich

Forwards: *Jim Carson, Tom Chorske, Greg Dornbach, Craig Janney,*
Mike Kelfer, Steve Leach, Lane MacDonald, Max Middendorf,
Paul Ranheim, Dan Shea, Mike Wolak, Scott Young

The 1986 IIHF World Junior Championships were played in four different cities in Ontario, Canada—London, Oshawa, Niagara Falls, and Hamilton—between December 26, 1985 and January 4, 1986. Eight teams participated: Canada, Czechoslovakia, Finland, the Soviet Union, Sweden, Switzerland, the United States, and West Germany. The management group of the United States Junior National Team consisted of Art Berglund, general manager; Dave Peterson, head coach; Ben Smith and Terry Christiansen, assistant coaches; Mike Schroeder, public relations; Denny Kovach, trainer; Gene Barcikoski, equipment manager; and myself as team physician.

Special awards to (L-R): Steve Leach, Greg Dornbach, and Paul Ranheim.

On Saturday, December 21, the team assembled in Detroit, where we practiced for three days. We had a nice Christmas Eve dinner and traveled to London, Ontario, on Christmas Day. We played the Soviets in our first game of the tournament on Thursday, December 26. We lost 7–2.

The next morning we traveled by bus to Hamilton, where we played the Czechoslovakian team that evening. It was a much better game for us, and we won 6–2.

Saturday, December 28, was a day off. After a late-morning practice we spent the day resting and relaxing. The next day we faced Canada. It was another tough game for us, and it ended 5–2 in favor of the Canadians.

On Monday, December 30, we took a bus to Oshawa to play Finland. It was a bad day for us. We not only lost a close game 7–5, but our goalie, Mike Richter, had a hard time playing because of a sore foot. After the game, I checked it out and noticed inflammation and a cut on the fifth toe of his right foot. He also had some tenderness and swelling in the lymph nodes of his right groin. It was bad news for our team. Mike could be out for the rest of the tournament. To make things even worse, he had a history of allergy to penicillin and intolerance to other antibiotics.

After the game, we returned to Hamilton and Mike stayed in bed with his right foot elevated. Our Denny Kovach kept the wound clean and frequently applied Betadine solution.

Tuesday, December 31, was a day of rest. It was New Year's Eve, and a nice dinner was arranged for the boys that evening. Later that night the management group had a glass of champagne and toasted to good health and good luck in the next three games.

On New Year's Day we played West Germany. Alan Perry replaced Mike Richter in the goal and played very well. Our defensemen, especially Brian Leetch and Eric Weinrich, did an excellent job protecting Alan and our net. We won the game 4–1. Afterward, I checked on Mike's foot. The wound looked better, and there was less swelling and tenderness in his lymph nodes.

The next morning we traveled by bus to Niagara Falls to play Switzerland. Luckily, the two games in which Mike couldn't play were also our easiest. In fact, since we didn't expect a tough game against the Swiss, we left Denny home to take care of Mike.

Our whole team played very well, and we won easily, 11–3. Everyone was happy about starting the New Year with two good wins. On the bus ride back to Hamilton, the boys were in excellent spirits.

Friday, January 3, was a free day. After practice, I checked on Mike again. There was a good improvement. The wound had started healing nicely, and there was no further swelling or tenderness in his lymph nodes. Mike was permitted to get up and move around a little bit more.

On Saturday, January 4, we played Sweden in our last game of the tournament. It was an important game for us. If we won by four or more goals, we would win the bronze medal. By then, Mike's foot had improved significantly and he begged me to let him play. Alan Perry had played very well in the last two games, but I knew that our team spirit would be even higher if Mike was back in goal. After consulting with the coaching staff, we decided to let him play. That gave a big boost to our team, and we played very well. Mike was excellent in goal, and late in the last period

we were winning 5–0. But then, in the last minutes of the game, Sweden scored a goal. Everybody held their breath, crossed their fingers, and hoped for no more Swedish goals. Finally the buzzer sounded. The score was 5–1 in favor of the American boys! We'd won the game by four goals and earned the bronze medal! That last game was definitely our best. Every player skated with great enthusiasm and determination.

The Soviets won the gold medal, the Canadians won the silver, and we took home the bronze. It was an emotional moment to see those bronze medals put around the necks of our players. Special awards were also presented to our team captain, Steve Leach, and assistant captains Greg Dornbach and Paul Ranheim.

On the morning of Sunday, January 5, we boarded a plane for home. It was a happy flight. Everybody told interesting, humorous stories, and laughter filled the plane. Those boys had good reason to be happy because they had written a special page in the history of USA Hockey—the first United States Junior Hockey team to bring home a medal from an IIHF World Championship.

The coaching staff did an excellent job, but a lot of credit also goes to Steve Leach, Greg Dornbach, and Paul Ranheim for keeping a positive attitude and high spirits throughout the games. Congratulations to all of you boys! You were great!

1986 United States National Hockey Team: World Championships, Moscow, USSR.
Row 1 (L-R): Mike Richter, Bryan Erickson, General Manager Art Berglund, Captain Mark Johnson,
Head Coach Dave Peterson, Aaron Broten, Chris Terreri. Row 2: Myself, Administrative Assistant Dave McNab,
Peter McNab, Ed Olczyk, Randy Wood, Doug Brown, David H. Jensen, Jim Johnson, Scott Sandelin,
Phil Housley, Assistant Coach Jeff Sauer, Team Physician Dr. Harvey O'Phelan. Row 3: Trainer Chris Ipson,
Jim Sprenger, Brian Williams, Alfie Turcotte, John Carter, Guy Gosselin, Clark Donatelli, Tony Granato,
Brett Hull, Richie Dunn, Equipment Manager Bob Webster. Not pictured: Tom Barrasso. Photo by James Lipa.

21

Chernobyl Explodes

IIHF World Championships, Moscow, USSR, 1986

Team Roster

In goal: *Tom Barrasso, Mike Richter, Chris Terreri*

Defense: *Richie Dunn, Guy Gosselin, Phil Housley, Jim Johnson, Scott Sandelin, Jim Sprenger*

Forwards: *Aaron Broten, Doug Brown, John Carter, Clark Donatelli, Bryan Erickson, Tony Granato, Brett Hull, Brian Johnson, Mark Johnson, Peter McNab, Ed Olczyk, Alfie Turcotte, Brian Williams, Randy Wood*

The 1986 IIHF World Championships were played in Moscow, USSR, from April 12 to 28. Eight teams participated: Canada, Czechoslovakia, Finland, Poland, Sweden, the Soviet Union, the United States, and West Germany.

Art Berglund returned as general manager of the US team, with Dave Peterson as head coach, Jeff Sauer as assistant coach, and Dave McNab as administrative assistant. Chris Ipson served as trainer, Bob Webster as equipment manager, Dr. Harvey O'Phelan as orthopedic consultant, and myself as the team physician.

At the Bolshoi Opera House in Moscow with Dr. O'Phelan (right).

On Sunday, April 6, the team assembled in New York at the LaGuardia Marriott Inn Hotel. The next day, we took a bus to JFK Airport and boarded a Finnair flight to Helsinki, Finland. We arrived in Helsinki on Tuesday morning, April 8, and made arrangements for getting our Soviet visas with the help of our Finnish friends.

Then, because of a strike at Helsinki Airport, we took a bus to Turku and flew to Moscow from there. We arrived in the early afternoon of Thursday, April 10, and checked into the Hotel Intourist.

Friday, after practice, we got our identification cards and spent the afternoon sightseeing. Our Dr. O'Phelan had never been to Moscow before. I knew Harvey very well. He came frequently to the University of Minnesota Student Health Service to

Butsy Erickson (left) and Clark Donatelli with Soviet schoolchildren.

check on injured hockey players and other student athletes. I learned a lot from him over the years, and we became close friends. Since our hotel was only one block from Red Square, we decided to go there. I had been to Moscow twice before and knew my way around to a certain extent. When we arrived at Red Square, Harvey was impressed with the Kremlin Wall and Saint Basil's Cathedral. After a brisk walk in the

cool spring air, we were ready for bed.

On Saturday, April 12, the World Championships started. We played our first game against Finland. It was a good game, but we lost 5–4.

Sunday, at breakfast, I told Harvey about my good friend Dr. Oleg Belakovski, chief medical officer for the Soviet Red Army Sports Club Medical Center in Moscow. We planned to call him later and make an appointment to visit him at his office.

Later, after a light morning skate, we had some free time. It was a nice, sunny day, so we decided to walk to the Bolshoi Theatre. That big, beautiful opera house was closed, but on the door was a schedule listing the performances for the following week. We noticed that Verdi's opera *La traviata* was to be performed on Saturday, April 19, at 7:00 p.m. Since there wasn't a game scheduled that day, we were quite interested in seeing that beautiful opera.

In the afternoon we played Poland in our second game of the tournament. It was an easier game for us, and we won 7–2.

Monday, April 14, was a day of rest. Early that morning I called Dr. Belakovski and told him we had a free day. Harvey and I would like to visit with him, I explained, at his medical center that afternoon, a proposition he gladly accepted. Soon after lunch, Harvey and I were in a taxi on our way to the medical center.

Dr. Belakovski was very happy to see us and gave us a tour of the medical facilities. The x-ray equipment was not exactly the most modern, but apparently they were satisfied with it. After the tour, we enjoyed tea and cookies in Dr. Belkovski's office. As is the Russian custom, first we lifted a glass of vodka and toasted to a long-lasting, wonderful friendship. After a lengthy discussion about the latest trends in treating hockey injuries and a few more glasses of vodka, a service car and driver took us back to our hotel. It was an interesting experience to see how the Soviets took care of their athletes.

On Tuesday, April 15, we played West Germany and won 9–2.

The next day, our opponent was Sweden. The very fast-skating Swedes won the game 5–2.

Thursday, April 17, was a day off. My good friend Robert Ridder had arrived in Moscow. Mr. Ridder had been the general manager of the United States Olympic Team that won the silver medal in 1952 and 1956 and still served as a consultant to USA Hockey. I introduced Harvey to Robert, and the three of us spent the day strolling around Moscow and reminiscing about the days when Robert and I were in Moscow with Herb Brooks and the rest of the United States National Team in 1979. Later that evening, all three of us enjoyed a nice dinner at our hotel.

On April 18 we played Czechoslovakia. We played well, but lost 5–2.

After our afternoon practice on Saturday, April 19, my old friend—and KGB agent—Valery from Leningrad showed up. He needed some tape for his wife. She was a ballet dancer and had problems with her ankles. He knew that we would have good athletic tape, so he asked for a few rolls. I gave him two rolls and said, "Valery, you can get all the tape you want after our games are finished if you can help my friend Harvey get a nice fur hat."

Valery said, "No problem! I know very well where to get a nice fur hat for your friend." We arranged to meet again on Tuesday, and Valery left. Then Harvey and I got ready for our trip to the opera that evening. The Bolshoi Theatre was large and beautifully decorated inside. We had great seats and enjoyed the

With Dr. O'Phelan (right) at Dr. Belakovski's office in Moscow.

performance very much. It was a special evening.

The next morning, Sunday, April 20, I got a telegram from my cousins in Riga, Latvia, that said they were coming to visit me in Moscow on Monday. That afternoon we played Canada. It was a good, hard game that ended 4–2 in their favor.

Monday, April 21, was a day of rest. Practice was held late that morning. Just afterward, my cousins Gunars and Ilmars showed up. Both of them were a few years younger than I. Gunars was an electrical engineer and Ilmars was a veterinary doctor. I invited them for lunch at our hotel, and we discussed the idea of shopping at the dollar shop. In those years, in the larger cities of the Soviet Union, there were shops where you could buy things only with US dollars. Those shops had better-quality merchandise than you could find in the usual stores. We spent the whole afternoon at the Hotel Russia dollar shop, just south of Red Square. We finished just in time for my cousins to catch the train back home.

After a light morning practice on Tuesday, April 22, Valery came back, and the three of us took a taxi to find a nice mink hat for Harvey at a shop Valery knew. We thanked Valery for his help, and I told him to come to our locker room right after the game on Sunday, April 27. Then I would give him all the tape we had left. The day had been very successful, and everybody was pleased.

At six o'clock that evening we played the Soviets. It was a very tough game for us, and we lost 5–1. It was also our last game of the preliminary round. With only two wins and four points, we were relegated to the consolation round with Czechoslovakia, West Germany, and Poland.

On Wednesday, April 23, we played West Germany in our first game of the final round. We won 5–0. Just before I left the arena, my old friend Erik Konecki arrived with a group of friends from Dortmund, Germany. He told me that they were staying at the Hotel Cosmos and invited me to lunch there the next day. He said that I should speak German as I approached the hotel so as not to draw attention to myself. I said, no problem, my German language is very good.

The next morning, after practice, Harvey and I went to meet Erik at the Hotel Cosmos. Harvey didn't speak German very well, so when we got out of the taxi, I told him just to say, "*Wunderschön, wunderschön,*" which means "very nice, very nice," in German. That maneuver worked very well, and we had no trouble.

Erik took us to his room, where we had a glass of good German wine before lunch. The dining room was much nicer than the one at the Intourist Hotel, and we enjoyed our lunch very much. Afterwards we walked down to a little amusement park nearby and talked about the tournament games. Soon it came the time for us to return to our hotel. We had difficulties getting a taxi. Nobody wanted to drive to our hotel. Finally, the one driver who was willing to take us there drove so terribly fast that we thought he was going to kill us. I told him in Russian to slow down, which helped a little. When we got to our hotel, I didn't give him a tip for such a crazy ride.

On Friday, April 25, we played Poland. We had

beaten them 7–2 in the preliminary round and were expecting an easy game. However, Poland was playing to avoid relegation to the B pool. It was a close, hard-fought game, but we won 7–5.

Saturday, April 26, was our last free day in Moscow. Everyone was in a good mood because of our victories against West Germany and Poland.

On Sunday, April 27, we played Czechoslovakia in our last game of the tournament. By then the result was no longer important. Even if we lost, we couldn't finish lower than sixth place. If we won, we still wouldn't get a medal. All that we wanted was to avoid injuries. It was a very friendly game, but we lost 10–2.

After the game, I looked for Valery to give him the tape, but I didn't see him anywhere. Finally, after we came back from doping control, he was waiting for me with his big sunglasses on. He hugged me and said, "George, sorry I am late. I had a terrible night, but we will always be friends, we will always be friends." He was unusually emotional and kept repeating the words *We will always be friends.*

I told him to calm down and said, "Sure, sure, Valery. We will always be friends. Being a little late is no big deal." Then, I gave him a box full of athletic tape. He was very happy but kept repeating that we would always be friends. I couldn't understand what was going on with him.

After everything was packed, we took a bus to Moscow Airport to board a plane to Turku, Finland. It was a good flight, and we arrived in the late afternoon. At the Turku Airport, people said, "Are you glowing? Are you glowing?" At first we didn't understand what they were talking about. Then one woman said, "Well, didn't you hear? The Chernobyl Nuclear Power Plant exploded last night!" No, no. Nobody in Moscow had told us anything like that. Now I understood why Valery was so upset and kept repeating *We will always be friends.*

The Chernobyl power plant was near the city of Pripyat in Ukraine, about one hundred miles northwest of the capital city, Kiev. Turku—and Finland in general—was not in danger of falling nuclear debris, but Poland and even the southern part of Sweden had already reported traces of nuclear contamination.

We stayed in Turku overnight and flew back to New York the following morning. Oh, boy, were we happy when we could board the plane, return home, and not worry about the problems of Chernobyl. The flight was nice and smooth. We arrived late in the afternoon and stayed overnight at the LaGuardia Marriott Inn. The next morning, Tuesday, April 29, the newspapers provided more information about Chernobyl, and we felt very relieved as we boarded our plane home to Minneapolis.

1987 United States National Junior Hockey Team: World Championships, Czechoslovakia.
Row 1 (L-R): Robb Stauber, Lee Davidson, Greg Brown, Brian Leetch, Captain Scott Young, Mike Kelfer,
Mike Wolak, Tom Fitzgerald, Ed Krayer, Pat Jablonski. Row 2: Equipment Manager Gene Barcikoski,
Assistant Coach Terry Christensen, Todd Copeland, Chris Biotti, Adam Burt, Marty Nanne, Bob Corkum,
General Manager Art Berglund, Head Coach Dave Peterson, Assistant Coach Ben Smith, Dave Capuano,
Darren Turcotte, Mike Posma, Mike Hartman, Bobby Reynolds, Trainer Denny Kovach, myself.

22

Blizzard on the Way Home

IIHF World Junior Championships, Czechoslavakia, 1987

Team Roster

In Goal: *Robb Stauber, Pat Jablonski*

Defense: *Chris Biotti, Greg Brown, Adam Burt, Todd Copeland, Brian Leetch, Mike Posma*

Forwards: *Dave Capuano, Bob Corkum, Lee Davidson, Tom Fitzgerald, Mike Hartman, Mark Kiefer, Ed Krayer, Marty Nanne, Bobby Reynolds, Darren Turcotte, Mike Wolak, Scott Young*

The IIHF 1987 Junior World Championships were scheduled from December 26, 1986, to January 4, 1987, in Czechoslovakia. The games were played in four different cities: Piešťany, Nitra, Trenčín, and Topoľčany. The eight teams competing were Canada, Czechoslovakia, Finland, Poland, the Soviet Union, Sweden, Switzerland, and the United States. The US National Junior Team management staff was the same as the staff of the previous year's junior championships in Canada: General Manager Art Berglund, Head Coach Dave Peterson, Assistant Coaches Ben Smith and Terry Christiansen, Trainer Denny Kovach, Equipment

Manager Gene Barcikoski, and myself as team physician.

On Friday, December 19, the team assembled at JFK Airport in New York City. USA Hockey had arranged a sponsorship agreement with Finnair to transport our team and equipment. Accordingly, we flew via Finnair from New York to Helsinki, changed planes, and continued on to Vienna, Austria. We landed in Vienna in the early afternoon of Saturday, December 20 and checked into the Hotel de France, our home for the next five days as we got acclimated, practiced, and played one exhibition game.

After morning practice and lunch on Sunday, December 21, we went for a walk to the Christmas market across the street from City Hall. There we met our Finnish friends Pentti Katainen, general manager of the Finnish National Junior Team, and Dr. Juhani Ikonen, the Finnish team physician.

A wonderful friendship had developed between us since the 1985 World Junior Championships in Finland. In fact, I still exchange cards with Dr. Ikonen every year. Our trainer, Denny Kovach, also had become great friends with Pentti Katainen. All of us were happy together, walking around that lovely Christmas market, kidding each other about our teams and joking around. We also ran into Glen Sonmor, longtime hockey coach at the University of Minnesota. He was also happy to join our group, and we all had a nice, relaxing first day in Vienna.

On Monday, December 22, we played an exhibition game against the Austrian National U22 team. It was an easy game, and we won 7–1.

The next morning we had a productive two-hour practice. After lunch, everybody went Christmas shopping downtown. There were so many beautiful things to buy that Denny came back to our hotel with a large bag over his shoulder.

Wednesday, December 24, we practiced after breakfast. Since it was Christmas Eve day, everyone went last-minute Christmas shopping in the afternoon. That evening we had a delicious Christmas Eve dinner and a very nice party at our hotel. It was our last day in Vienna, and everyone enjoyed it very much.

The next morning, Christmas Day, we took a two-hour bus trip to Piešt'any and checked into the Balnea Grand Hotel. It was a nice, large hotel. The teams from Finland, Switzerland, and Russia were also there. We got our credentials, completed our registration, and spent the rest of the day relaxing.

On Friday, December 26, the 1986 IIHF World Junior Championships began. Our first game was against Finland. We played well, but the Finns had a very good team and they won 4–1.

Saturday morning, right after breakfast, we took a bus to Nitra to play the host country, Czechoslovakia. Our team played very well and won 8–2. After the game we returned to our hotel and ate dinner. Everyone was happy about the win.

Sunday, December 28, was a day off. After the morning practice, most everyone went sightseeing downtown. Denny, Geno, and I went window shopping and found some shops with beautiful crystal vases. We didn't buy anything, but we planned to return on our last free day.

At the Christmas Market in front of the City Hall (L-R): Gene Barcikoski, Denny Kovach, Lou Barcikoski, Glen Sonmor.

Christmas shopping with our Finnish friends (L-R): Glen Sonmor, myself, Pentti Katainen, Denny Kovach, Lou Barcikoski, Finnish Team Trainer, Dr. Juhani Ikonen.

On Monday, December 29, we had a short practice after breakfast and then took a bus to Trenčín, where we played Poland. We beat them easily, 15–2. We ate dinner after the game and returned very happy.

The next morning we congratulated our Finnish friends on beating the Soviets 5–4 the night before. They were very happy and said that they were keeping their fingers crossed for us as well. That morning's practice lasted only forty-five minutes. After lunch we took a bus to Topoľčany for our game against Switzerland. It was another easy game for us, ending 12–6 in our favor. We stayed for dinner and then returned by bus to our hotel in Piešťany.

There were no games on Wednesday, December 31. After a short morning skate we were free the rest of the day. Hotel management held a nice New Year's Eve dinner for our team that Denny and I almost missed because we got stuck in the elevator for about ten minutes. After dinner, we celebrated with our Finnish friends and had a very enjoyable New Year's Eve.

On New Year's Day, 1987, we ate a late breakfast and had a light skate before lunch. We played Canada at 7:00 p.m. It appeared that our boys were a little more tired from their New Year's Eve celebration than the Canadians were, and we lost 6–2.

After a light practice on Friday, January 2, we traveled to Topoľčany for our game against the Soviets. Our team played very well, and we beat them 4–2. Needless to say, it was a big mood lifter for the boys.

Saturday, January 3, was our last day of rest before playing our final game and heading home. At breakfast, Art Berglund told us that there was a problem with our travel arrangements: Finnair didn't have a flight on Monday morning from Vienna to Helsinki. Consequently, the only way to catch our transatlantic flight home from Helsinki was to fly from Vienna to Frankfurt, Germany—via Austrian Airlines—at 7:00 a.m. Monday morning and then take a Finnair flight from Frankfurt to Helsinki at 9:40 a.m. to reconnect with our original flight back to JFK. However, since we didn't have a deal with Austrian Airlines like we did with our sponsor, we were going to be charged prohibitively for our equipment. To stay within our budget, Ben Smith, Denny Kovach, Gene Barcikoski, associate coach for Boston College Steve Cedorchuk who happened to be traveling with us at the time, and I would leave immediately after the game on Sunday evening and take the equipment by bus. Then we'd all meet at the Frankfurt Airport and continue together from there.

Meanwhile, it was also our last day for shopping, so Denny, Geno, and I went downtown to buy the vases we'd seen.

Sunday morning, soon after breakfast, everyone started packing the bus for the trip to Trenčín for our game against Sweden at 4:00 p.m. Perhaps due to all the confusion and sudden, last-minute changes, we didn't play very well and lost 8–0. Immediately after the game we loaded all the equipment onto the bus and left for Frankfurt. Since we needed to arrive at the airport at least one hour before our flight to Helsinki the following morning, we'd hired two drivers to alternate straight through the night.

We reached the Czechoslovakian–Austrian

border near Bratislava at about 10:00 p.m. As usual, it took almost an hour to cross. It was nearly midnight when we arrived in Vienna. From there, we planned to continue on to Salzburg, where we would cross the Austrian–German border and continue on through Munich, Augsburg, Ulm, Stuttgart, and Darmstadt and then to the Frankfurt Airport.

Soon after we left Vienna, light snow started falling. Then, as we got closer to Salzburg, it got heavier and heavier. We listened to the road report, which didn't sound very good.

We arrived at the Austrian–German border near Salzburg at about 2:00 a.m. Our drivers took a break and had a cup of coffee. Meanwhile, I talked to the German border guards and asked to get a road report for the drive to Frankfurt via Munich, Ulm, Stuttgart, and Darmstadt. They were very helpful and told me that it was snowing quite heavily near Ulm and driving would be very slow.

As we crossed into Germany at about 2:30 a.m., it started snowing harder and harder. Heavy snow had accumulated on the road, and driving got much slower. Then we heard an announcement that the road between Augsburg and Ulm was closed. I suggested that we take the road to Nuremberg before we got to Munich, but our drivers said that they didn't know the way. I reassured them that I had traveled that road many times during my years in medical school and knew it very well. They asked me to sit next to them and tell them where to go. From that moment on, I was the navigator.

Shortly before we got to Munich, blizzard conditions developed and the road signs were hard to see. Luckily, I recognized the sign to Nuremberg, and we turned. After about ten or fifteen miles, however, the snow became very wet, covering the road with heavy slush. Traffic was heavy, and driving was very slow. It was almost 7:00 a.m. when we got to Nuremberg, and we still had to take the road from Heilbronn to Darmstadt and then on to the Frankfurt Airport. Thankfully, after Nuremberg, the snowing stopped and the roads were clean, but traffic was extremely heavy. It was going to be impossible to get to the airport by 8:30 a.m. Art had given me the telephone number for the Finnair counter at the airport and told me to call them if we had any problems.

At about nine o'clock, we stopped at a gas station near Heilbronn and I called Finnair. They put Art on the phone, and told him about our troubles, explaining that we wouldn't make it until at least 10:30. He told me to take the next possible flight to Helsinki. They would wait for us there.

After Heilbronn, the traffic got thinner and we finally arrived at the airport shortly before 11:00 a.m. I went directly to the Finnair counter and was greeted by a very nice German girl. I told her that we needed to catch the next flight to Helsinki, but she said, "I'm sorry, there are no more flights to Helsinki today. You'll have to wait until tomorrow morning." But when she saw how tired and unhappy we were, she said, "Just a minute, I have an idea. I have a very good friend who works at the Lufthansa counter. Let's go talk to her. She may be able to help you."

So, we went to the Lufthansa counter and met

Marty Nanne with Denny Kovach.

another very friendly German girl. At this point, my German language skills and being a doctor who'd graduated from a German medical school helped a lot. I explained my situation, and soon we all started laughing and joking about the terrible bus ride from Trenčín. The Lufthansa girl said she would be glad to help and asked, "How many are you?" I told her that

we were five, but we had a lot of hockey equipment. The Finnair girl interjected and told me not to worry, she would take care of that. The only question was whether there were five empty seats. For a moment, the Lufthansa girl looked concerned, but then she started laughing again. She said, "I really don't have space for five of you in coach, I'll have to put you in first class." So, it was settled. I asked the Finnair girl to call Helsinki to let Art know that we'd be on the Lufthansa flight and to wait for them at JFK.

Meanwhile, Denny and Geno ran to our bus and started loading the equipment onto the Lufthansa counter. The Czechoslovakian drivers also helped, and I gave them a good tip.

When the equipment was finally loaded onto the plane and we had our boarding passes, I breathed a wonderful sigh of relief. I hadn't slept the night before, since I'd had to watch the road. That comfortable first-class seat was exactly what I needed for taking a good, long nap. Needless to say, all of us greatly enjoyed the flight back to New York.

At JFK, Geno sprang into action. He found several airport workers and showed them how to arrange the hockey bags in alphabetical order. When the boys arrived, everything was in perfect shape. Art and Dave shook their heads and asked how we'd done all of this. Geno said, "No sweat, you only have to know how to deal with people."

Unfortunately, that Monday afternoon not everyone could get a connecting flight home from JFK. Most of us took the bus to the LaGuardia Marriott Inn to wait until the following day. On the way, Art and Dave told us about the terrible last game in Piešt'any between Canada and Russia. In the third period, with the Canadians leading 4–2, a brawl had broken out. Both benches emptied, and the referees lost control. Everyone was fighting. They even turned the lights off in the arena, but nothing helped. The game was never finished.

Later, we got news that both teams were disqualified. The final standings were Finland in first place, Czechoslovakia in second, Sweden in third, the United States in fourth, Switzerland in fifth, and Poland in sixth. It was too bad for Canada, because they definitely would have won the tournament.

It was another memorable trip with the US National Junior Team. More than anything else, that all-night bus ride to Frankfurt will be remembered by the five of us for a long, long time and already has brought laughter to many of our friends. Ben, Denny, Geno, Steve, and I talk and laugh about it all the time.

1987 United States National Hockey Team: World Championships, Vienna, Austria.
Row 1 (L-R): Equipment Manager Bob Webster, Ed Olczyk, myself, Assistant Coach Ben Smith, Head Coach
Dave Peterson, General Manager Art Berglund, Assistant Coach Jeff Sauer, Captain Mark Johnson, Trainer
Denny Kovach. Row 2: Craig Wolanin, Tom Kurvers, Ron Wilson, Brian Lawton, Jim Johnson, Bryan Erickson,
Chris Terreri, Team Physician Dr. Harvey O'Phelan. Row 3: Bob Carpenter, Scott Young, Clark Donatelli, Aaron
Broten, Craig Janney. Row 4: Administrative Assistant Dave McNab, Kevin Stevens, Brian Leetch, Tony Granato,
Bob Brooke, Jim Carson, Gordie Roberts, John Vanbiesbrouck, Mike Richter.
Not pictured: Lane MacDonald.

23

The Pravda Cup, Leningrad, USSR, 1987 and IIHF World Championships, Vienna, Austria, 1987

Team Roster

In Goal: *Mike Richter, Gary Kruzich*

Defense: *Greg Brown, Ian Kidd, Don McSween, Jeff Norton, Tim Thomas, Eric Weinrich*

Forwards: *Wally Chapman, Clark Donatelli, Scott Fusco, Tony Granato, Jim Johannson, Brad Jones, Bob Kudelski, Kevin Miller, Paul Ranheim, Kevin Stevens, Marty Wiitala, Brian Williams, Scott Young*

The 1987 IIHF World Championships in Vienna, Austria, were set for April 17 through May 2. However, USA Hockey had also accepted an invitation to play in the Pravda Cup in Leningrad, USSR, from March 31 to April 6. The Pravda Cup was the national B team tournament, so USA Hockey sent a select group of talented younger players to get some international experience.

The management group was General Manager Art Berglund, Head Coach Dave Peterson, Assistant Coaches Ben Smith and Doug Palazzari, Trainer Denny Kovach, Equipment Manager Bob Webster, Orthopedic Consultant Dr. Harvey O'Phelan, and myself as team physician.

When I learned that we were going to spend seven days in Leningrad prior to the World Championships, I was very concerned. I remembered, of course, what had happened to the US National Junior Team in 1974. Since then, the water in Leningrad had not improved. The threat of bad diarrhea from the water-borne parasite *Giardia lamblia* still existed. I called Centers for Disease Control in Atlanta for advice. They told me that giardiasis could be prevented if, on top of the usual safety measures, every member of our team took a 250 mg capsule of tetracycline every morning. This preventive treatment was to begin two days before arrival in Leningrad and continue every day while there.

I told Dr. O'Phelan what had happened to our team in 1974 and relayed the advice from the CDC. We informed Art Berglund about this potential hazard and got permission to buy the necessary medications: 300 tetracycline capsules of 250 mg each to cover the team and staff for nine days.

On Saturday, March 28, the Pravda Cup team assembled at the Finnair terminal of New York's JFK Airport. We arrived in Helsinki the next day and took a bus to the Klaus Kurki Hotel. At lunch, I explained the water problems in Leningrad and detailed the safety precautions to prevent severe diarrhea. To ensure that each team member got his daily tetracycline capsule, we decided to give them out at breakfast. A sign describing necessary precautions was also posted in the bathroom of each hotel room. It all worked very well, and we went the entire trip without a single case. That afternoon we practiced from 4:30 until 6:00 p.m. Afterwards, everyone was ready for dinner and a good night's rest.

On Monday morning, March 30, we practiced from 9:00 to 10:00 a.m. and then flew to Leningrad after lunch. In Leningrad, we checked into our hotel and completed registration for the Pravda Cup.

On Tuesday, March 31, we played Sweden in our first game of the tournament. We won 9–2.

Wednesday, April 1, was our day off. Harvey went to visit an American friend who worked at the diplomatic service in Leningrad, while Denny Kovach and I joined a group of players who took a bus to visit the Catherine Palace, former summer residence of Russian tsars, redesigned by the famous baroque architect Francesco Bartolomeo Rastrelli in 1751.

As soon as we entered the Catherine Palace, everyone was given a pair of fleece overshoes to wear throughout the tour. The most impressive room was the Great Hall, covered with gilded carvings and sculptural ornamentation, that runs the entire width of the palace. After spending more than an hour admiring the Great Hall and other extremely richly decorated rooms, we didn't have much time to visit the grounds. The early spring weather was not ideal for walking outside, anyway, so we returned to the bus for the trip back to Leningrad. Nonetheless, it was a special experience that we will remember for the rest of our lives.

On Thursday, April 2, we played the Soviets. It was a good, close game, but we lost 4–3.

The next day, we played Czechoslovakia. It was another hard game for us, and we lost 4–2. In the evening, a group of my old high school and hockey friends arrived from Riga, Latvia. I invited them to dinner at our hotel, and we made arrangements to meet again the next morning, after practice.

Saturday, April 4, was a day of rest. After breakfast and a light practice, the team decided to visit the world-famous Hermitage Museum. Harvey joined the team, but I joined my friends from Riga. I was especially happy to see my close friend Dr. Janis Kveps, known as John. He was the team physician for the Riga Dinamo, as well as the Latvian National Team. John had been in Leningrad many times before and was an excellent guide.

First we went to see the famous Smolny Cathedral and Convent, also designed by Rastrelli. Then we walked downtown, stopping on the way to admire Peter Clodt's four sculptures comprising "The Taming of a Horse," one on each corner of the Anichkov Bridge across the Fontanka River. After that we visited Saint Isaac's Cathedral, which took forty years to build under the direction of French architect Auguste de Montferrand.

After such an extensive walk, I invited our group to dinner. John suggested a nice restaurant, where we enjoyed a typical Russian meal of pork roast with red cabbage. I very much enjoyed walking and dining with my old high school friends. Ludvig Skrodelis, for instance, was my best high school buddy, with whom I shared a school bench for our last four years. Dr. Ruta Grapmane was my high school sweetheart. We graduated the same year. I entered the field of medicine and she started in the dental school at the University of Latvia in Riga. I have developed a wonderful friendship with John over the last forty years. He is a very talented man: an excellent physician and a popular singer who speaks several languages. When I visit my hometown of Riga, he is always the first one I always contact. After our lovely dinner, my friends took the train back to Riga and I returned to our hotel.

On Sunday, April 5, we played an early afternoon game against West Germany. It was the same old story, trouble with the West Germans. We played well, but we couldn't seem to score and lost the game 5–4.

Monday, April 6, was our last game of the Pravda Cup. We played Finland and managed to end the tournament with a 6–6 tie. Immediately after the game we took a bus to the Leningrad airport and flew to Helsinki. After a short flight of less than an hour, we checked back into the Klaus Kurki Hotel.

On Tuesday morning, April 7, we ate a late breakfast before most of the players from the United States Select Team and Assistant Coach Doug Palazzari flew home. The rest of us flew to Zürich at 5:55 p.m. The World Championships were set to begin in Vienna in ten days, but first we would play a three-game exhibition schedule in the Swiss towns of Davos, Biel, and Lugano.

At the Smolni Cathedral and Monastery with my Latvian friends from Riga, Latvia (L-R): Mrs. Skrodelis, myself, Dr. Ruta Grapmane, Dr. John Kveps, Ludvig Skrodelis.

We landed in Zürich at 8:50 p.m. and took a bus to Davos. It was late when we finally arrived, and the winding mountain roads had caused a few jitters, so everybody was ready for bed immediately after dinner.

On Wednesday, April 8, a new group of team members arrived from the United States, along with Assistant Coach Jeff Sauer and Administrative Assistant Dave McNab. We spent the day on a light practice and relaxation.

Team Roster

In Goal: *John Vanbiesbrouck, Mike Richter, Chris Terreri*

Defense: *Bob Brooke, Jim Johnson, Tom Kurvers, Brian Leetch, Gordie Roberts, Ron Wilson*

Forwards: *Aaron Broten, Bob Carpenter, Jim Carson, Clark Donatelli, Bryan Erickson, Tony Granato, Craig Janney, Mark Johnson, Brian Lawton, Lane MacDonald, Ed Olczyk, Kevin Stevens, Craig Wolanin, Scott Young*

On Thursday, April 9, we practiced after breakfast and got ready for the first game with our newly assembled team. We played Switzerland that evening and lost 5–4. Our play wasn't very good.

The next day, we practiced again and rested. The players who'd just arrived needed more time for acclimatization.

On Saturday, April 11, we had a light practice after breakfast, ate lunch, and took a bus to Biel for a rematch against Switzerland at eight o'clock that night. This time we played a bit better, but we still lost 4–3.

On Sunday morning we took a bus to Lugano. It was a long but very scenic ride across the whole of Switzerland, from the northern border with France to the south where it borders Italy. On the way we stopped for lunch in Interlaken, a beautiful resort town with a magnificent view of the Jungfrau peak. After lunch we traveled through the Andermatt region, known as the crossroads of Switzerland, and passed through the St. Gotthard Tunnel to Bellinzona, arriving in Lugano in the afternoon. Lugano is a beautiful city on the shores of a lake by the same name. The people there speak Italian.

After we checked into the Hotel Cadro Panoramica, the boys needed a little rest to get ready for yet another game against Switzerland that evening. We'd played them twice in the last three days and had started to adapt to their style. Our own game was also improving, and we won that night, 7–5. Unfortunately, Scott Fusco injured his knee and had to be sent home.

After our last exhibition game we had two days off in Lugano for rest and relaxation. On Monday, April 13, we practiced after breakfast and spent the afternoon sightseeing.

Denny, Harvey, and I went for a walk with a group of players along the southern shore of Lake Lugano. When we arrived at the border with Italy, there were signs for both countries. In fact, you could stand with one foot in Switzerland and the other in Italy. That, of course, was a great place for taking all kinds of funny photos.

We returned to our hotel for a five o'clock reception hosted by the Swiss Ice Hockey Federation. It was a great event that everyone very much enjoyed.

Tuesday, April 14, was our last day in Lugano. We slept in and had a late breakfast. After practice, Harvey, Coach Sauer, and I went for a short walk in the park, where the tulips and narcissus were showing their beautiful spring colors. Later, we ate dinner at a mountainside restaurant with a panoramic view of Lake Lugano. Everyone enjoyed the dinner, but we had to get to bed early before a very long bus ride to Vienna the following day.

On the morning of Wednesday, April 15, we boarded the bus to Vienna. The winding mountain roads were very picturesque, especially in the San Bernardino Pass, one of the highest roads in all Europe. At lunchtime we arrived in Vaduz, Liechtenstein. Soon after that, we entered Austria near Feldkirchen and continued over the Tyrolean Alps to Innsbruck, Salzburg, Linz, and on to Vienna. It was late in the evening when we finally checked into the Vienna

Marriott Hotel.

On Thursday, April 16, we stayed at the rink after our morning practice to get our credentials. At lunch I talked to the team about doping control and reemphasized that they were not to take any medications, supplements, or vitamins before checking with me.

That afternoon, Harvey and I went for a walk in City Park, famous for its gilded bronze monument to Johann Strauss Jr., right across the street from our hotel. It was a nice, sunny spring afternoon with forsythia bushes in full blossom and large flowerbeds covered with red and yellow tulips. It was a nice way to relax before the World Championships started.

Friday, April 17, was the start of the tournament. Eight teams participated: Canada, Czechoslovakia, Finland, Sweden, Switzerland, the United States, the Soviet Union, and West Germany.

After a light morning practice, Harvey and I went sightseeing in downtown Vienna. For Harvey, it was a nice welcome back. He had spent some time at the University of Vienna and had even married a girl whose parents came from Austria. However, that was many, many years ago, and Vienna looked a little different to him now. I had been to Vienna several times recently and knew my way around very well. We very much enjoyed walking around that beautiful city.

In the evening, we played Canada in our first game of the tournament. It was a hard-skating game that ended 3–1 in favor of the Canadians.

Saturday morning, after practice, Lane MacDonald complained of dizziness and severe fatigue that he'd been experiencing for the past two or three days. I advised him to rest for the afternoon and not dress for the four o'clock game against Sweden.

The boys had played a tough game against Canada the day before and couldn't keep up with the fast-skating Swedish team that evening. We lost 6–2.

Easter Sunday, April 19, was a day off for everybody. Early in the morning, I checked on Lane MacDonald. He still wasn't feeling well, but he wasn't feverish, so I ordered him to rest until I checked on him again the next morning.

After breakfast I met Dr. Gabor Czaszar, from Budapest, and we went across the street for walk in the City Park with Harvey. It was a nice Easter Sunday. We all sat down on a bench, and Dr. Czaszar told us all about a hockey doctors' conference in Budapest to be held in June of the following year, organized by the IIHF.

We decided to go to lunch at the cozy Rathskeller, next to the opera house. While we were eating, Dr. Czaszar told us more about Budapest and invited us to visit. We thanked him for the invitation, but explained that even on days of rest, one of us always stayed with the team. Only I would be able to go. So, we made plans for me to go to Budapest on Friday morning, April 24, and return to Vienna the next day. Over the next two days I gathered information about train times to Budapest and made plans with Dr. Czaszar.

Dr. Czaszar returned to Budapest that afternoon, but Harvey and I found a little Viennese café with nice piano music. We enjoyed it very much while having a cup of coffee and apple strudel, a typical Viennese pastry.

On the border point at Lake Lugano. Aaron Broten (left) in Switzerland and Denny Kovach in Italy.

On Monday, April 20, Lane still didn't feel well. In fact, he had a fever and a sore throat. So, I examined his throat and the lymph nodes on his neck. The para-cervical lymph glands, on the side of the neck, were markedly swollen, often a sign of infectious mononucleosis. I contacted a local laboratory and scheduled an appointment. Early the next morning, Lane's test results showed that his complete blood count was consistent with mononucleosis, and we sent him home.

In the early afternoon game, the West Germans defeated Finland. We played the Soviets that evening. It was a very hard game for us, and we lost 11–2.

On Tuesday, April 21, West Germany pulled off a major upset, beating Canada 5–3. Suddenly there was talk about West Germany advancing to the medal, with Canada relegated to the consolation round.

Our game against Finland was later that afternoon. We hoped for our first tournament win, but it didn't happen. Finland's goalie played very well, and we lost 5–2.

Wednesday, April 22, was a day of rest. After breakfast, Harvey and I went to a travel agency, where I got my tickets to Budapest. When we returned to our hotel, everybody was talking about a scandal involving the West German team. Finland had filed a protest regarding the eligibility of West German player Miroslav Sikora. If tournament officials determined at the next directorate meeting that the West German team had acted illegally, they would be penalized and lose all of their points from the previous games. Still, I was a little skeptical about the value of the Finnish protest. The president of the IIHF was a West German,

Dr. Günther Sabetzki, from Düsseldorf. I found it hard to believe that he would let a player compete without the proper credentials. In any case, the IIHF Annual Congress was scheduled for June 1987. Very likely, a final decision would come at that time.

Meanwhile, Harvey and I decided to have dinner at my favorite Viennese restaurant, the Czardasfürstin. After we entered the restaurant, I noticed that my musician friends, Julius Horwatch and his son, Harry, were still playing with the band there. Harvey liked the restaurant very much, and after a glass of good Kremser Schmidt white wine, we started looking over the menu. Harvey was going to try the roast venison with lingonberries, while I ordered the Gypsy schnitzel, which is like Wiener schnitzel with some mushrooms and a little paprika. After a while, the musicians came out to our table and played some of our favorite tunes. We enjoyed our dinner and the music very much and returned to our hotel in a very relaxed mood.

On Thursday morning, April 23, news circulated about a potential bomb threat in the arena, the Stadthalle. The arena was searched thoroughly, but nothing was found.

On Friday, April 24, I got up early to catch the 7:45 a.m. train to Budapest. When I arrived there at 11:00 a.m., Dr. Czaszar was at the station to welcome me. We drove his car up to Gellért Hill, which offers a wonderful view of the whole city. The Danube River flows in from the northwest, continues through the middle of the city, and flows down to the southwest. On the right bank of the Danube is the old, hilly part

The Parliament building in Vienna.

In Budapest, by Mathias Church with Dr. Gabor Czaszar.

of the city called Buda. Historic Buda Castle, beautiful Matthias Church, and Fisherman's Bastion are on that side. Across the river is Pest, with the majestic parliament building and elegant shopping district around Váci Street.

After taking in the panoramic view, we walked down to the old castle and stopped at a small restaurant near Matthias Church. There we sat in a little courtyard in front of the restaurant and enjoyed a delicious Hungarian salami sandwich with a glass of wine. Gabor told me all about the upcoming hockey doctors' conference, scheduled for June 1988, in Budapest, and then we returned to his car.

We drove over the Elisabeth Bridge to the Pest shopping area and went to Vörösmarty, a well-known pastry shop, beautifully decorated with crystal chandeliers and elegant marble countertops, to pick up a cake to take home with us. After visiting with the owners, we drove to Gabor's apartment in a residential district south of the city center. Gabor's wife, Klari, had prepared an excellent fish soup for lunch, and we discussed our plans for the afternoon and evening. They suggested that we first return to the elegant shopping area at Vaci Street in Pest and then go to dinner at an old Hungarian restaurant with traditional music in the Castle District of Buda.

Our plans worked very well, but when we went to dinner, Gabor had to park his car in a special parking lot. The old Hungarian restaurant was on a very narrow, steep street, and parking the car there would be impossible. The building itself was built partially into the hillside, and the interior was very cozy. I ordered the paprika chicken, and all of us enjoyed a glass of very popular Szürkebarát white wine from the Badacsony region. Soon Gabor, Klari, and some other guests started singing along with the band as they played popular Hungarian melodies. We had a wonderful evening and were still humming those fantastic tunes on our way home.

On Saturday morning, after an early breakfast, I thanked Gabor and Klari for their hospitality, and he took me to the railway station, where the train to Vienna was scheduled to depart at 9:00 a.m. I arrived back in Vienna at 12:15 p.m. and went to our hotel to check with Harvey about the condition of the team. Everything was fine, and we started preparing for our game against Switzerland at 4:00 p.m.

Meanwhile Harvey told me that he had noticed an advertisement for the Johan Strauss Jr. operetta *The Gypsy Baron* at the Volkstheater on Wednesday, April 29, and had bought two tickets for the evening performance since we didn't have a game. I was very happy about his decision, and we went to the arena in a very positive mood.

Things got even better when we beat Switzerland 6–3 in an easy game. Everyone's spirits were high because we'd won our last two games, with only one game left in the preliminary round.

Sunday, April 26, was our day off. In the last two games, the boys had played very well and deserved some good relaxation time. So management arranged to take us all out for lunch in the charming suburb of Grinzing. On Sundays, especially, many Viennese take the streetcar there to spend the day relaxing in the many beer and wine cafes of that picturesque old village. We had reservations at one of the larger garden restaurants. As soon as we entered, we were greeted by Schrammel musicians. Everyone relaxed with a glass of beer and enjoyed a good Austrian lunch. After a while, a group of us walked around the village and returned to our hotel in the late afternoon. It was a day well spent relaxing and enjoying the beautiful spring weather.

Monday, April 27, was our last game of the preliminary round. We had a light morning practice before our game against Czechoslovakia at 4:00 p.m. Everyone was relaxed because we were safe from being relegated to the B pool and had no chance to advance to the medal round. The outcome was unimportant. It was a good skating game, but we lost 4–0, joining Finland, West Germany, and Switzerland in the consolation round.

We played Finland first, on Tuesday, April 28. We played well but lost 6–4.

After practice the next day, Harvey and I went downtown because I wanted Harvey to see the most beautiful baroque church in Vienna, the Franciscan Church. After that, we walked past Saint Stephen's Cathedral to the oldest restaurant in Vienna, the Griechenbeisl, which reportedly opened in about 1450. When we got to the ancient, towerlike building, we had to walk through narrow, winding hallways to get to our dining hall. Harvey said, "George, if there's a fire, we'll never get out of here."

I said, "Harvey, in five hundred years they haven't had a fire. Why should it be today?"

We were not very hungry, so I only had a sandwich and a glass of beer. Later that night we went to the operetta, which had many beautiful melodies. We enjoyed the show very much.

On Thursday, April 30, Harvey and I went for our usual walk before lunch. We passed the Vienna Opera House and noticed that Puccini's opera *Madame Butterfly* was scheduled for Friday evening, May 1, our last free day. We agreed it would be a nice way to complete our trip to Vienna. The only tickets left were in the second balcony, but that was fine with us.

That evening, we played West Germany and won 6–3.

On Friday, everybody went shopping after practice. Harvey and I went to our favorite little café, where we listened to nice piano music while enjoying some Viennese pastries and coffee. When we returned to our hotel, we got ready for the opera.

As we entered the charming, white marble front hall of the opera house, I saw that Harvey was quite impressed by the beautiful interior. We climbed up the stairs to the second-floor balcony and found our seats in the front row. We had a great view of the stage. At the intermission, we walked down to the Great Hall and enjoyed a glass of champagne. We liked the show very much and returned to our hotel in a very happy mood.

On Saturday, May 2, we played Switzerland in our last game in the tournament. It was a good game for us, and we won 7–4. With a record of 4–6–0, we knew that we would stay in the A pool, but we didn't know our final placement because the West German case was going to be reassessed at the IIHF Congress in June. After that meeting, the final standings were determined and we were notified that the United States had finished in seventh place.

On Sunday morning, May 3, we flew from Vienna to Frankfurt, Germany. There, we transferred to our Lufthansa flight to New York. Eight hours later, everyone was happy to be back in the US.

The five-week trip was full of some very interesting episodes. Since we spent most of our time in Vienna, my favorite city in the world, and my very close friend Dr. Harvey O'Phelan was able to join us, it will stay in my memory as one of the nicest trips I've ever taken.

US National Hockey Team at Canada Cup Tournament, 1987. Row 1 (L-R): John Vanbiesbrouck, Bobby Carpenter, Joel Otto, Rod Langway, Head Coach Bob Johnson, General Manager Lou Nanne, Assistant General Manager Craig Patrick, Mike Ramsey, Mark Johnson, Bob Mason, Tom Barrasso. Row 2: Gary Suter, Ed Olczyk, Dave Ellett, Kevin Hatcher, myself, Assistant Coach Ted Sator, Business Manager Larry Johnson, Assistant Coach Doug Woog, Bob Brooke, Curt Fraser, Chris Nilan, Chris Chelios. Row 3: Trainer Dave Smith, Corey Millen, Joe Mullen, Kelly Miller, Wayne Presley, Aaron Broten, Pat LaFontaine, Phil Housley, Trainer Skip Thayer, Equipment Manager Joe Murphy.

1987 Canada Cup

Team Roster

In Goal: *Tom Barrasso, John Vanbiesbrouck, Bob Mason*

Defense: *Chris Chelios, Dave Ellett, Kevin Hatcher, Phil Housley, Rod Langway, Mike Ramsey, Gary Suter*

Forwards: *Bob Brooke, Aaron Broten, Bobby Carpenter, Curt Fraser, Mark Johnson, Pat LaFontaine, Corey Millen, Kelly Miller, Joe Mullen, Chris Nilan, Ed Olczyk, Joel Otto, Wayne Presley*

The 1987 Canada Cup tournament was played in six different Canadian cities: Calgary, Alberta; Halifax, Nova Scotia; Hamilton, Ontario; Montreal, Quebec; Ottawa, Ontario; and Sydney, Nova Scotia. Games also took place in Hartford, Connecticut, and Lake Placid, New York, in the United States. Six teams participated: Canada, Czechoslovakia, Finland, Sweden, the United States, and the Soviet Union.

Team USA was administered by General Manager Lou Nanne, Assistant General Manager Craig Patrick, Business Manager Larry Johnson, Head Coach Bob Johnson, Assistant Coaches Ted Sator and Doug Woog, Trainers Skip Thayer and Dave Smith, Equipment Manager Joe Murphy, Orthopedic Surgeon Dr. Pat

Smith, Administrative Assistant Sue Thomas, Public Relations Manager Patty Connelly, and myself as team physician.

On August 3, 1987, the US team assembled in Minneapolis. Players were quartered at the Bloomington Marriott Hotel, and practices were held at the Bloomington Ice Garden.

On Tuesday, August 4, physical examinations began at 9:00 a.m., followed by afternoon practice from 3:00 to 6:00 p.m. After that, training camp continued for the next several days, with two-hour practice sessions held twice daily. On Monday, August 10, the last day of training camp in Minneapolis, we practiced in the morning and went golfing at the Minikahda Club in the afternoon.

On Wednesday, August 12, we embarked on a six-game exhibition schedule: four games against Team Canada and two games against the US Olympic team. Our first destination was Montreal. We flew from Minneapolis to Detroit, changed planes, and continued to Montreal, where we stayed at the Holiday Inn La Seigneurie. After a short rest at the hotel, we practiced at the Montreal Forum, ate dinner, and went to bed.

The next day we had a light morning practice and took a bus to Ottawa for our first exhibition game against Team Canada. It was a good, evenly played game, but we lost 3–2. We took the bus back to Montreal.

On Friday we slept in and had a late breakfast. At 11:00 a.m. we took a bus to Lake Placid for a game against the US Olympic team. Our boys played well,

and we won 3–1. After an enjoyable dinner with the Olympic team players and coaches we returned to Montreal by bus.

There were no games on Saturday or Sunday. We practiced at the Montreal Forum but had the afternoons and evenings off.

On Monday, August 17, we had a light skate after breakfast and a pregame meal at 1:30 p.m. We played Team Canada that night and lost 6–2.

On Wednesday night we played Team Canada again at the Montreal Forum. This time, it was a more evenly played game that ended 7–6 in favor of the Canadians. After dinner, we took a charter flight from Montreal to Halifax. We landed at 1:50 a.m. and took a bus to the Citadel Halifax Hotel, where we checked in at about 8:00 a.m. on Thursday morning. After a short and restless sleep, we played Team Canada for the third time in four days. We were very tired and lost badly, 11–2.

On Friday, August 21, right after breakfast, we took a bus to Halifax Airport, where we boarded a flight to Boston. From the Boston airport we went by bus to Hartford and checked in at the Sheraton Hartford Hotel. Finally, we had the afternoon free for rest and relaxation. On Saturday and Sunday we practiced in the mornings, but had the afternoons and evenings off.

On Monday, August 24, we had a light morning skate followed by a pregame meal in preparation for our final exhibition game. We played well and beat the US Olympic team 5–2, finishing with a record of 2–4–0. We'd beaten Team USA twice, but we dropped all four games to Team Canada. In any case, we now had three days' rest before the 1987 Canada Cup officially began.

After the game we had a nice surprise. Our good friend Mr. Paul Haenni had arrived from Bienne, Switzerland. Mr. Haenni was an executive with a prestigious Swiss watch manufacturer and a longtime friend and supporter of Team USA. He'd come with a special surprise for the members of our administrative group: beautiful women's Gucci watches for each of them. Later, we all enjoyed a nice dinner with Mr. Haenni. It was a very pleasant way to end our exhibition schedule.

For the next three days we stayed in Hartford, practicing two hours per day. On Friday, August 28, the 1987 Canada Cup tournament began. We played Finland in our first game at the Civic Center Coliseum in Hartford. Those three days of practice and rest were clearly good for our team. Our playmaking skills were sharp, and we beat the Finns 4–1 on two goals from Pat LaFontaine and a goal each from Joe Mullen and Wayne Presley.

Immediately after the game, we took a bus to the airport and flew to Hamilton, Ontario. We landed at 12:15 a.m. and checked into the Royal Connaught Hotel. Thankfully, there were no games on Saturday or Sunday, so the boys had a chance to practice some more and rest.

On Monday, August 31, we held a pregame skate at 10:30 a.m. and prepared for our game against Sweden. The boys were sharp once again, and we won

John Vanbiesbrouck leading the team for the last game of the tournament.

5–2 on goals from five different players and a solid performance by John Vanbiesbrouck in goal.

Tuesday was a day off. It also happened to be my wedding anniversary, so I called Velta. It was wonderful to hear my wife's loving voice on the other end of the phone. After a late breakfast, we practiced at 1:00 p.m. and relaxed the rest of the day.

On Wednesday we had a pregame skate at 10:00 a.m. followed by our pregame meal at 1:00. We played Team Canada that night in front of a crowd of seventeen thousand fans. Pat LaFontaine and Corey Millen each scored a goal for us, but Canada's Mario Lemieux scored a hat trick—assisted twice by Wayne Gretzky—and we lost 3–2.

Last game of the tournament versus Czechoslovakia in Sydney.

On Thursday, September 3, we got up early and took a bus to the Toronto airport, where we boarded a prop plane back to Hartford at 8:55 a.m. We landed in Connecticut just an hour and a half later and checked into the Sheraton Hartford Hotel. After a late breakfast, the boys took a short rest. Later, we practiced at the Coliseum and rested again in the afternoon to prepare for the hard day ahead of us.

The next day, Friday, September 4, we had a one-hour pregame skate followed by a pregame meal at 1:00 p.m. We played the Soviets that night. As expected, we had a tough time. The smooth-passing Soviets—led by the legendary KLM Line centered by Igor Larionov with Vladimir Krutov and Sergei Makarov on the wings—were dominant, and we lost 5–1. Afterward, dinner at our hotel wasn't served until 11:30 p.m., so everybody got to bed very late.

On Saturday, September 5, after a short night's rest, we ate a quick breakfast and boarded a bus to the Boston airport. We flew from Boston to Halifax, landing at 3:00 p.m., and changed planes for a one-hour flight to Sydney, Nova Scotia. Once there, we took a bus to Keddy's Motor Inn, where we finally checked in at about 8:30 p.m. after twelve hours of travel. After dinner, everybody was ready for bed.

On Sunday, after a late breakfast, we practiced and prepared for our final game of the tournament, which was against the Czechs at 6:30 p.m. It was a good, close game that ended 3–1 in favor of Czechoslovakia.

On Monday, September 7, we flew from Sydney to Montreal and then on to Minneapolis. Suddenly, the 1987 Canada Cup—with its grueling travel schedule—was over. Team USA, with only four points total on wins against Sweden and Finland, finished in fifth place. We'd had a tremendous defensive showing, allowing a mere fourteen goals in five games, but we'd only managed to score thirteen goals ourselves. We didn't have the offensive firepower to compete with the top teams.

Canada won the cup, two games to one over the Soviets, who placed second. Sweden finished in third place and Czechoslovakia in fourth place. Finland, the only winless team, rounded things out in sixth place.

I was mainly happy that we didn't suffer any serious injuries. Sure, we'd had the usual training camp strains and soreness, followed by some cuts and bruises, but we'd only had two real problems. At practice in Montreal on August 18, a puck had hit Scot Kleinendorst's left foot, hard. X-rays showed an undisplaced fracture of his first metatarsal bone, and a posterior splint cast was applied. Bryan "Butsy" Erickson suffered a groin strain at training camp in Minneapolis that was re-aggravated at practice on August 22 in Hartford. Unfortunately, both players were released for further treatment and ultimately missed the tournament.

After returning home, most of the players enjoyed a week or so off before reporting to their respective NHL teams for preseason training camp. Corey Millen and I, however, joined the US Olympic team a few days later. Both of us looked forward to a new chapter and new challenges.

In Calgary with 1988 US Olympic Hockey Team (L-R): Clark Donatelli, Al Bourbeau, Pete LaViolette, Greg Brown, Kevin Miller, John Blue, Dave Snuggerud, Eric Weinrich, Guy Gosselin, Kevin Stevens, myself, Mike Richter, Tom Chorske, Steve Leach, Corey Millen, and Todd Okerlund.

25

15th Olympic Winter Games

Calgary, Canada, 1988

Team Roster

In Goal: *John Blue, Mike Richter, Chris Terreri*

Defense: *Greg Brown, Guy Gosselin, Peter Laviolette, Brian Leetch, Jeff Norton, Eric Weinrich*

Forwards: *Allen Bourbeau, Clark Donatelli, Scott Fusco, Tony Granato, Craig Janney, Jim Johannson, Steve Leach, Lane MacDonald, Corey Millen, Kevin Miller, Todd Okerlund, Dave Snuggerud, Kevin Stevens, Scott Young*

The 1988 Olympic Winter Games were held in Calgary, Alberta, Canada from February 14 to 28. Twelve teams competed for medals in the hockey tournament, seeded into two divisions. Group A consisted of Sweden, Canada, Finland, Switzerland, France, and Poland. Group B contained the Soviet Union, Czechoslovakia, West Germany, the United States, Austria, and Norway.

The US management group was Art Berglund, general manager; Keith Blase, assistant general manager; Dave Peterson, head coach; Ben Smith and Jack Blatherwick, assistant coaches; Dave Carrier, trainer; Bob Webster, equipment manager; Mike Schroeder, public relations; Dr. Tom Mahoney, orthopedic surgeon; and myself as team physician.

Seventy-nine players were invited to tryout camp in Greensboro, North Carolina, in July 1987. After final cuts, the players and coaches assembled in Lake Placid, New York, in early August. I served as the US team physician at the 1987 Canada Cup tournament from August 3 to September 7 and was therefore unable to be with the US Olympic team during that time. Coincidentally, after the first week of training camp in Lake Placid, the US Olympic team played several exhibition games, including two games against the Canada Cup roster of Team USA, with whom I was traveling. I joined the 1988 US Olympic team in Lake Placid on Tuesday, September 15, 1987, after they'd returned from a ten-day training camp in Finland.

The next day, we played the Springfield Indians, of the American Hockey League, and won easily, 8–2.

On Thursday and Friday we practiced in Lake Placid before embarking on an eight-game road trip against eight different NHL teams. We kicked things off Saturday night in Albany against the New York Rangers. It was a much tougher game, and we lost 6–5. We also lost the next two games—by one goal each—to the Philadelphia Flyers and Buffalo Sabres, with scores of 3–2 and 4–3, respectively.

On Tuesday, September 23, we flew to Washington, D.C., where we practiced that afternoon. The next day, President Ronald Reagan hosted our team at a White House reception in the Rose Garden.

It was a sunny autumn day, and all of us felt very honored. Coach David Peterson presented President Reagan with a US Olympic team jersey, and everybody was in a very festive mood. The next night, we played the Washington Capitals and lost 3–2.

On Saturday, after breakfast, we boarded a plane to Detroit for a game against the Red Wings. The boys played hard, and we finally notched our first victory against an NHL team, winning by a score of 3–1.

On Sunday, September 27, we flew to Minneapolis, where we practiced at the Metropolitan Sports Center for the next two days. On Tuesday evening we played the Minnesota North Stars. That night, the puck didn't bounce right for us and we lost 4–2.

On Thursday, October 1, we traveled to Salt Lake City, where we played the Calgary Flames the next day. It was a very even game, but the Flames won 5–4 in overtime.

On Saturday, after a light skate in the morning, we flew to San Diego, where we spent the next four days. That evening we played the Los Angeles Kings. It was a good, hard game that we lost 6–4.

The next three days we enjoyed some much-needed rest and relaxation. We'd played a whirlwind eight games in eight cities in fifteen days, ending with a record of just 1–7–0. We practiced in the afternoons and enjoyed leisurely trips to the famous San Diego Zoo, as well as the beautiful beaches, in our free time.

On Wednesday, October 7, I returned to Minneapolis to resume my work at the University of Minnesota Student Health Service for the next month. Meanwhile, the team continued on to Lake Placid and

September 24, 1987, at the White House reception (L-R): Kevin Stevens, Guy Gosselin, John Blue, Brian Leetch, Scott Young, myself, Mike Richter, President Ronald Reagan, Tony Granato, Jeff Norton, and Allen Bourbeau.

Chris Terreri in Warroad, MN. January 10, 1988.

stayed on the East Coast until November 10, when they returned to Minneapolis. During that span, Team USA beat the Canadian Olympic team 4–2 and posted impressive victories against the University of Maine, 4–1; Northeastern University, 8–2; Providence College, 10–2; Boston University, 6–3; University of Massachusetts at Lowell, 6–2; University of New Hampshire, 15–4; Boston College, 12–3; University of Vermont, 9–1; and Harvard University, 15–3.

Upon returning to Minneapolis, the boys played the University of Minnesota at our home rink, the Metropolitan Sports Center, and won 5–1. During the next four days in Minneapolis, we practiced in the morning and spent the afternoons resting and relaxing.

We played five games in the next three weeks, compiling a record of 2–2–1 in that span, beating Bowling Green and Michigan State, losing to the Canadians twice, and tying Michigan State 3–3 at a second game in Detroit.

On Wednesday, November 25, we flew to Los Angeles, where we stayed for five days, practicing, resting, and relaxing. It was a nice Thanksgiving break.

We played the Canadian team twice more, on November 28 and 29, tying them the first time 5–5 and beating them the next time 2–1.

On Monday, November 30, we flew to Kalamazoo, Michigan. The next morning we had a light practice, and we played Western Michigan University that evening. The boys were very relaxed, and we easily won 3–2.

On December 2 we traveled to Madison, Wisconsin, where we stayed for the next seven days. On Monday, December 7, we played the University of Wisconsin and won 7–3. The next two days we spent in preparation for an eight-game series against the Soviet Select Team, to be played from December 10 through 22 in eight different US cities.

In the end, we finished with a record of 6–1–1 against the Soviets, including huge wins in Uniondale, New York, by a score of 13–2, and St. Louis, Missouri, by a score of 9–1. We'd won an impressive six games in thirteen days against our rival Soviets, outscoring them 49–22 in the process. After such good work, the boys were given a very well-deserved six-day break for Christmas.

On Monday, December 28, the team reassembled in Minneapolis for three days of practice. On New

Olympic festivities at Lake Louise.

Year's Eve we played the hometown team, University of Minnesota, beating them 10–3 at Mariucci Arena. After that we held three more days of practices before flying to Chicago on Monday, January 4, for a game against the University of Illinois—Chicago Circle. It was an easy game for us, and we won 10–1.

The next morning, we flew to Duluth to play the UMD Bulldogs, whom we beat that evening 9–4. With no immediate games on the schedule, we stayed in Duluth for four days and held practice there.

Right after practice on Saturday, January 9, we traveled by bus to Warroad, Minnesota, for the traditional game against the Warroad Lakers. Oh, my God! It was so terribly *cold* in Warroad. The next morning, in honor of our backup goalie, someone had spelled out, "75 BELOW ZERO IN WARROAD AND CHRIS TERRERI IS STILL ALIVE" on a large outdoor sign. That evening we beat the Lakers 13–3.

The next morning we took a bus to Grand Forks, North Dakota, where we defeated the University of North Dakota 12–2.

On Tuesday, January 12, we took a flight back to Minneapolis, where we practiced for two days. On Thursday we again played the Canadian Olympic team at the MSC in Bloomington. That game was much tougher than any previous match we had in the last two weeks, and we lost 6–4.

The next morning we boarded a plane for Detroit and practiced there in the afternoon. On Saturday, at Joe Louis Arena, we played another game with the Canadian Olympic team, which they won 5–1. On Sunday, January 17, we traveled from Detroit to Toronto, where another game against the Canadian Olympic team was scheduled. That game was closer, but the Canadians won 6–5.

On Tuesday, January 19, we flew to Colorado Springs and played Colorado College. That was an easy game for us, and we won 12–4. The next day, after practice, the boys completed their drug testing at the medical center.

On Thursday, January 21, I received sad and surprising news from USA Hockey when they informed me about a new rule. The US Olympic Committee had determined, apparently, that a team physician couldn't serve more than three terms. Since I'd previously served as team doctor in Grenoble, Sapporo,

Lake Placid, and Sarajevo, I couldn't do so in Calgary. It was a huge disappointment and an unceremonious end to my service to the 1988 US Men's Olympic Hockey Team. USA Hockey offered to cover my round-trip ticket from Minneapolis to Calgary, if I would like to attend the Winter Games as a spectator, but room and board would be at my own expense. I couldn't stay with the team in the Olympic Village, nor would I have passes to the games.

On Friday, January 22, I said a sad good-bye to the boys and the rest of staff and flew back to Minneapolis.

After a few days back in Edina, I ran into my good friends and neighbors Rick and Eddie Feslers. As the three of us were chatting, I told them about my misfortune with the US Olympic team. Rick said, "George, Eddie and I have organized a trip to the Olympic Games. If you'd like to be our main speaker at a few breakfast and dinner meetings, we'd be happy to have you join us. We already have tickets for the US hockey games. Come and stay with us. We'll take care of you. You buy your plane ticket, and we'll take care of the rest." Without hesitation, I accepted their invitation.

The Feslers had frequently organized trips to special events. For the Olympic Games in Calgary, they led a group of about thirty people. On Saturday, February 13, Rick introduced me to the group at breakfast at the Marlborough Hotel in Calgary and I said a few words. Soon after that, we went to the opening ceremonies at McMahon Stadium. For the first time in my life, I was a spectator at the Winter Olympics. Later that evening, as I watched Team USA's game against Austria from the stands, I felt strange and disoriented, sitting in the crowd instead of standing behind the bench. To be honest, I didn't quite know what to do with myself. Luckily, it was a wide-open, high-scoring game, which the United States won 10–6.

Two days later, on Monday, February 15, Team USA played Czechoslovakia. Amazingly, the US opened the game by scoring goals on each of our first three shots, leading 3–0 just six minutes into the game. The Czechoslovakians battled back, however, and pulled away in the third period, winning by a final score of 7–5. After such an incredible start, it was a sudden and shocking loss.

The next day I called Dr. Herbert Goba, my classmate from medical school in Riga, Latvia, who was practicing psychiatry in Calgary. He came to pick me up in his car, and we spent nice afternoon together with his wife, Rhonda, at their home.

On Wednesday, February 17, I rejoined the Feslers and their group. That night we ate an early dinner before Team USA's game against the Soviets. It was a hard game for the boys, which they lost 7–5 on a dominant performance by Soviet defenseman Slava Fetisov, who led his team with two goals and three assists. With a record of 1–2–0 so far, Team USA would have to win

With Rick Fesler in Canmore, Alberta.

its next two games to even have a chance of advancing to the medal round.

Luckily, the game against Norway was much better. The team played very well and established a solid lead from the start on two early goals by Lane MacDonald. Norway tried to battle back, but the third period belonged to Corey Millen, who scored twice for a 6–3 win. It was a very pleasant bus ride back to our hotel as I told stories about that game and compared it to past American victories.

On Saturday, February 20, Dr. Goba took me on a trip to Lake Louise and Banff. It was a nice, sunny day and I took many pictures, especially of the hot-air balloons taking off from and sailing over the frozen lake. Then we enjoyed a wonderful lunch at the elegant Château Lake Louise restaurant. On the way back to Calgary we stopped at the majestic Fairmont Banff Springs Hotel, which the locals justifiably call "Canada's Castle in the Rockies." It is indeed an impressive, château-like building at the foot of a big mountain. We rested in the main lounge for a little while, but then it was time to return to Calgary. It was a wonderful day in the splendor of the Canadian Rockies.

On Sunday, February 21, Team USA played West Germany in a do-or-die game. It was Team USA's last game of the preliminary round. If they didn't win by at least two goals, they wouldn't advance. They played well, but the West German goalie, Karl Friesen, was stellar and they didn't score on him until the third period. The game ended 4–1 in favor of West Germany, and the United States was relegated to the consolation round with Austria and Norway.

The next morning we had a breakfast meeting at the Marlborough Hotel where I spoke to the group. I tried to cheer them up by telling stories about games when our opponents couldn't score, like when we played the Czechoslovakians at the 1972 Olympics in Sapporo, Japan. I also spoke the next night, at the Rimrock Inn in Banff, where I highlighted my experiences at previous Olympic Games. We all had a good laugh and enjoyed our dinner.

The next afternoon, the United States played Switzerland for seventh place. Switzerland scored first, just nineteen seconds into the game, on a long shot by Peter Jaks, but Team USA scored the next five goals and never looked back. In the end, it was an easy game, which the Americans won 8–4, finishing with a tournament record of 3–3–0.

On Saturday, February 27, we had our last breakfast meeting at the Marlborough Hotel, where I gave my farewell talk.

The next morning, right after breakfast, I went to the bobsled track and was lucky to meet Janis "John" Kipurs, from Latvia, who'd won the gold medal with his teammate, Vladimir Kozlov, in the two-man bobsled the day before. At that time, Latvia was occupied by the Soviet Union, so Latvian Olympic athletes were forced to compete for the USSR. In any case, it was nice to meet John and congratulate him on his gold medal.

Meanwhile, Finland had beaten the Soviets 2–1 in the final game of the medal round. Most importantly, the two points from that win gave the Finns a total of seven points for the tournament and the silver medal. Excitedly, I went to congratulate my good friends Dr. Juhani Ikonen, the Finnish team doctor, and Pentti Katainen, their general manager, who were both very much in a celebratory mood. The Soviets still took the gold, with eight points, since they'd only lost one game, and Sweden took the bronze medal, with six points, followed by Canada, West Germany, and Czechoslovakia. Team USA had finished in seventh place, but they could be proud of the fact that Cory Millen—with six goals and five assists—had finished fourth among the top scorers. Only Vladimir Krutov, Igor Larionov, and Slava Fetisov, all from the Soviet Union, had finished with more points than Corey.

After the excitement on the last day, I had dinner with Rick and Eddie. I thanked them for inviting me to join them. They thought my stories about previous Olympic Games at our breakfast and dinner meetings had been very entertaining and informative for the group.

The next morning, as if to underscore the fact that I was no longer traveling with Team USA, I got bad news regarding my return flight to Minneapolis, which had been scheduled to depart on Tuesday, March 1. Because so many Olympic teams and fans were leaving Calgary at the same time, for destinations all over the world, I couldn't get a flight out until Thursday, March 3. Even then, I would have to fly to Chicago first and then back to Minneapolis.

Eventually, I made it home, returning to Minnesota with mixed feelings. The trip had been bittersweet. On one hand, I was grateful for the chance to watch the boys play and see the culmination of those many months of hard work. On the other hand, I was sad not to have been with those boys behind the bench, in the locker room, on the bus rides, and at the hotel. They'd all meant so much to me over the last several months that it was difficult not to be there with them—and *for them*—during the games. In any case, life goes on, and I vowed only to remember the nice things I'd experienced.

1989 United States National Junior Team: World Championships, Anchorage, Alaska.
Row 1 (L-R): Jason Glickman, Mike Lappin, Mike Modano, David Emma, Jeremy Roenick, Captain Adam Burt,
Mark Richards. Row 2: Myself, Assistant Coach Kevin Constantine, Tony Amonte, Rodger Sykes, Tom Pederson,
Assistant Coach Dean Blais, General Manager Art Berglund, Head Coach Steve Cedorchuk, Steve Heinze,
Peter Ciavaglia, Neil Carnes, Public Relations Representative Mike Schroeder, Trainer Britta Nielsen.
Row 3: Ted Crowley, Joe Sacco, John LeClair, Bill Guerin, Tom Dion, Shaun Kane, Barry Richter,
Equipment Manager Gene Barcikoski.

26

It Sure Was Cold

IIHF World Junior Championships, Anchorage, Alaska, 1989

Team Roster

In Goal: *Jason Glickman, Mark Richards*

Defense: *Adam Burt, Ted Crowley, Tom Dion, Shaun Kane, Tom Pederson, Barry Richter, Rodger Sykes*

Forwards: *Tony Amonte, Neil Carnes, Peter Ciavaglia, David Emma, Steve Heinze, Bill Guerin, Mike Lappin, John LeClair, Mike Modano, Jeremy Roenick, Joe Sacco*

The 1989 IIHF World Junior Championships were held in Anchorage, Alaska, from December 26, 1988, through January 4, 1989. Eight teams competed: Canada, Czechoslovakia, Finland, Norway, Sweden, the United States, the Soviet Union, and West Germany.

The administrative group for the United States was General Manager Art Berglund, Head Coach Steve Cedorchuk, Assistant Coaches Dean Blais and Kevin Constantine, Trainer Britta Nielsen, Equipment Manager Gene Barcikoski, Public Relations Manager Mike Schroeder, and myself as team physician.

The team assembled in Colorado Springs on Sunday, December 18, and was quartered at the dormitory of the US Olympic Training Center. After dinner, we took a bus to the Air Force Academy Fieldhouse, where we had a light practice. Over the next two days we practiced twice daily.

On Wednesday, December 21, we had a one-hour morning practice and played the Air Force Academy that night. We won 5–4.

After seeing the team in action, team administrators, coaches, and others agreed that this year's roster was loaded with talent. It was led by experienced veterans who'd played in the World Junior Championships in Moscow one year earlier, including Jeremy Roenick, the team's leading scorer in 1988, Mike Modano, David Emma, John LeClair, Ted Crowley, Jason Glickman, and team captain Adam Burt. The other players, too, were very highly regarded. All we had to do was keep our fingers crossed and hope for a little bit of luck.

After an early breakfast on Thursday, December 22, we took a bus to the Denver Airport and boarded a plane to Anchorage, Alaska. We landed at 3:30 p.m. and checked in at the Sheraton Anchorage Hotel.

The next day, we practiced at Sullivan Arena and played an exhibition game against a Soviet team. We played well, scored first, and led 1–0 after the first period. The Soviets took the lead, but we tied the score 2–2 midway through the third period. With about five minutes to go in the game, however, the Soviets scored again and beat us 3–2. Nonetheless, it was a good game that gave us confidence that we could play with the best teams in the tournament.

We had Saturday morning, December 24, free, and everybody went into town for some last minute Christmas shopping. We practiced from 3:15 to 4:45 p.m., and had a nice Christmas Eve dinner afterward.

On Christmas Day we had a late breakfast and practiced in the early afternoon. During the rest of the day we explored Anchorage and enjoyed its colorful Christmas decorations.

On Monday, December 26, the tournament began. The opening ceremony, with the presentation of each team's flag, preceded our first game at 7:30 p.m. After the procession and customary speeches, we played Finland. We knew that it would be a difficult game because the Finns always play hard, disciplined hockey. They'd also won the bronze medal in the last World Junior Championships.

We started very well and were leading 4–1 after the first period. The second period was scoreless, but in the third period Finland launched an intense attack. In a mere fifteen minutes they scored four straight goals and went ahead 5–4. Then, in the last minute of the game, Jeremy Roenick, who'd already scored two goals, tied the game. We'd salvaged one point with a tie that could be very important in the final standings.

The next day we took on the Soviets. We played with great discipline, and within the first five minutes John LeClair scored on a power play. The Soviets tied it up late in the period, which ended 1–1. At the beginning of the second period we got a high-sticking penalty, and the Soviets scored on the ensuing power play. That slowed us down a bit. The Soviets scored again, and the period ended 3–1. In the last period,

It sure was cold in Anchorage.

the Soviets scored yet again, but with about five minutes to go in the game, John LeClair scored his second power-play goal. The game ended 4–2 in favor of the Soviets.

Wednesday, December 28, was our day off, so we made a trip to see the Portage Glacier. At that time of year, daylight is very short. Therefore, we had to be in place to see the glacier by noon. It was interesting, but the sky was overcast and there was not enough light to take a good picture. I took some photos, but they did not turn out. It was an unusual experience, however, and everyone enjoyed it very much. Late that afternoon, we practiced for an hour and a half. Afterwards, the boys were ready for a good sleep.

The next day we played Canada. It was a very tough game for us. The Canadians played an extremely physical game and beat us 5–1.

On Friday, December 30, we faced Czechoslovakia. We played very well, forechecking the Czechoslovakians in their own zone and disrupting their smooth passing game. The puck bounced right for us, and we beat them 5–1. It was our first big win. Everyone was very happy.

Saturday was New Year's Eve. We didn't have a game, but we got the good news from Davos, Switzerland, that the United States Select Team had won the Spengler Cup by beating Canada 8–1 in the finale.

On New Year's Day we played West Germany in the early afternoon. It was no contest. David Emma scored four goals, Jeremy Roenick added a hat trick and one assist, Mike Modano had five points with two goals and three assists, and John LeClair added two more goals and two assists. Four other players scored a goal each for a final score of 15–3. Everybody was happy to start the year with such an impressive victory.

The next day we played Norway. We started quick and hard, scoring three goals in the first fifteen minutes. In the last five minutes of the first period, however, we suffered some defensive lapses and the Norwegians scored twice to tighten the score. Then, in the second period, Mike Modano scored a hat trick and John LeClair scored two goals. The period ended 8–4 in our favor which broke Norway's resistance, and we easily added four more goals in the final period, winning 12–4.

We played Sweden on Wednesday, January 4, the last day of the tournament. They came into the game with only one loss, to the Soviets, and were in contention for the gold medal. We knew it would be a tough game, and it was. We had great difficulty keeping pace with the very fast-skating Swedes, and they won 3–1.

When we got back to the hotel, we started packing immediately for our flight back home at midnight. The banquet and award presentations were scheduled for the evening. In the last game of the tournament, the Soviets beat Canada to win the gold medal with twelve points and a record of 6–1–0. Sweden took the silver medal, and Czechoslovakia won the bronze. We finished in fifth place and were very content with our performance, especially that of Jeremy Roenick and Mike Modano, who finished first and second in scoring with sixteen points and fifteen points, respectively.

Soon after the awards ceremony, we left for the airport to catch our overnight flight to Seattle. We didn't get much sleep because we landed at 5:00 a.m. and had to change planes to Denver. We finally made it home at about two o'clock in the afternoon. It was nice to be home again, especially when we heard that it had gotten so cold in Anchorage that they'd canceled all outgoing flights the next day. We felt very lucky to have gotten out of Anchorage in time.

I will definitely always remember the World Junior Championships in Anchorage as a very exciting tournament with some great, high-scoring victories and a close loss to the Soviets.

*US National Hockey Team at 1989 World Championship in Stockholm, Sweden. Front row
(L-R): Cleon Daskalakis, Assistant Coach Larry Pleau, Assistant Coach Craig Patrick, Ed Olczyk,
John Vanbiesbrouck, Pat LaFontaine, General Manager Art Berglund, Head Coach Tim Taylor, Robb Strauber.
Middle row: Trainer Tom Woodcock, Trainer Mark Aldrich, Tom Kurvers, Jack O'Callahan, Dave Snuggerud,
Greg Brown, Jeff Norton, Brian Leetch, Scott Young, Phil Housley, Equipment Manager Bob Webster,
Equipment Manager Skip Cunningham. Top row: Corey Millen, Brian Mullen, Dave Christian, Paul Fenton,
Tom Fitzgerald, Doug Brown, Kelly Miller, Tom Chorske, Randy Wood, Tom O'Regan.
Not pictured: Orthopedic Surgeon Dr. Jim Schaffausen and myself.*

27

Problems in Stockholm

IIHF World Championships, Stockholm and Södertälje, Sweden, 1989

Team Roster

In Goal: *John Vanbiesbrouck, Cleon Daskalakis, Robb Stauber*

Defense: *Greg Brown, Phil Housley, Tom Kurvers, Brian Leetch, Jeff Norton, Jack O'Callahan*

Forwards: *Doug Brown, Tom Chorske, Dave Christian, Paul Fenton, Tom Fitzgerald, Pat LaFontaine, Corey Millen, Kelly Miller, Brian Mullen, Tom O'Regan, Ed Olczyk, Dave Snuggerud, Randy Woods, Scott Young*

The 1989 IIHF World Championships were played in Stockholm and Södertälje, Sweden, from April 15 through May 1. Management for Team USA was Art Berglund as general manager, Tim Taylor as head coach, Larry Pleau and Craig Patrick as assistant coaches, Tom Woodcock and Mark Aldrich as trainers, Skip Cunningham and Bob Webster as equipment managers, Dr. Jim Schaffhausen as orthopedic surgeon, and myself as team physician.

On Sunday, April 9, we departed for Helsinki, Finland. We landed around noon on Monday, April 10, and took a bus to Turku, where we checked into the Seurahuone Hotel. We practiced at 4:00 p.m., ate dinner afterward, and went to bed.

The next morning, we slept in and ate a late breakfast. We practiced that afternoon and again later that evening.

April 28, 1989, in Stockholm, Sweden. The US Hockey team is boarding the Gustafsberg *for a boat ride in the Archipelago of Stockholm.*

On Wednesday, April 12, we practiced for an hour in the morning and prepared for an exhibition game against Finland. We were not yet acclimated and lost 9–3.

The next morning, we took a bus to the airport and flew to Stockholm. The uneventful flight was less than an hour in length, and we checked into the Park Hotel and rested for the afternoon and evening.

On Friday, April 14, Dr. Schaffhausen and I attended a meeting for team doctors at which IIHF officials outlined new doping control procedures, rules, and regulations. The team practiced from 3:30 to 4:45 p.m. and then settled in for a good rest.

On Saturday, April 15, the World Championships started. Our opponent in the first game was the Soviet Union. To be honest, we were a little surprised by the unnecessarily rough play by some of the Soviet players. Slava Fetisov, who'd crosschecked Jimmy Johnson in the face at Prague in 1985, high-sticked Corey Millen in the face, causing a large laceration above Corey's left upper eyelid. Fetisov got a five-minute major for high-sticking and drawing blood. Meanwhile, I took Corey to the first-aid room and gave him twelve stitches to close the wound. It was an unpleasant game, which the Soviets won 4–2 on the strength of two goals and one assist from future Detroit Red Wings star Sergei Fedorov.

The next day we played the host team, Sweden. We played well, but as always, the Swedes were excellent skaters and we had difficulty keeping up, especially in the third period. They scored three goals in the final ten minutes and beat us 4–2.

On Monday, April 17, we had a day off. We practiced from 10:00 to 11:45 a.m. and went shopping and sightseeing in the afternoon.

Tuesday was a tough day for us. We faced the always-strong Canadian team at 12:30 p.m. The boys skated hard, but we were no match for the Canadians.

On the Gustafsberg, *we were greeted by friendly musicians.*

Steve Yzerman scored a hat trick, and we lost the game 8–2.

On Wednesday, April 19, we practiced early. After lunch, a bus took us to Södertälje, a suburb of Stockholm, for our 4:00 p.m. game against Czechoslovakia. It was perhaps our best total team performance, as we outshot the Czechs 40–24. Young Dominik Hašek was stellar in goal, however, and we lost 5–4, unable to slip the tying goal past "The Dominator," as he would later come to be known. After the game, we returned to Stockholm for dinner and a restful night.

Early the next morning I got a telephone call from the chairman of the IIHF Medical Committee. He told me that Corey Millen's urine, provided the night before for random testing, showed traces of an illegal drug. Oh, my God—what a blow!

Before giving the news to our coach and general manager, I went to see Corey to ask if he had taken anything that might be illegal. He answered, "Doc, not again!"

I said, "What do you mean, 'not again'?"

He said, "Doc, don't you remember? Back in November 1983, when we were preparing for the Olympics in Sarajevo, Dr. Leach called me and asked if I'd taken any steroids. My urine had tested positive. I told him at the time that everyone in my family has elevated testosterone levels. It's a genetic condition. If I do any weight training, I puff up so bad I can't fit into my clothes. Dr. Leach ordered more tests and said it would be okay."

I said, "So you were the one! Yes, I remember!"

As Team USA was preparing for the 1984 Winter Olympics, Dr. Leach had told me that someone on the roster had tested positive for steroids, but he wouldn't give me the name. Dr. Leach had ordered more tests to further investigate the matter. It *appeared* that the player might have taken steroids, but his high testosterone levels could have been *endogenous*, produced by the body itself. That player was Corey Millen! Now I had to act quickly.

I told the entire story to Tim Taylor and Art Berglund, and we tried to get proof about Corey's steroid status from the US Olympic Committee Medical Department, who'd previously helped to clear Corey from similar allegations at the 1984 Winter Games. The IIHF Anti-Doping Committee decided, however, that Corey was banned from competition, effective immediately, pending further tests. In fact, the Tournament Directorate removed all of our goals from the last two games, officially listing the score versus Canada as 8–0 and against Czechoslovakia as 5–0. The scoring changes didn't affect our standings, but it was a difficult blow to lose Corey for rest of the tournament. Luckily for Corey, as further tests were conducted over the next three months, he was vindicated and his elevated testosterone levels were proven to be endogenous.

In any case, on Friday, April 21, we played an afternoon game against West Germany in Södertälje. Everyone was upset about the unfair decision, and the boys were really pumped up. We scored the first three goals and beat the West Germans 7–4.

Saturday was a day of rest. After practice, Dr.

Schaffhausen and I went downtown for a beer to forget all the unpleasant developments.

The next day we played Finland. Once again, we jumped out to a 3–0 lead, but the Finns tied it up and the game ended 3–3.

On Monday, April 24, we didn't have a game, so we enjoyed a late, leisurely breakfast. We practiced from 12:00 to 1:15 p.m., ate lunch, and walked around Stockholm Harbor. It was a nice, sunny spring day, and I enjoyed seeing the big ships and the government buildings, including Stockholm City Hall. After such a long walk in the fresh air, I was ready for dinner and a good night's rest.

On Tuesday, April 25, we played Poland in our last game of the preliminary round. It was an easy game for us, but in the last period our goalie, John Vanbiesbrouck, took a puck in the left jaw. "Beezer" went down hard, and I knew that it could be bad. He was replaced by backup goalie Cleon Daskalakis, and we took him to the first-aid room. I applied ice packs to his injured jaw to minimize swelling and hemorrhaging. Then, immediately after the game, I took him to Karolinska Hospital for x-rays. There was, indeed, a fracture on the left side of his mandibular ramus (jawbone), but displacement was minimal. Still, there was no way that he could play any more. We'd won the game 6–1, but we lost another excellent player. The next morning, Johnnie flew home to get the necessary treatment as soon as possible.

Meanwhile, we'd ended the preliminary round with five points and were relegated to the consolation round with Finland, West Germany, and Poland. That

afternoon we played our second straight game against Poland in our first contest of the consolation round. The boys were quite emotional and dedicated the game to John. We skated hard and fast and won the game 11–2.

We didn't have a game the next day, so after breakfast I met with a group of team doctors to discuss protective equipment that could further improve player safety. That afternoon we received an invitation for the entire team to take a boat tour the next morning.

On Friday, April 28, right after breakfast, we took a bus to Stockholm Harbor, where we boarded a large tour boat named *Gustafsberg*. Musicians greeted us upon our arrival, and there was friendly atmosphere in and around the boat. Peter Wallin, a Stockholm native and former New York Ranger, was assigned as our team guide and host. He became very good friends with Dr. Schaffhausen, and they had a lot of fun together. It was such a wonderful change of scenery, out on the Baltic Sea that borders Stockholm, among the thousands of islands that make up the Stockholm archipelago.

At 7:30 p.m. that evening we played West Germany. We played very well but suffered another injury when Eddy Olczyk took a high stick in his left eye. We won the game 4–3, but I had to take Eddy to the hospital to diagnose what turned out to be a minor corneal abrasion. We were lucky it was minor and returned to our hotel much relieved.

Saturday, April 29, was our last free day. The souvenir hunters among us shopped in downtown

Stockholm. The weather was quite nice, and all of us enjoyed strolling along the waterfront.

On Sunday, April 30, we played Finland in our last game of the tournament. We not only lost 6–2, but also suffered even more injuries. Kelly Miller sprained his right wrist, Paul Fenton re-aggravated a previously strained abdominal muscle, Randy Wood sprained his right knee, and Tom Kurvers took a hard puck to his left foot, which became so sore that he could no longer skate.

At times like this, it was good to have an orthopedic surgeon with us. After the game, we took Tom to the hospital for x-rays. Dr. Schaffhausen was sure that Tom had a compression fracture of his left tarsal navicular bone (his instep). He wanted to recheck Tom's foot and follow up with him as soon as they got back to Minneapolis.

Monday, May 1, was the last day of the tournament. We'd finished our games and spent the forenoon packing our luggage. The final standings were Soviet Union, gold medal; Canada, silver medal; and Czechoslovakia, bronze medal. We finished in sixth place with a record of 4–5–1.

After the games were over, we attended the tournament banquet at City Hall. It was a very well-organized dinner, followed by the awards ceremony, but the mood was not very happy because the Swedes, as host team, hadn't won a medal.

The next morning, after a late breakfast, we took the bus to the airport and boarded Finnair flight 105 to JFK Airport in New York. We landed later that day at about 4:00 p.m. and continued on to Minneapolis.

I was happy to be home and happier still to have had Dr. Schaffhausen on hand at the tournament. In the midst of so many medical problems, it was comforting to have someone else with whom to discuss various treatment options. Dr. Schaffhausen's wisdom and experience were invaluable assets and much appreciated.

One day, not long after I'd returned home, I received a phone call from Japan from my good old friend Helmut Balderis. Helmut had left Riga Dinamo in 1985 and gone to Japan to work as a player-coach. After a bitter falling-out with Coach Viktor Tikhonov after the 1980 Olympics, Helmut had been shunned by Soviet sports authorities and never played in the Olympics again, despite his amazing talents. By the summer of 1989, however, glasnost reforms were well underway and the Iron Curtain was falling. The Soviet Union's grip on its hockey players had begun to loosen, and some of them were migrating to teams in the NHL. Helmut was ready to join them.

I'd always known, of course, that Helmut dreamed of playing for a team in the NHL—we'd talked about it years ago in Schönbrunn Park in Vienna, when we'd first met—but he'd never considered defecting out of fear for his family's safety and the political ramifications. Under the weakening Soviet system, however, he no longer needed to worry. He could play in the NHL without fear of repercussions. Knowing my connection to the Minnesota North Stars, he thought they were the obvious choice. Of course, I was happy to help. I hung up the phone and called North Stars General Manager Jack Ferreira. With the NHL entry

Walking along the harbor area of Stockholm, with Stockholm's City Hall in the background.

draft rapidly approaching, there was no time to waste.

Jack knew Helmut well from the 1980 Soviet team in Lake Placid and other Soviet national teams of the late 1970s and early 1980s. In fact, Jack had seen Helmut play in Montreal and was very impressed. And, of course, Helmut's accomplishments spoke for themselves: Soviet League Player of the Year in 1977, Soviet League top scorer in 1977 and 1983, a career total of 333 goals in Soviet League play, and three world championships in international competition. Jack's only concern was Helmut's age. Jack wanted to be sure that Helmut, at thirty-six years old, still had what it takes.

After some discussion, Jack and the Minnesota North Stars decided the risk, if any, was worth it, and on June 17, 1989, Helmut Balderis became the oldest player ever drafted by an NHL team. He was chosen in the 12th round with the 238th overall selection.

Before offering a contract, however, and flying Helmut to the United States for tryouts, Jack Ferreira still wanted to see him perform in person. So, on Monday, August 14, Jack and I flew to Riga, Latvia, where Helmut was practicing, unofficially, with his old team, Riga Dinamo. We landed the following day and met with the president of the Latvian Sports Association, who believed that Helmut would make an excellent "sports ambassador" to the United States and was in full support of Helmut joining the NHL. Arrangements were made for us to watch Helmut practice on Thursday, August 17.

Helmut hadn't played professionally in Europe since 1985, but he looked as good as ever. He was the same powerful, fluid skater I'd always known, but Jack was particularly impressed with Helmut's dazzling puck-handling skills. "I love his hands," said Ferreira, clearly sold on the prospect of Helmut joining his team. Now the work began to secure Helmut's visa and making travel arrangements. This was a very difficult process since the Latvian officials I needed to speak with were awake and working while I slept, and vice versa.

On September 1, however, we finally secured Helmut's visa, and he left for the United States the following day. Meanwhile, I bought a plane ticket to New York to meet him there, help get him through passport control, and accompany him back to Minneapolis. He arrived in the United States on Sunday, September 3, and by the end of the day he resided in Jimmy Craig's former bedroom in the basement of my house in Edina. After a few short days of getting settled and acclimated, Helmut was off to Kalamazoo, Michigan, for tryouts and training camp, which began Thursday, September 7.

Helmut performed well throughout training camp, despite the sometimes overzealous attempts of younger rookies to beat him up and intimidate him with their rough, physical style of play. Helmut was unfazed by their antics, of course, and easily made the roster, ending up on a line with his former rival from the 1980 Olympics, Neal Broten. Broten was more than happy to play *with* Balderis, rather than against him, and often commented on Balderis's unparalleled ability to see the ice and thread passes unexpectedly through the defense. In contrast to fellow rookie Mike

Modano, who already had a reputation for blasting shots from anywhere and everywhere, Balderis was a precise and deliberate playmaker. Almost immediately, he was a hit with Minnesota's knowledgeable hockey fans, who often chanted, "Hel-mut, Hel-mut," in unison as he carried the puck.

Needless to say, it was particularly gratifying to me to help my dear old friend and countryman realize his dream to play in the NHL. I was happy to play such a vital role in making it happen. In some ways, I felt a bit like a proud father. I will never forget, especially, when Helmut scored two goals against the Toronto Maple Leafs on November 12 and was named the first star of the game. I was as happy for him as I've ever been for any player.

US team members for 1989 Spengler Cup tournament held in Davos, Switzerland.

Spengler Cup

Davos, Switzerland, 1989

Team Roster

In Goal: *John Blue, Matt DelGuidice*

Defense: *Josh Caplan, Jim Hughes, Paul Marshall, Brian McColgan, Andy Otto, Bill Schafhauser*

Forwards: *Bob Crawford, Rich Costello, Rick Erdall, Bryan Erickson, John Fritsche, Ed Galiani, Mike Hiltner, Andy Janfaza, Mark LaVarre, Steve McSwain, John Messuri, Skeeter Moore, Tom Sasso, Sean Toomey*

The Spengler Cup, one of the oldest and most prestigious hockey tournaments in Europe, has been held in Davos, Switzerland, on the days between December 26 and New Year's Eve, since 1923. The tournament was founded by Dr. Carl Spengler, who wished to promote international sports competition and donated the first cup, and Dr. Paul Müller, president of the Davos Hockey Club. Davos was an early hockey hotbed in Switzerland and natural home to the event. The Davos Hockey Club was founded in 1921: Dr. Müller was always very interested in international competition, and Dr. Spengler was a major supporter of the club.

US Team Captain Ed Galiani receiving the Spengler Cup for fourth place.

The Spengler Cup President Alfred Gfeller getting ready to present the Spengler Cup trophies to each team.

Throughout the 1920s there were many good hockey teams in Europe. In the United Kingdom, for example, both Oxford and Cambridge Universities had very strong clubs, albeit largely stocked with Canadian students. The Berlin Skating Club in Germany and LTC–Prague in Czechoslovakia were also formidable teams.

Oxford University won the first Spengler Cup in 1923 and three times more that first decade, sharing the cup with LTC–Prague in 1932 when the two teams played to a 0–0 tie and were declared co-champions after an overtime session failed to produce a winner. The Berlin Skating Club won the Spengler Cup three times in the first ten years, as did LTC–Prague. Host team HC Davos won the cup just once in the first decade of competition, but six times in the 1930s and 1940s. Soviet and Czechoslovakian teams dominated play in the mid-to-late twentieth century, winning all but one cup between them from 1962 to 1983. In 1988, the USA Selects won the Spengler Cup and were invited back the following year. Four other teams rounded out the field: Färjestad Bollklubb (BK) from Sweden, Spartak Moscow, Team Canada, and the host team, Davos Select.

The US team for the sixty-third Spengler Cup was staffed by General Manager Dave Peterson, Head Coach Bill Flynn, Assistant General Manager Rene Duperret, Trainer Bob Edrzejek, Equipment Manager Jim Dunn, and myself as team physician.

Since the coach, assistant general manager, and most of our players played for professional or semipro hockey teams in Europe, we all assembled on Sunday, December 24, in Davos, where we were quartered at the Kongress Hotel. We held a light practice from 5:00 to 6:00 p.m. and enjoyed Christmas Eve dinner at our hotel afterward.

On Christmas Day we practiced from 9:30 to 11:00 a.m. and again from 4:00 to 5:00 p.m. In the evening we walked around town and admired the Christmas decorations.

The tournament began on Tuesday, December 26. The format, as is customary, consisted of one set of round-robin games, with the top two teams squaring off in a championship game for the cup. Four teams competed each day, while one team had the day off. We didn't play on the first day. In the opening game, Spartak Moscow beat Team Canada 4–1. Later that night, Färjestad BK beat Davos Select 7–5.

On Wednesday, December 27, we played Davos Select in our first game of the tournament. We played very well and won 9–3. My good friends from Zürich, Hardy Spillman and Ausma Vanags, were at the game. It was great to see them again. After the game, we all went out to dinner.

The next day, I walked around the charming Alpine town of Davos with Hardy and Ausma. Later that afternoon, they took the train back to Zürich and I returned to the hotel to get ready for our evening game against Spartak Moscow. It was a tough game for us, and we lost 7–3.

On Friday, December 29, we again played in the evening game. Since I had the afternoon free, I visited the dentists for whom my daughter, Brigita, had worked as a hygienist in 1977. One of them, Dr. Prader, was very much involved with the Spengler Cup organization and told me some interesting stories about the cup's history. One year, for example, when the tournament was still played outside, it snowed very hard during the championship game. Play was interrupted frequently for snow removal, but still they couldn't keep up. At one point, the goalie for Dukla Jihlava, the Czechoslovakian team, couldn't find the puck in the snow and stepped on it accidentally, knocking into his net. Dukla Jihlava lost the game, which many fans found quite upsetting, since they were clearly the better team.

We played Team Canada that night. We got off to a slow start, and by late in the second period we were behind 6–2. Then things turned around, and we scored six unanswered goals for a 8–6 victory. After we'd fallen behind, the spectators cheered us on and the boys responded. It was an unbelievable game!

Going into our final game on Sunday, December 30, against Färjestad BK from Sweden, we still had a shot at finishing in second place and advancing to play for the cup. It was a beautiful, sunny day with the bright sun low in the sky. The game started well enough for us, and after the second period the score was tied 3–3. Then came some bad luck for us. In the third period, our defensive goal was at the east end of the rink, looking west. The sun was shining through the window very brightly, practically blinding our goalie. Our skaters, too, were bothered by the sun and had difficulty making good plays. The Swedes, on the other hand, seemed to have no trouble and scored three straight goals to win the game 6–3. All of

us were in shock! The Swedes finished second, Team Canada took third, and we finished in fourth place.

The next day was New Year's Eve, with the championship played at noon between Spartak Moscow and Färjestad BK. Spartak Moscow won the game 5–3 and took home the 1989 Spengler Cup. The awards ceremony followed the final game, and each team received a cup trophy that varied in size according to its placement. We left Davos in the early evening and celebrated New Year's in Zürich.

On Monday, January 1, 1990, the players and coaches returned to their European teams, and Dave Peterson and I returned to Minneapolis. It was an interesting experience despite our failure to win the Spengler Cup.

1990 Women's World Ice Hockey Championship, March 19-25, Ottawa, Canada.
Front row (L-R): Kelly Dyer, Maria Dennis, Heidi Chalupnik, Lisa Brown, Tina Cardinale, Kimberly Eisenreid, and Mary Jones. Middle row: Equipment Manager Kulraj Sidhu, Assistant Coach Karen Kay, Head Coach Don MacLeod, Jeanine Sobek, Sue Merz, Julie Sasner, Cindy Curley, Beth Beagan, Sharon Stidsen, Kelly O'Leary, Assistant General Manager Lynn Olson, Trainer Debbie White-Lyons, and myself.
Top row: General Manager Robert Allen, Judy Parish, Kelley Owen, Lauren Apollo, Yvonne Percy, Shawna Davidson, and Cammi Granato.

The First Women's World
Championships

Ottawa, Ontario, Canada, 1990

Team Roster

In Goal: *Kelly Dyer, Mary Jones*

Defense: *Lauren Apollo, Kelly O'Leary, Kelley Owen, Judy Parish, Yvonne Percy, Sharon Stidsen*

Forwards: *Beth Beagan, Lisa Brown, Tina Cardinale, Heidi Chalupnik, Cindy Curley, Shawna Davidson, Maria Dennis, Kimberly Eisenried, Cammi Granato, Sue Merz, Julie Sasner, Jeanine Sobek*

The first IIHF Women's World Championships were held from March 19 to 25, 1990, in Ottawa, Ontario. Eight teams participated, divided into two groups. Group A featured Canada, Sweden, Germany, and Japan. Group B contained the United States, Finland, Switzerland, and Norway. Each team would play a series of round-robin games within its own group, with the top two teams from each group advancing to the medal round.

The selection process for the United States women's team started with numerous tryout camps in October 1989. They were held in Massachusetts, Michigan,

Minnesota, and New York. The management group consisted of General Manager Robert Allen, Assistant General Manager Lynn Olson, Head Coach Don MacLeod, Assistant Coach Karen Kay, Trainer Debbie White-Lyons, Equipment Manager Kulraj Sidhu, and myself as team physician.

On Thursday, March 15, the team assembled in Lake Placid, New York, for three days of practice before leaving for Ottawa. We flew to Ottawa on Sunday, March 18, and checked into the Skyline Hotel. That afternoon we completed our accreditation formalities and attended a welcome reception. The first directorate meeting, where rules and regulations were discussed, took place on Sunday evening. IIHF Technical Director Roman Neumayer asked how much physicality should be allowed. In short, would the tournament be checking or non-checking? After some lively discussion, the matter was put to a vote. Canada, the United States, and Switzerland voted against body checking, but Sweden, Finland, Germany, Norway, and Japan voted in favor of body checking. The vote was 5–3 in favor of checking!

On Monday, March 19, the tournament began. Early that morning I attended the team physicians' meeting. The chief medical officer for the event, Dr. Rudy Gittens, reviewed on-site medical services and explained necessary procedures. We were all also informed that random doping control tests would be administered throughout the tournament.

At 1:00 p.m. we played Switzerland in our first game. It was an easy game, which our girls won 16–3. No games were scheduled the next day, and since all of the teams were quartered at the Skyline Hotel, I had a chance to meet and talk to the other team doctors.

On Wednesday, March 21, we faced Norway at 1:00 p.m. It was another very easy game, and we blanked the Norwegians 17–0. After dinner, Roman Neumayer and I decided to attend the game between Sweden and Japan because both teams had voted in favor of body checking. The game was hilarious. Those big, strong Swedish players relentlessly checked the smaller Japanese players, sending them sprawling and rolling all over the ice. Roman turned to me and said, "George, this is ridiculous! This isn't hockey, it's a circus!"

After the game, Roman called a directorate meeting to discuss an immediate rule change. The others agreed, and body checking was eliminated midtournament for the remainder of the games. The more skillful US and Canadian teams had always played without checking, and both countries were happy to have it officially removed for the World Championships.

The next day we played Finland. This was a much different game. Finland had one very fast skater on their team. They all played a good, strong game, but we won 5–4.

Friday, March 23, was another day off. I went for a walk with our team manager, Robert Allen, and the chairman of the tournament, Walter L. Bush Jr. It was a very windy day, however, and after taking a few pictures, we returned to our hotel.

The round-robin games for both groups were finished. In Group A, Canada finished first and Sweden

Walter L. Bush, Jr., the IIHF Vice President and chairman of the Women's Hockey Committee,
was a major force in organizing the first IIHF Women's World Championship Games in Ottawa, Canada in 1990.
He also persuaded the IOC to include Women's Ice Hockey as a sport for the Olympic Winter Games in 1998
in Nagano, Japan.

Happy winners of the silver medal for the first Women's World Championship in Ottawa, Ontario, Canada.

second. In Group B, the United States placed first and Finland second. Therefore, we played Sweden—the second-place team in the other group—in a semi-final game on Saturday, March 24. During a tough game against Finland, our girls were very focused and played excellently. The final result was a 10–3 win for Team USA.

In the evening game, Canada defeated Finland 6–5, setting up the gold-medal game between the US and Canada on Sunday, March 25.

The gold-medal game featured a much higher level of play than most of the other games in the tournament. The skillful Canadian team played a good, strong game and won 5–2, taking the first-ever IIHF Women's World Championship. Team USA took silver, and the Finnish team won the bronze by beating their Swedish counterparts. A banquet and award ceremony followed that evening, and several of our players won individual awards. Cindy Curley was the tournament scoring leader, with twenty-three points on eleven goals and twelve assists. Kelly Dyer was recognized as the best goaltender in the tournament and Cindy Curley and Kelly O'Leary were named to the tournament all-star team.

On Monday morning, March 26, we said goodbye to each other. Most of our team returned to their East Coast college teams. Only Kelly Owen, Jeanine Sobek, Lynn Olson, Walter Bush, and I boarded the plane for Minneapolis.

It had been an interesting tournament and a landmark event—the first World Championship in women's ice hockey. Though we didn't win the gold medal, we were very proud of our girls, who represented the nation so well.

Walter L. Bush, Jr., (left) president of USA Hockey, and Frank Gallagher, vice president of USA Hockey, presented a silver medal to me as well in 1992.

In those early years, medals were presented only to the players. Those rules were changed in 1992. After that, administrators, coaches, and staff members—including team physicians—were also given medals. Later, a silver medal was also presented to me. It will always be a special memento of a very special team and a very special time.

1990 United States National Hockey Team: World Championships in Bern, Switzerland. Row 1 (L-R): Bill Pye, Neal Broten, Mark Johnson, Tom O'Regan, Head Coach Tim Taylor, Jon Casey, General Manager Art Berglund, Captain Jim Johnson, Greg Brown, Jeff Norton, John Blue. Row 2: Trainer Skip Thayer, Bobby Reynolds, Danton Cole, Kip Miller, Assistant Coach Mike Eaves, myself, Assistant Coach Ben Smith, Ed Galiani, Steve McSwain, John Fritsche, Trainer Dave Carrier. Row 3: Equipment Manager Bob Webster, Joel Otto, Guy Gosselin, Dan Keczmer, Mike Modano, Paul Ranheim, Chris Dahlquist, Kevin Stevens, Joe Sacco, Equipment Manager Steve Latin. Missing from picture: Team Physician Dr. Harvey O'Phelan, Director of Player Personnel Dave Peterson, Public Relations Representative Mike Schroeder.

30

IIHF World Championships

Bern and Fribourg, Switzerland, 1990

Team Roster

In Goal: *Jon Casey, John Blue, Bill Pye*

Defense: *Greg Brown, Chris Dahlquist, Guy Gosselin, Jim Johnson, Dan Keczmer, Jeff Norton*

Forwards: *Neal Broten, Danton Cole, John Fritsche, Ed Galiani, Mark Johnson, Steve McSwain, Kip Miller, Mike Modano, Tom O'Regan, Joel Otto, Paul Ranheim, Bobby Reynolds, Joe Sacco, Kevin Stevens*

The 1990 IIHF World Championships took place in Bern and Fribourg, Switzerland, from April 16 through May 2. Eight teams participated: Canada, Czechoslovakia, Finland, Norway, Sweden, the United States, the Soviet Union, and West Germany.

The USA Hockey management group was Art Berglund as general manager, Dave Peterson as director of player personnel, Tim Taylor as head coach, Ben Smith and Mike Eaves as assistant coaches, Skip Thayer and Dave Carrier as trainers, Bob Webster and Steve Latin as equipment managers, Mike Schroeder

Dave Carrier and Bob Webster (right) at the Neuschwanstein castle.

in public relations, Dr. Harvey O'Phelan as orthopedic surgeon, and myself as team physician.

On Saturday, April 7, the team assembled for the first time at the TWA Airlines counter at New York's JFK Airport. Our flight left for Zürich, Switzerland, at 6:25 p.m. It was a smooth, uneventful flight, and we arrived at 9:45 the next morning.

From the Zürich Airport, we took a bus to Füssen, Germany, where we were quartered in the dorms at the German National Hockey Training Centre for the next two days.

On Monday, April 9, we practiced after breakfast and had the remainder of the day for rest and relaxation. On Tuesday, after practice, we toured the picturesque Neuschwanstein Castle, which sits high on a hill overlooking the village. Commissioned by the "Fairytale King," Ludwig II of Bavaria, the castle is most famous for inspiring Disneyland's Sleeping Beauty Castle. After touring the lush interior for an hour or so, we walked back down the winding road to our dorm. Some players were lucky enough to jump on a farmer's large horse-drawn wagon headed down the hill, but he only had room for a few. For the rest of us, the long walk downhill was horrible. My quads were aching for three or four days afterward. Some of the players were also hurting.

The next day we took a bus to Augsburg, where we played our first exhibition game against West Germany. We were still a little tired from the flight, as well as from that walk down the hill, and we lost 1–0.

Right after the game I met a German friend from Augsburg, Erich Reinhardt. We arranged to meet in

The "rescue squad" for some players walking down the hill.

Bern on Wednesday, April 25, but I didn't have much time to talk because we had to get back to Füssen.

On Thursday, April 12, we played the West German National Team in Garmisch-Partenkirchen. This time we were better rested and won the game 5–4. That victory gave us a little more confidence, and everybody was in a much better mood.

On Friday, April 13, we took a bus to Bern, Switzerland. It was a pleasant spring day with pleasant scenery en route. We arrived at about 2:00 p.m. and checked into the Hotel Bern. We had a light practice later that afternoon. The next day we got our credentials and practiced some more. Sunday, April 15, was a day of rest and relaxation.

On Monday, April 16, the 1990 IIHF World Championships started. We traveled to Fribourg, a nice university city about twenty miles southwest of Bern, to play Czechoslovakia in our first game. After having played just two exhibition games together, we were no match for the very smooth-skating Czechoslovakian team and lost 7–1. After the game, we returned to Bern and tried to get a good night's rest.

On Tuesday, April 17, we had a late practice in the morning and played Canada at 4:30 p.m. We played better than the day before, but the Canadian defense was very solid and we lost 6–3.

Wednesday, April 18, was our day off. Clearly, we needed a good rest before we faced the mighty Soviets. After practice, I went downtown with our trainer, Skip Thayer, to do some window shopping. There was a watch store on every corner, but we were especially impressed with a very fine leather goods shop.

On Thursday, April 19, we returned to Fribourg to play Russia at 7:00 p.m. It was a very difficult game for us that ended 10–1 in favor of the Soviets.

Luckily, we didn't have to travel the next day, since we were to play Sweden in Bern at 4:30 p.m. All throughout the game, I kept my fingers crossed that we would avoid any injuries. It was the last tough game for us. The next three games would be much easier. Still, we needed all of our players in good health. The fast-skating Swedes were very effective in front of our net, however, and they beat us 6–1.

Saturday, April 21, was a day off for our team, but I had to go to Fribourg for the IIHF Medical Symposium entitled "Injury Prevention in Ice Hockey by Correct Protective Equipment." Several doctors from different countries presented papers.

Since our goalie at the 1989 IIHF World Championships in Stockholm, John Vanbiesbrouck, had suffered a broken lower jawbone, I presented a paper entitled "Head Injuries and Protective Facemasks for Goalies in Ice Hockey."

In the afternoon, a group of doctors, including Daniele Mona from Switzerland, Patrick Bishop and Derek Mackesy from Canada, Jaroslav Tintera from Czechoslovakia, and I joined another group from the symposium to visit La maison du Gruyère, the world-famous Gruyère cheese factory. It was a very interesting—and delicious—experience.

On Sunday, April 22, we played West Germany. It was a much better game for us, and we won 6–3. After the game I met my old hockey buddy Erik Konecki, who had arrived from Dortmund, Germany. I told him that his friend from Augsburg, Erich Reinhardt, was arriving on Wednesday, April 25. Konecki had played for the Augsburg Ice Hockey Club in the late 1940s and had known Reinhardt since then.

On Monday, April 23, Dr. Harvey O'Phelan arrived, which was a big relief for me. I felt much more comfortable with him around. After Harvey rested for a while, I briefed him about the health situation of some of our players and said that I hoped that the hard part of the tournament was over. At 4:30 p.m. that day we played Norway. Our boys were quite relaxed, and we won the game 9–4.

On Tuesday, April 24, we didn't have a game.

Harvey and I walked downtown after practice and had lunch at the well-known Kornhauskeller. I told Harvey that Erich Reinhardt and his wife, Ingrid, were coming the next day. Since we had Thursday off, I thought we all might drive to Thun, about fifteen miles south of Bern, to see Erik Konecki, whom Harvey remembered well from our time in Moscow in 1986 at the Cosmos Hotel.

We played Finland in our last game of the preliminary round on April 25. The game wouldn't affect our standing because we'd lost our first four games. Even with a win, we couldn't qualify for the medal round. Still, the boys played hard and we won the game 2–1. We finished the preliminary round with four losses and three wins and joined Finland, West Germany, and Norway in the consolation round.

On our day off, Harvey and I met Erich and Ingrid Reinhardt after practice, and we all drove to Thun, a beautiful tourist town on Lake Thun, to visit Erik Konecki. The drive took just fifteen minutes, but Harvey and I were very uncomfortable at first. Erich drove a big, powerful new BMW 740 and went about eighty-five or ninety miles per hour! Harvey didn't like it at all, so I told Erich, in German, "We think it's a very nice car, but we would appreciate it if you slowed down a little bit." Erich happily complied, and we had no further problems after that.

After finding Erik Konecki, we all went for a walk along the shores of the lake and ate lunch at a local *Gasthaus*. During lunch we also made plans for our next free day, Saturday, April 28. I thought a trip up to Grindelwald to see the Jungfrau peak would be

interesting. Everybody liked that idea. Shortly after lunch we returned to Bern because Harvey and I had tickets for the ballet *Romeo and Juliet* that evening.

A game against West Germany.

On Friday, April 27, we played West Germany at 8:00 p.m. We had some time for shopping after lunch, so I told Harvey that Skip Thayer and I had found some nice shops downtown. We went to the leather goods store that had caught my eye and each of us bought a pair of shoes.

After dinner, the bus took us to the arena to play West Germany in the first game of the consolation round. We played well and won 5–3.

The next morning, after practice, Erich and

Myself with a group of medical conference participants at Fribourg, visiting the cheese factory of Gruyères.

Ingrid were waiting for us at our hotel. Harvey and I were quick to get ready, and soon we were on our way to the Grindelwald.

We picked up Erik Konecki in Thun and, after driving another fifteen miles south, we arrived at the charming tourist town of Interlaken. South of it, you can see the Jungfrau peak quite well. From Interlaken our road headed uphill. The scenery was beautiful, with many old, interesting farmhouses and meadows full of different colored flowers. As we arrived in Grindelwald, the sun was shining and we had an excellent view of the mountain. We walked around the picturesque Alpine village, took many photos, and found a nice little restaurant for lunch. Walking in the fresh, clean mountain air had given us a good appetite, and we very much enjoyed our lunch. I felt bad that we could not stay much longer and enjoy the wonderful mountain scenery, but Harvey and I had to be back by 4:00 p.m. for a reception at the United States Embassy at 5:30 p.m.

After Harvey and I returned to our hotel, everyone got ready for the reception. At about 5:15 p.m., a bus took us to the embassy. There were several dignitaries from USA Hockey and the IIHF present. It was a very nice reception, and I met and talked to many people of different professions. After the reception, Harvey and I joined Walter Bush and Bob Allen for dinner at a local restaurant. Dinners with Walter Bush are always very enjoyable because he tells so many funny stories about various tournaments. It was a full day of different and very interesting events.

On Sunday, April 29, we had a late practice after breakfast, and afterwards Harvey and I walked downtown. We took some pictures and admired how clean the town was.

Our game against Norway was scheduled for 6:00 p.m. It was an easy game for us, and we won 4–1. At the game we met our good friend Paul Haenni. We told him that Monday was a day off, and he invited the whole team to visit his watch factory.

On Monday morning, April 30, a bus took us to Paul Haenni's watch factory in Biel, the French-speaking town where few people spoke English. Paul himself led the tour through different sections of the factory and explained to us how some of the watch parts were made and how they were put together. It was extremely interesting, and the boys enjoyed the tour very much. Afterward, we returned to our hotel in Bern and invited Paul to join us for dinner. At dinner we thanked him for inviting us and explaining how his factory operated. Art Berglund, our general manager, presented Paul with a white United States pullover. He was so happy about it that he wore it the entire evening.

After dinner we watched the Canada–Russia game on TV. Canada had difficulties facing the smooth-passing Soviets and lost 7–1.

Tuesday, May 1, was our last game of the World Championships, against Finland. Our boys felt very relaxed, and we won 3–2. Our record was 6–4–0, which was good for fifth place. All of us were satisfied with our performance, as the top four teams were outstanding.

Wednesday, May 2 was the last day of the

tournament. Two big games were scheduled: Russia versus Czechoslovakia and Canada versus Sweden. The Soviets won against the Czechoslovakians, 5–0, for the gold medal. Canada lost to Sweden, 6–4, and the Swedes got the silver medal. The bronze medal was awarded to Czechoslovakia.

During the awards ceremony, the goalie for the Russian team, Artūrs Irbe, won the best goalie award. Irbe was a Latvian who played for the Riga Dinamo in his country and had been drafted by the Minnesota North Stars in 1989. I therefore went to congratulate him and brought him to our table, where he could meet and talk to Jon Casey, the current North Stars goalie. It was a nice banquet, with a friendly atmosphere among all players and management personnel.

The next morning, Thursday, May 3, a bus took us to the Zürich Airport, and at about noon our flight left for New York. The flight was very smooth, and after about nine hours we were home again. The 1990 World Championships were over, leaving us with many nice memories to be recalled in later days.

April 28, 1990 in Grindelwald (L-R): Erich Reinhardt, Ingrid Reinhardt, Erik Konecki, and myself.

Art Berglund presenting a white US pullover to Paul Haenni (left).

EPILOGUE

During the days of the 1990 IIHF Championships in Bern and Fribourg, it never came to my mind that it could be my last tournament with the United States National Team.

But it happened that, at the IIHF Congress in June 1990, I was selected as a new member for the IIHF Medical Committee. The chairman of the Committee told me that I would now be observing the games, registering and reporting all serious injuries, and overseeing doping control. I would therefore have to take a neutral stance and could no longer serve as a team physician.

Yes, it opened another interesting chapter in my life, but I very much missed being together with the players. Besides my family, the camaraderie that I developed with all those players throughout the years has been the greatest blessing in my life.

It's something you cannot buy for a million dollars, and I will cherish those relationships for as long as I live.

2003 recipient of Paul Loicq Award for outstanding contributions to the sport of ice hockey, the IIHF, and the hockey family worldwide.

2010 University of Minnesota "M" club Hall of Fame induction.

2010, daughters Sylvia and Brigita with USA Hockey Hall of Fame plaque.

2010 HOF induction. Front row (L-R): Dick McGlynn, Craig Sarner, Tom Mellor, myself, Keith Christiansen, Murray Williamson. Standing (L-R): Pat Williamson, Frank Sanders, Don Mellor, grandson Bill Kelly, daughter Sylvia Lawver, Evie Christiansen, Rebecca Naslund, Paula McGlynn, daughter Brigita Kelly, Ron Naslund, Sylvia's husband Joe Lawver, Nan Curran, Mike Curran, and Michael Nanne. Sitting on the monument (L-R): granddaughters Heidi Kelly, Gigi Lawver with friend Grace Mayer.

AWARDS

*The Order of the Three Stars from
the President of the Republic of Latvia,
on November 17, 2001.*

The Gold Olympic Pin, from the President of the Latvian Olympic Committee
on November 19, 2001.

Paul Loicq Award from IIHF, on May 9, 2003.

A Testimonial Dinner with several honorary plaques and gifts, arranged by
US National, Olympic, and University of Minnesota Hockey Alumni, on
September 1, 2004.

The Distinguished Achievement award from USA Hockey and the Excellence
in Safety award from the Safety and Protective Equipment Committee of USA
Hockey, on June 11, 2005.

Inducted into the University of Minnesota "M" Club Hall of Fame on
September 9, 2010.

Inducted into the US Hockey Hall of Fame, October 21, 2010.

INDEX

JIM CRAIG

Dr. Nagobads, his wife Velta, and his family have been a huge part of my success. I was very lucky to be part of his family and learned so much from him. He was not only a doctor, a mentor, an assistant coach, an interpreter, and a best friend to me, but he was there for everyone. He was universally loved by everyone through the years as their second "Father."

-Jim Craig-

Jim Craig with the Nagobads family in Minnesota. Jim lived in the Nagobads's basement in 1980 during training for the 1980 Olympics. L to R: daughter Brigita, myself, Jim, my wife Velta, daughter Sylvia.

LOU NANNE

No team has ever had a more caring, competent, and considerate doctor.
Besides that, he was the best stitch artist in hockey.

-Lou Nanne-

2013 event with Murray Williamson, Lou Nanne, and myself.

MIKE NANNE

*My very good friend, the late Mike Nanne, who served with me on many
US Equipment Certification Committees.*

PRAISE FOR GOLD, SILVER, & BRONZE

He was more than a doctor, he was a friend and an advisor, a man of deep convictions and with a stout and generous heart. Doc was everyone's friend.

-Lou Vairo

I was fortunate to play on three teams coached by Dr. Nagobads.
Doc has always been special to me and our friendship has continued through the years. He's a kind, humble, and selfless person who always put the team first. Congratulations, Doc on a truly wonderful effort reflecting on an amazing career.

-Tom Mellor

Dr. Nagobads is simply put: the most unselfish, unassuming, humble, and nicest person you will ever meet in your life. Once you meet "Nagy" you will love him and never forget him.

Dr. Nagobads was much more than a team doctor. He was an invaluable asset to USA Hockey for forty-three years – especially in earlier times during the Iron Curtain Days when the term "Ugly American" was coined. He was a big time ambassador for USA Hockey due to his being so highly regarded by the whole international community.

As I said, "Doc" was much more than a team doctor. He was at times a coach, a friend, a confidant, a travel guide, an interpreter, and a facilitator.

-Gary Gambucci

"Few off-ice people can match Doc's contributions to American hockey.
It's a joy to know him."

-Roger Godin, former director/curator, United States Hockey
Hall of Fame

Over the many years I've known "Dr. Noggy" personally, through USA Hockey and the International Ice Hockey Federation, I have found his professional approach along with his kind and friendly way in all situations to be outstanding. All players, staff, and administrators owe a sincere "thank-you" and express our gratitude to Dr. Nagobads, a true "hockey guy" and friend to us all. He is someone who has moved our sport upward for the benefit of everyone who can participate in all the pleasures of ice hockey.

-Walter Bush, Jr.

Doctor Nagobads was a father figure, a mentor, a role model, and a moral compass to more than a thousand young and impressionable USA hockey players during his nearly fifty plus years of service to USA hockey.

Nagy was "all in." He not only took care of us physically but also supported us emotionally. He didn't treat us any differently than he treated his own children; supportive and encouraging at times, stern and resolute at other times. On occasion, he would chastise those of us who needed it, but in the end the good doctor was always proud of us, win or lose.

What distinguished Doctor Nagobads from all others, was his sincerity, compassion, and genuine concern for the welfare of those in his care.

-Richard A. McGlynn,USA Olympic Team, 1972, USA National Team, 1971, USA National Team, 1972

Doc, one of a kind. A hero to thousands of young men and women over the years. Still going strong, travelling the world at the age of ninety-two. A dear friend and mentor for fifty-four years. The finest gentleman I have ever known.

-With gratitude from Len Lilyholm

Gary Gambucci

HALL OF FAME

Dr. V. George Nagobads

I am writing this letter to recommend that Dr. V. George Nagobads be nominated for selection into the United States Hockey Hall of Fame.

For the better part of the past forty-three years (including service with the IIHF), the one constant denominator for all of our US National and Olympic teams has been the humble Dr. Nagobads. Whenever the rich tapestry of American international hockey history is woven, Dr. Nagobads is, without a doubt, one of its most significant components.

All of us athletes who were privileged to play during the "Nagy Era" owe him a big debt of gratitude for always reminding us that the achievement of making the US team was an honor, but also came with certain responsibilities. He always made sure that we realized we were not only representing our country, but also our family, friends, and neighbors back home.

Dr. Nagobads was always a vital part of every team he was with—intimately in lockstep with his players through many successes as well as many heartbreaking losses.

Dr. Nagobads was not only a very skilled, compassionate, and dedicated physician as our team doctor—he was so much more! It was not uncommon for Nagy, in addition to his medical skills, to also double as our tour guide, interpreter, negotiator, historian, mentor, facilitator, and even as an assistant coach when the circumstances warranted it.

Perhaps the best kept secret of the 1980 Olympic Team is the fact that right before the game started, Herbie gave Doc his stopwatch and told him, "Doc, you're in charge. I don't want any line out there for more than forty-five seconds!"

True to international hockey, the mighty Russians were outskated in the critical third period—a period they always dominated.

Having personally had the good fortune to have had Nagy as a doctor both at the University of Minnesota and also with four US teams, I can state unequivocally that whenever a player had a problem, one call to Dr. Nagobads and you became his only priority—whether it was the administering of stitches (which he was certainly one of the best at doing), or staying up with you all night to make sure there were no complications from a concussion. His largesse was further evidenced by the fact that many times he assisted athletes from competing countries when necessary, this endearing him to the whole international community.

Dr. Nagobads's concern for both his players and his dedication to US hockey, while legendary, came at a price. Consider, if you will, through all the years, the number of Christmases and other special occasions that Nagy forfeited being with his family because he felt his boys needed him.

While many of his virtues have already been extolled, it bears repeating that his great knowledge and understanding of European customs and Communism proved invaluable on many occasions, especially before the collapse of the Berlin Wall. As many of his teams navigated through strange airports, austere customs agents, and foreign lands, there was no one better to have by your side than Dr. Nagobads. He had an acute appreciation of their quirky customs and political agendas.

Furthermore, the selection of the gracious doctor will be the most popular induction in the history of US hockey. Why? Simply because Dr. Nagobads has not only had a powerful and enduring impact on all of us players whose lives he has touched, but also because his friendship, compassion, and dedication to a noble cause, along with his unwavering commitment to each player whose life he touched, will never be equaled again.

The term "Lifetime Achievement" comes to mind as I reflect back on all the years the good doctor spent in the service of USA Hockey.

The time has come to recognize his unconditional dedication and his long-standing years of service.

Dr. George Nagobads' selection into the US Hockey Hall of Fame is LONG OVERDUE.

Warmest personal regards,

Gary Gambucci
(2007 Inductee)